Weight Watchers

Quick Start
Programme Cookbook

For information about the Weight Watchers Classroom
Programme, contact:
Weight Watchers UK Limited
11-12 Fairacres
Dedworth Road
Windsor
Berkshire SL4 4UY
Telephone: Windsor 856751

Art Director: Roger Judd
Photography: Barry Bullough
Home Economist: Ann Page-Wood
Styling: Carol Pastor
Kitchen equipment by courtesy of:
China and Cutlery, from Dickins and Jones Regent Street, W1 and
Lawleys 154 Regent Street, W1
Materials and wallpaper, from Osborne and Little 304 Kings Road, SW3
Tablecloths and napkins, from Descamps, 197 Sloane Street, Knightsbridge
Kitchenware, glass dishes, chinese bowls and wok, from David Mellor 4 Sloane Sq SW1
Line Drawings: Marilyn Day

British Library Cataloguing in Publication Data
Weight Watchers Quick Start Programme Cookbook
    1. Reducing diets – Recipes
    I. Weight Watchers
    641.5'635   RM222.2

First published in Great Britain in 1986 by New English Library, Mill Road, Dunton
Green, Sevenoaks, Kent, a division of Hodder & Stoughton Ltd.

Photoset by South Bucks Photosetters Ltd, Beaconsfield, Bucks
Printed and bound by Hazell, Watson & Viney Ltd, Aylesbury, Bucks

ISBN: 0 450 06147 7

Creole Sauce (P79)

Weight Watchers®
Quick Start
Programme Cookbook

NEW ENGLISH LIBRARY

A NOTE FROM WEIGHT WATCHERS

The Weight Watchers Organisation started in the United States in 1963 and now has over 2000 classes in the United Kingdom. So how can Weight Watchers help you with something new when it has been giving the same message for the past 22 years?

It can. The Organisation has spent more time on research than any other in this field and has used the services of the most eminent specialists to constantly update its method.

The philosophy of Weight Watchers, like its method, is sensible and unspectacular. It won't shock you into action, but rather will guide you through a series of graded steps to permanently acquired skills. Once you have learned to cope with the small problems which prevented you from controlling your weight effectively, you will see that your whole attitude begins to change.

But what of food? Well, food is there to be enjoyed and we will never tell you to skip a meal or to go hungry! Instead we will guide you, at first with very structured steps, to learn how to build a sensible daily and weekly food plan. We will show you which are the better choices to make, both in terms of food and of cooking techniques.

An exercise routine is not part of a Weight Watchers class, but that is not to say we don't approve of exercise. It's just that we believe physical activity should be an essential part of a person's life, but tailored to that person and in his or her own good time. We will give you advice on how to become fit according to your own strength and likes and dislikes, from small changes to your lifestyle such as walking up the stairs instead of taking the lift, to including four or five half-hour visits to your local swimming pool if that's what you enjoy.

Looking good and feeling good is an important part of losing weight, so we give members a booklet packed with tips and advice on grooming.

Weight Watchers will also make you feel at home from your first day in class. You will not have to face the whole group 'on your own', hoping for the best!

We have the best trained lecturers, the soundest method, and the most friendly classes. All you have to do is turn up! Week by week we can show you how to reach your goal and achieve lifetime membership which offers you lasting care and attention by checking your weight monthly.

We know you will enjoy using this book, whether you are a member of Weight Watchers or trying to control your weight on your own. Weight Watchers Magazine, published every other month, is another source of delicious recipes and weekly menus, as well as fashion, beauty and feature articles.

Anyone who is in any doubt about their health, who is currently under a doctor's care, or who is or who becomes pregnant, should consult their doctor before starting or continuing on the Weight Watchers Food Plan or any weight reducing diet.

CONTENTS

INTRODUCTION

THE FOOD PLAN

This book has been arranged for you to use as the basis of a complete weight loss programme. Whether you are a member of Weight Watchers, or simply want to lose a few pounds, this book can help you because we have included all the information you need to use the Food Plans and recipes.

The Weight Watchers Quick Start Programme is simpler and more flexible than ever before and offers the added advantage of a quicker start to weight loss. The Programme uses what are known as 'Exchange Lists'. For all categories of food, i.e. Fruit, Vegetables, Milk, Bread, Fats and Protein, there is an 'Exchange List'. This means that if you do not like a food on an Exchange List you may choose another from that same list.

To help you we have included a typical week's Menu Plan for each of the four steps in the Quick Start Programme. These steps are:

QUICK START 1 – the first step. This offers a balanced diet which allows women to have 1000 calories each day, men 1400 calories and teenagers 1500 calories. Quick Start 1 will give you a good start with a quick weight loss and should be followed for one week.

QUICK START 2 – the second weekly step. The number of Protein Exchanges that you have each day has been increased and the other Exchange Lists are slightly less restricted.

QUICK START 3 – the third weekly step. Your total number of daily Exchanges has been increased and there is more variety. Additionally, we have included a number of foods in an 'Optional' Exchange List which will provide interest and variety to your meals. Women now take 1100 calories, men 1500 and teenagers 1600.

FULL EXCHANGE PLAN – the fourth step. This is the Plan you will follow to reach your goal weight. It has been designed to provide a wide variety of nutritious foods and allows women 1200 calories each day, men 1600 and teenagers 1700. The Plan is so full of choices and so flexible that it can fit your individual needs and your lifestyle quite easily.

HOW TO USE THIS BOOK

In the first section of this book are Menu Plans, Exchange Lists and recipes related to the first three steps and a Menu Plan and Exchange Lists for the Full Exchange Plan. Beside each food listed within the Menu Plans, we tell you how many Exchanges you are using from your daily allowance. Note that men and teenagers are allowed slightly more of certain foods than women and these are indicated at the top of the Exchange Lists.

The recipes which follow are related to the Full Exchange Plan and have been divided into the same food categories as the Exchange Lists: Fruit, Vegetables, Milk, Bread, Fat and Protein. To show you how to use the Optional Exchange List, a recipe section using foods from this List is also included.

As well as Programme Exchange information to help you fit each recipe into your daily Food Plan, we also include calorie counts.

VEGETARIAN FULL EXCHANGE PLAN

The number of non-meat-eaters has increased in recent years and the Quick Start Programme allows for this with a special Plan. This book includes a typical Full Exchange Vegetarian Menu Plan and some delicious non-meat recipes.

FAST FINISH PLAN

Finally, since many people following a weight loss programme find it difficult to lose the last few pounds, we have provided a 'Fast Finish' Menu Plan to help speed up your weight loss. This Plan should only be followed when you are within 7lbs of your goal weight.

IMPORTANT NOTE

All the Menu Plans in this book have been devised to provide a nutritionally balanced diet. *Do not eat less* than indicated on the plans or your diet will not provide you with sufficient nutrients to remain healthy.

GENERAL INFORMATION

ARTIFICIAL SWEETENERS

Many of our recipes include sweetening in the form of small amounts of sugar and honey. If you prefer to take artificial sweeteners, you may do so. The correct equivalent amounts will be listed on the packages.

CALORIES

The general principle is that a woman who wants to maintain her weight should take approximately 1500 calories a day (1800 for a man or teenager). A woman who wants to lose weight should take approximately 1000–1200 calories a day (1600 for a man, 1700 for a teenager).

Each day's calorie intake should be spread over 3 meals which should include a wide variety of nutritious, healthy foods. Snacks can be fitted into your plan as long as they form part of the total calorie count and are not in addition to it.

If you are in any doubt at all about the state of your health, you MUST consult your doctor before embarking upon any weight loss regime.

WEIGHING

Be careful when weighing and measuring ingredients used in the recipes. Accuracy not only ensures successful recipes but also leads to good weight control for yourself. We recommend that you use the Standard British measuring jugs and spoons and a good dietary scale. Keep them always to hand somewhere in the kitchen near your work surface.

When using measuring spoons for ingredients in a recipe, always make sure they are level by using the back of a knife to level them off. Remember, 1 teaspoon equals 5 ml and 1 tablespoon equals 15 ml. Don't forget that careless weighing and measuring adds calories which in turn add weight.

SHOPPING

BREAKFAST CEREALS – Sugar coated cereals add unnecessary calories to your diet. When buying, choose only those that are not coated.

FATS AND OILS – Oils and margarines that are high in polyunsaturated fats are generally better for you. Find out which these are from the labels which will be clearly marked.

FISH – Buy fresh, frozen, smoked or canned. Fish may be canned in oil, tomato sauce or, wherever possible, brine since it is lower in calories. Drain well before eating.

FRUIT – You may choose fresh, frozen, dried or canned fruits, but buy only canned fruits packed in natural fruit juice with no added sugar. Some fruits, including oranges, grapefruit, strawberries, blackcurrants and many more, have more vitamin C in them than others.

MILK – Buy fresh or longlife liquid skimmed milk or low-fat dry powder.

COOKING PROCEDURES

MEAT AND POULTRY – Always buy the leanest joints and cuts of meat possible. When a recipe calls for minced meat, buy lean casserole cuts, removing any remaining fat, and mince yourself.

Meat and poultry skin is a source of concentrated fat and should be removed, whenever possible, before cooking.

When roasting or grilling meat, cook on a rack so that any fat and rich juices can drip away during cooking.

Meat shrinks when it is cooked. As a guideline, 4oz of raw meat yields approximately 3oz when cooked.

VEGETABLES – Vegetables and salads should be bought as fresh as possible to ensure their best flavour and texture.

When preparing vegetables for cooking, scrape or peel very thinly, removing any discoloured leaves or woody stems. Cut into equal pieces and cook briskly in a small amount of boiling, lightly salted water. Drain well while still crisp, but tender.

Keep salad vegetables in a salad crisper in the refrigerator and prepare them at the last moment in order to keep them crisp.

PASTA AND RICE – ¾oz dry pasta or rice will yield approximately 2oz when cooked.

MARGARINE AND OIL – Use either for sauteing vegetables, chicken, eggs, fish, liver and veal. Why not try stir frying? This quick and easy method of cooking will retain much of the colour, flavour, texture and nutrients of your food.

HERBS AND SPICES – Herbs and spices add flavour and interest to your food and you can't beat fresh mint, chives, parsley etc. picked from your own garden or window-sill pots. Dried herbs are convenient, though, and you can retain their strength by storing away from light. If you're using fresh herbs, you'll need approximately four times the amount of dried.

Try experimenting with spices. Delicious combinations are nutmeg with cauliflower or cabbage, cinnamon with courgettes, allspice with red cabbage and carrots and cloves with beetroot, spinach and mushrooms.

Many of our recipes can be adapted for use in slow cookers and micro-wave ovens. Since there is no single standard that applies to all micro-wave ovens, experiment with your own unit and follow the manufacturer's advice for timing.

Non-stick pans are an invaluable cooking aid for low-fat and fat-free cooking.

METRIC CONVERSION TABLE

Liquids		Solids	
		¼ oz	7 g
		½ oz	15 g
¼ fl oz	7 ml	1 oz	30 g
½ fl oz	15 ml	2 oz	60 g
1 fl oz	30 ml	3 oz	90 g
2 fl oz	60 ml	4 oz	120 g
3 fl oz	90 ml	5 oz	150 g
4 fl oz	120 ml	6 oz	180 g
5 fl oz	150 ml	7 oz	210 g
6 fl oz	180 ml	8 oz	240 g
7 fl oz	210 ml	9 oz	270 g
8 fl oz	240 ml	10 oz	300 g
9 fl oz	270 ml	11 oz	330 g
10 fl oz	300 ml	12 oz	360 g
11 fl oz	330 ml	13 oz	390 g
12 fl oz	360 ml	14 oz	420 g
13 fl oz	390 ml	15 oz	450 g
14 fl oz	420 ml	16 oz (1 lb)	480 g
15 fl oz	450 ml	17 oz	510 g
16 fl oz	480 ml	18 oz	540 g
		19 oz	570 g
20 fl oz (1 pt)	600 ml	20 oz (1¼ lb)	600 g
24 fl oz	720 ml	24 oz (1½ lb)	720 g
30 fl oz (1½ pts)	900 ml	28 oz (1¾ lb)	840 g
32 fl oz	960 ml	32 oz (2 lb)	960 g
		36 oz (2¼ lb)	1 kg 80 g
35 fl oz	1 l	40 oz (2½ lb)	1 kg 200 g
40 fl oz (2 pts)	1 l 200 ml	48 oz (3 lb)	1 kg 440 g
45 fl oz (2¼ pts)	1 l 250 ml	56 oz (3½ lb)	1 kg 680 g
50 fl oz (2½ pts)	1 l 500 ml	64 oz (4 lb)	1 kg 920 g
60 fl oz (3 pts)	1 l 800 ml	68 oz (4¼ lb)	2 kg 40 g
70 fl oz (3½ pts)	2 l	72 oz (4½ lb)	2 kg 160 g
80 fl oz (4 pts)	2 l 250 ml	80 oz (5 lb)	2 kg 400 g

Quick Start 1 Menu Plan

	MONDAY		TUESDAY		WEDNESDAY	
BREAKFAST	4fl oz (120ml) grapefruit juice	1	4fl oz (120ml) orange juice	1	4oz (120g) fruit salad	1
	2½oz (75g) cottage cheese	1	¾oz (20g) cereal	1	1 boiled egg	1
	1 slice bread	1	¼ pint (150ml) skimmed milk	½	1 slice bread	1
					1 teaspoon margarine	1
LUNCH	1 oz (30g) Cheddar cheese, grated	1	2oz (60g) canned tuna on shredded lettuce grated carrot and sliced green pepper	2	5oz (150g) low-fat soft cheese	2
	1 hard-boiled egg	1		1	mixed salad	2
	mixed salad	2	2 teaspoons low calorie mayonnaise	1	1 slice bread	1
	2 teasooons salad dressing	1	1 medium apple	1	1 teaspoon margarine	1
	1 medium orange	1			½ medium grapefruit	1
DINNER	3oz (90g) turkey	3	4oz (120g) lamb's liver	4	3oz (90g) chicken	3
	3oz (90g) broccoli	1	1 teaspoon vegetable oil for cooking liver	1	3oz (90g) spinach	1
	mixed salad	1	2 grilled tomatoes	2	3oz (90g) carrots	1
	1 teaspoon vegetable oil with wine vinegar	1	3oz (90g) French beans	1	1 teaspoon margarine	1
	1 slice bread	1	3oz (90g) mushrooms	1	1 medium pear	1
	1 teaspoon margarine	1	1 slice bread	1		
	4oz (120g) fruit salad	1	1 teaspoon margarine	1		
			1 medium pear	1		
SNACKS OR DRINKS TO BE USED THROUGHOUT THE DAY	½ pint (300ml) skimmed milk	1	¾ pint (450ml) skimmed milk	1½	½ pint (300ml) skimmed milk	1
	5fl oz (150ml) low-fat natural yogurt	1			5fl oz (150ml) low-fat natural yogurt	1

IMPORTANT NOTES

This Plan is designed for Women. For Men and Teenagers, increase amounts as indicated on each exchange List.

If you do not like the suggested Menu Plan, substitute something else from the Exchange List. Do not exceed or fall below the stated daily total.

Seasonings, stock cubes, condiments and artificial sweeteners may be taken in reasonable amounts.

Select up to 10 calories a day of diet products such as drinks etc. Water, unlimited.

Tea or coffee may be used in reasonable amounts, with or without skimmed milk from the daily snacks or drinks on your menu plan.

Do not have more than 7 eggs weekly or more than 4oz hard cheese weekly.

Liver is a good source of iron; have a main meal once a week.

Amounts given for meat, fish and poultry are cooked weights.

Amounts given for fruit are fresh, frozen or canned.

NOTE: All Exchanges do not have the same weight, for example, 1 Exchange of low-fat soft cheese is 2½oz, but 1 Exchange of chicken is only 1oz.

FRUIT DAILY EXCHANGES

Women	3
Men	4
Teenagers	4

One Exchange

Apple, 1 medium
Fruit salad, 4oz
★Grapefruit, ½ medium or 4 oz
★Grapefruit juice, 4fl oz
★Honeydew Melon, 2" wedge or 5oz chunks
★Orange, 1 medium
★Orange juice, 4 fl oz
Pear, 1 medium
Pineapple, ¼ small

★Fruits marked with an asterisk are good sources of Vitamin C. Select at least one daily.
Rhubarb is low in calories and may be used freely at any time.

VEGETABLE DAILY EXCHANGES

Women	2 or more
Men	2 or more
Teenagers	2 or more

One Exchange

of raw or cooked vegetables is 3oz. Do have at least 6oz daily, preferably more.
Broccoli
Brussels Sprouts
Cabbage
Carrots
Cauliflower
Celery
Courgettes
Cucumber
Green beans
Lettuce
Mushrooms
Onions
Peppers
Radishes
Spinach
Spring Onions
Tomatoes

THURSDAY	
1 medium orange	1
¾oz (20g) porridge oats, cooked with water	1
¼ pint (150ml) skimmed milk	½
2oz (60g) canned tuna	2
mixed salad	2
2 teaspoons salad dressing	1
1 slice bread	1
2 teaspoons low-fat spread	1
1 medium apple	1
4oz (120g) smoked mackerel	4
3oz (90g) green beans	1
3oz (90g) broccoli	1
1 teaspoon margarine	1
4oz (120g) pineapple	1
¼ pint (150ml) skimmed milk	½
5fl oz (150ml) low-fat natural yogurt	1

FRIDAY	
½ medium grapefruit	1
2½oz (75g) cottage cheese	1
crispbreads up to 80 calories	1
2 hard-boiled eggs	2
mixed salad	2
2 teaspoons salad cream	1
1 slice bread	1
1 teaspoon margarine	1
4oz (120g) fruit salad	1
3oz (90g) chicken	3
3oz (90g) broccoli	1
3oz (90g) carrots	1
1 teaspoon margarine	1
1 medium baked apple	1
½ pint (300ml) skimmed milk	1
5fl oz (150ml) low-fat natural yogurt	1

SATURDAY	
2″ wedge honeydew melon	1
¾oz (20g) cereal	1
¼ pint (150ml) skimmed milk	½
5oz (150g) low-fat soft cheese	2
mixed salad	2
2 teaspoons salad dressing	1
1 slice bread	1
1 teaspoon margarine	1
1 medium apple	1
4oz (120g) grilled rump steak	4
3oz (90g) courgettes	1
1 medium tomato, halved and grilled	1
mixed salad	1
2 teaspoons salad dressing	1
1 medium pear	1
¼ pint (150ml) skimmed milk	½
5fl oz (150ml) low-fat natural yogurt	1

SUNDAY	
4oz (120g) pineapple	1
1oz (30g) Cheddar cheese	1
1 slice bread	1
2oz (60g) chicken	2
3oz (90g) cauliflower	1
3oz (90g) carrots	1
1 slice bread	1
1 teaspoon margarine	1
4oz (120g) fruit salad	1
3oz (90g) canned sardines	3
mixed salad	2
4 teaspoons salad dressing	2
1 medium orange	1
½ pint (300ml) skimmed milk	1
5fl oz (150ml) low-fat natural yogurt	1

MILK DAILY EXCHANGES

Women...................... 2
Men.......................... 2
Teenagers.................... 3

One Exchange
Milk, skimmed, 10fl oz (½ pint)
Milk, low-fat dry, 1oz
Buttermilk, 10fl oz (½ pint)
Yogurt, low-fat natural, 5fl oz (¼ pint)

BREAD DAILY EXCHANGES

Women...................... 2
Men.......................... 4
Teenagers.................... 4

One Exchange
Bread, any type, 1 slice (1oz)
Cereal, ready to eat, not sugar coated, ¾oz
Cereal, uncooked, ¾oz
Crispbreads, up to 80 calories

FAT DAILY EXCHANGES

Women...................... 3
Men.......................... 3
Teenagers.................... 3

One Exchange
Low-fat spread, 2 teaspoons
Margarine (high in polyunsaturates), 1 teaspoon
Mayonnaise, low-calorie, 2 teaspoons
Salad Dressing, low-calorie, 4 teaspoons
Salad Dressing, any type, 2 teaspoons
Vegetable Oil, 1 teaspoon

PROTEIN DAILY EXCHANGES

Women...................... 6
Men.......................... 8
Teenagers.................... 8

One Exchange
★Beef, 1oz
Cheese, low-fat soft, 2½oz
Cheese, hard, 1oz
Chicken, 1oz
Egg, 1
Fish, 1oz
★Lamb, 1oz
Liver, 1oz
★Pork, 1oz
Turkey, 1oz
Veal, 1oz

★Limit these meats to a combined total of 4oz weekly.

■ = Daily Exchanges

11

— Garden Salad —

SERVES 4

140 CALORIES PER SERVING

8oz (240g) mixed salad greens, e.g. lettuce,
watercress, young spinach

6oz (180g) tomatoes, cut into wedges

3oz (90g) radishes, sliced

3oz (90g) spring onions, chopped

2 eggs, hard-boiled and cut into quarters

4 tablespoons blue cheese salad dressing

Mix salad greens, tomato wedges, radishes and spring onions in salad bowl and arrange egg segments on top. Serve with dressing.

Each serving provides: ½ Protein Exchange, 2 Vegetable Exchanges, 1½ Fat Exchanges

— Courgette-Mushroom — Bake

SERVES 4

270 CALORIES PER SERVING

4 teaspoons olive oil

3oz (90g) onion, chopped

2 garlic cloves, crushed

9oz (270g) courgettes, thinly sliced

3oz (90g) mushrooms, sliced

3oz (90g) red pepper, seeded and chopped

½ teaspoon basil

¼ teaspoon each salt and pepper

4 eggs

4oz (120g) Cheddar cheese, grated

Preheat oven to 400°F, 200°C, Gas Mark 6. Heat 3 teaspoons oil in large frying pan, add onion and garlic and saute until onion is transparent. Add courgettes, mushrooms, red pepper and seasonings and, stirring constantly, saute until vegetables are tender-crisp, about 5 minutes. Remove from heat. Beat eggs, add 2oz (60g) cheese and the sauteed vegetables and stir to combine. Grease a baking dish with remaining teaspoon oil, transfer vegetable mixture to dish and sprinkle with remaining 2oz (60g) cheese. Bake 25 to 30 minutes, or until mixture is puffy and brown and a knife inserted in centre comes out clean.

Each serving provides: 2 Protein Exchanges, 1½ Vegetable Exchanges, 1 Fat Exchange

— Quick Tomato Sauce —

SERVES 4

60 CALORIES PER SERVING

1lb (480g) canned tomatoes

8 fresh basil leaves or ½ teaspoon dried

6 parsley sprigs or 1 teaspoon parsley flakes

4 teaspoons olive oil

1 tablespoon chopped onion

½ teaspoon salt

1 small garlic clove, crushed

pinch each oregano and freshly ground pepper

Place all ingredients in blender and puree until smooth. Transfer to a saucepan and bring to the boil. Reduce heat, cover and simmer for 10 minutes.

Each serving provides: 1 Vegetable Exchange, 1 Fat Exchange

— Yogurt-Mint Dip —

SERVES 2

40 CALORIES PER SERVING

5fl oz (150ml) low-fat natural yogurt

2 tablespoons finely chopped mint leaves

1 teaspoon lemon juice

pinch each white pepper, cayenne pepper and salt

Combine all ingredients and mix well. Cover and refrigerate until required. Serve as a dip for raw vegetables.

Each serving provides: ½ Milk Exchange

— Vegetable Soup —

SERVES 2

55 CALORIES PER SERVING

1 teaspoon vegetable oil

2 tablespoons chopped onion

1 garlic clove, crushed

5oz (150g) each carrots and courgettes, thinly sliced

2 teaspoons chopped parsley

¼ teaspoon each thyme and salt

pinch pepper

¾ pint (450ml) water

Heat oil in non-stick saucepan, add onion and garlic and cook until onion is transparent. Add carrots, courgettes, parsley, thyme, salt and pepper. Cover and cook over low heat, stirring occasionally, until vegetables are tender, about 10 minutes. Add water and bring to the boil. Reduce heat to moderate and cook until vegetables are soft, about 20 minutes. Remove from heat and let cool slightly. Remove one cupful of soup from pan and reserve. Pour remaining soup into blender container and puree at low speed until smooth. Return to the pan with the reserved soup and cook, stirring constantly, until well mixed and hot.

Each serving provides: 2 Vegetable Exchanges, ½ Fat Exchange

●

— Tuna Salad with Lemon — French Dressing

SERVES 2

125 CALORIES PER SERVING

2 medium tomatoes, chopped

8 cos lettuce leaves, torn into ½-inch (1-cm) pieces

4oz (120g) drained canned tuna, flaked

1 tablespoon chopped spring onion

2 teaspoons olive oil

½ teaspoon French mustard

1 tablespoon lemon juice

1½ teaspoons each red wine vinegar and water

pinch each salt and pepper

2 teaspoons chopped parsley

Mix tomatoes, lettuce, tuna and spring onion in a salad bowl. Mix oil and mustard and whip until creamy. Add lemon juice, vinegar, water, salt and pepper and stir to combine. Pour dressing over tuna mixture and toss. Sprinkle with parsley before serving.

Each serving provides: 2 Protein Exchanges, 1½ Vegetable Exchanges, 1 Fat Exchange

●

— Sauteed Livers with — Vegetables

SERVES 2

250 CALORIES PER SERVING

2 teaspoons margarine

3oz (90g) onion, chopped

1 garlic clove, crushed

10oz (300g) chicken livers

1½oz (45g) green peppers, seeded and sliced

1 medium tomato, cut into 8 wedges

pinch salt

Heat margarine in frying pan, add onion and garlic and saute until softened. Add livers and saute over fairly high heat for 3 minutes. Add green pepper and saute for 2 minutes longer. Add tomato and saute until just heated through, season with salt and serve.

Each serving provides: 4 Protein Exchanges, 1½ Vegetable Exchanges, 1 Fat Exchange

●

Quick Start 2 Menu Plan

	MONDAY		TUESDAY		WEDNESDAY	
BREAKFAST	5oz (150g) strawberries	1	½ medium grapefruit sprinkled with cinnamon	1	4fl oz (120ml) orange juice	1
	¾oz (20g) cereal	1	1oz (30g) Cheddar cheese	1	¾oz (20g) cereal	1
	¼ pint (150ml) skimmed milk	½	melba toast, up to 80 calories	1	¼ pint (150ml) skimmed milk	½
LUNCH	2 eggs, poached, on 1 slice	2	5oz (150g) cottage cheese	2	3oz (90g) canned tuna, mixed	3
	bread, toasted	1	mixed salad	2	with 2 teaspoons mayonnaise	2
	1 teaspoon margarine	1	2 teaspoons mayonnaise	2	2oz (60g) cooked pasta	2
	2 grilled tomatoes	2	crispbreads, up to 80 calories	1	mixed salad	1
	mixed green salad	2	2 teaspoons low-fat spread	1	1 medium apple	1
	1 medium orange	1	2″ wedge honeydew melon	1		
DINNER	4oz (120g) fish	4	3oz (90g) chicken	3	3oz (90g) turkey	3
	3oz (90g) green beans	1	mixed salad	2	3oz (90g) cauliflower	1
	2oz (60g) mushrooms	½	4oz (120g) fruit salad	1	2 medium tomatoes	2
	mixed salad	1	5fl oz (150ml) low-fat natural	1	3oz (90g) Brussels sprouts	1
	2 teaspoons mayonnaise	2	yogurt		1 teaspoon margarine	1
	1 medium apple	1			4oz (120g) pineapple	1
SNACKS OR DRINKS TO BE USED THROUGHOUT THE DAY	¾ pint (450ml) skimmed milk	1½	½ pint (300ml) skimmed milk	1	¾ pint (450ml) skimmed milk	1½

IMPORTANT NOTES

This Plan is designed for Women. For Men and Teenagers, increase amounts as indicated on each Exchange List.

If you do not like the suggested Menu Plan, substitute something else from the Exchange List. Do not exceed or fall below the stated daily total.

Seasonings, stock cubes, condiments and artificial sweeteners may be taken in reasonable amounts.

Select up to 10 calories a day of diet products such as drinks etc. Water, unlimited.

Tea or coffee may be used in reasonable amounts, with or without skimmed milk from the daily snacks or drinks on your menu plan.

Do not have more than 7 eggs weekly or more than 4oz hard cheese weekly.

Liver is a good source of iron; have a main meal once a week.

Amounts given for meat, fish and poultry are cooked weights.

Amounts given for fruit are fresh, frozen or canned.

NOTE: All Exchanges do not have the same weight, for example, 1 Exchange of low-fat soft cheese is 2½oz, but 1 Exchange of chicken is only 1oz.

FRUIT DAILY EXCHANGES

Women.......................3
Men 4
Teenagers....................4

One Exchange
Apple, 1 medium
Berries, 5oz
Fruit salad, 4oz
★Gooseberries, 5oz
★Grapefruit, ½ medium or 4oz
★Grapefruit juice, 4fl oz
★Honeydew Melon, 2in wedge or 5oz chunks
★Orange, 1 medium
★Orange juice, 4fl oz
Pear, 1 medium
Pineapple, ¼ small
★Strawberries, 5oz

★Fruits marked with an asterisk are good sources of Vitamin C. Select at least one daily.
Rhubarb is low in calories and may be used freely at any time.

VEGETABLE DAILY EXCHANGES

Women............. 2 or more
Men .... 2 or more
Teenagers.......... 2 or more

One Exchange
of raw or cooked vegetables is 3oz. Do have at least 6oz daily, preferably more.
Bean Sprouts
Broccoli
Brussels Sprouts
Cabbage
Carrots
Cauliflower
Celery
Courgettes
Cucumber
Green beans
Leeks
Lettuce
Mushrooms
Onions
Peppers
Radishes
Spinach
Spring Onions
Tomatoes

THURSDAY	
2" wedge honeydew melon	1
2½oz (75g) cottage cheese	1
1 slice bread	1
1 hard-boiled egg, halved and spread with 1 teaspoon mayonnaise	1
1oz (30g) cheese, grated	1
mixed salad	2
1 medium pear	1
3oz (90g) grilled lambs liver	3
3oz (90g) onion, sauteed in 1 teaspoon vegetable oil	1
3oz (90g) potato, mashed with 1 teaspoon margarine	1
mixed green salad	1
4oz (120g) pineapple	1
5fl oz (150ml) low-fat natural yogurt	1
½ pint (300ml) skimmed milk	1

FRIDAY	
4fl oz (120ml) orange juice	1
¾oz (20g) cereal	1
¼ pint (150ml) skimmed milk	½
1oz (30g) hard cheese	1
2oz (60g) chicken	2
mixed salad with sliced tomatoes	3
2 teaspoons low-calorie mayonnaise	1
1 medium apple	1
3oz (90g) grilled veal fillet with 2 teaspoons margarine	3
	2
2oz (60g) cooked rice	1
3oz (90g) broccoli	1
4oz (120g) canned apricots	1
¾ pint (450ml) skimmed milk	1½

SATURDAY	
4oz (120g) fruit salad	1
2½oz (75g) low-fat soft cheese	1
1 slice bread	1
cheese omelette, made with 1 egg and 1oz (30g) Cheddar cheese	2
1 teaspoon vegetable oil	1
mixed salad with lemon juice and herbs	2
1 medium orange	1
3oz (90g) grilled fish	3
2 teaspoons margarine	2
3oz (90g) spinach	1
3oz (90g) green beans	1
2oz (60g) cooked rice	1
½ medium banana	1
5fl oz (150ml) low-fat natural yogurt	1
½ pint (300ml) skimmed milk	1

SUNDAY	
½ medium grapefruit	1
¾oz (20g) cereal	1
¼ pint (150ml) skimmed milk	½
2oz (60g) canned salmon	2
mixed salad	2
2 teaspoons mayonnaise	2
1 slice bread	1
1 teaspoon margarine	1
4oz (120g) fruit salad	1
2½fl oz (75ml) low-fat natural yogurt	½
4oz (120g) grilled lamb chop	4
1 medium tomato, grilled	1
3oz (90g) carrots	1
3oz (90g) cauliflower	1
2" wedge honeydew melon	1
½ pint (300ml) skimmed milk	1

MILK DAILY EXCHANGES

Women........................ 2
Men 2
Teenagers............... 3 to 4

One Exchange
Milk, skimmed, 10fl oz (½ pint)
Milk, low-fat dry, 1oz
Buttermilk, 10fl oz (½ pint)
Yogurt, low-fat natural, 5fl oz (¼ pint)

BREAD DAILY EXCHANGES

Women........................ 2
Men 4
Teenagers.................... 4

One Exchange
Bagel, small, ½ (1oz)
Bread, any type, 1 slice (1oz)
Cereal, ready to eat, not sugar coated, ¾oz
Cereal, uncooked, ¾oz
Crispbreads, up to 80 calories
Melba toast, up to 80 calories
Pasta, cooked, 2oz
Potato, 3oz
Rice, cooked, 2oz

FAT DAILY EXCHANGES

Women........................ 3
Men 3
Teenagers.................... 3

One Exchange
Low-fat spread, 2 teaspoons
Margarine (high in polyunsaturates), 1 teaspoon
Mayonnaise, 1 teaspoon
Mayonnaise, low-calorie, 2 teaspoons
Salad Dressing, low-calorie, 4 teaspoons
Salad Dressing, any type, 2 teaspoons
Vegetable Oil, 1 teaspoon

PROTEIN DAILY EXCHANGES

Women................... 6 to 7
Men .... 8 to 9
Teenagers............... 8 to 9

One Exchange
★Beef, 1oz
Cheese, low-fat soft, 2½oz
Cheese, hard, 1oz
Chicken, 1oz
Egg, 1
Fish, 1oz
★Ham, 1oz
★Lamb, 1oz
Liver, 1oz
★Pork, 1oz
Turkey, 1oz
Veal, 1oz

★Limit these meats to a combined total of 4oz weekly.

■ = **Daily Exchanges**

15

— Ham Spread or Dip —

SERVES 4

170 CALORIES PER SERVING

5oz (150g) low-fat soft cheese

4 teaspoons margarine

6oz (180g) ham, minced

2 tablespoons chopped spring onion

1 tablespoon spicy brown mustard

Place cheese and margarine in blender and puree until smooth. Add remaining ingredients and blend again until well mixed.

Each serving provides: 2 Protein Exchanges, 1 Fat Exchange

•

— Beef and Pasta — Casserole

SERVES 2

435 CALORIES PER SERVING

9oz (270g) minced beef

2 teaspoons vegetable or olive oil

3oz (90g) onion, chopped

2 garlic cloves, crushed

3oz (90g) mushrooms, sliced

1 tablespoon chopped parsley

1lb (480g) canned tomatoes, crushed

¼ teaspoon each basil, salt and pepper

pinch oregano

4oz (120g) cooked macaroni

1oz (30g) Cheddar cheese, thinly sliced and cut into strips

Shape beef into a patty and grill on rack, turning once, for about 7 minutes. Crumble beef and set aside. Heat oil in a saucepan, add onion and garlic and saute until onion is softened. Add mushrooms, parsley and crumbled beef and saute for about 5 minutes. Stir in tomatoes and seasonings and simmer, stirring occasionally, for 15 minutes. Preheat oven to 350°F, 180°C, Gas Mark 4. Stir macaroni into beef mixture and spoon into shallow flameproof casserole. Top with cheese strips and bake until mixture is heated through, 20 to 25 minutes. Place under hot grill until cheese is lightly browned, about 2 minutes.

Each serving provides: 4 Protein Exchanges, 1 Bread Exchange, 3½ Vegetable Exchanges, 1 Fat Exchange

•

— Potato-Vegetable Saute —

SERVES 2

120 CALORIES PER SERVING

2 teaspoons vegetable oil

2 tablespoons chopped onion

½ garlic clove, crushed

6oz (180g) peeled cooked potatoes, cut into cubes

1½oz (45g) each red and green pepper, seeded and cut into ½-inch (1-cm) squares

pinch each salt and pepper

Heat oil in frying pan, add onion and garlic and saute until onion is soft. Add potatoes and peppers and saute, stirring until potatoes are lightly browned and peppers are tender-crisp. Stir in salt and pepper and saute for 2 minutes longer.

Each serving provides: 1 Bread Exchange, 1 Vegetable Exchange, 1 Fat Exchange

•

— Noodle Salad —

SERVES 2

130 CALORIES PER SERVING

4oz (120g) cooked shell or bow pasta

6oz (180g) tomatoes, chopped

1½oz (45g) spring onions, chopped

1oz (30g) celery, chopped

2 teaspoons oil and vinegar salad dressing

pinch each salt and pepper

Place all ingredients in salad bowl and toss well. May be covered and chilled lightly in refrigerator if not for immediate use.

Each serving provides: 1 Bread Exchange, 1½ Vegetable Exchanges, 1 Fat Exchange

•

— Eggs with Tomato — Sauce

SERVES 1

335 CALORIES PER SERVING

1 teaspoon olive oil

3 tablespoons chopped onion

¼ garlic clove, crushed with pinch salt

8oz (240g) canned tomatoes, crushed

¼ teaspoon oregano

pinch pepper

2 large eggs

2oz (60g) long grain rice, hot

Heat oil in non-stick frying pan, add onion and saute until tender. Add crushed garlic and saute for about 30 seconds. Stir in tomatoes and seasonings, reduce heat to low and let simmer until mixture thickens slightly. Make 2 hollows in tomato mixture. Break eggs carefully into a cup, one at a time, and slip into the hollows. Cover pan and let simmer until eggs are set, 3 to 4 minutes. Slide eggs and sauce onto hot rice.

Each serving provides: 2 Protein Exchanges, 1 Bread Exchange, 3 Vegetable Exchanges, 1 Fat Exchange

•

— Crab and — Potato-Stuffed Peppers

SERVES 2

475 CALORIES PER SERVING

2 medium green peppers, cut lengthwise into halves, seeded and blanched

4oz (120g) thawed and thoroughly drained frozen crab meat, flaked

3oz (90g) Cheddar cheese, grated and divided

6oz (180g) onions, chopped and steamed

½ pint (300ml) skimmed milk

6oz (180g) cooked mashed potato

1 egg, beaten

2 teaspoons margarine, melted

parsley sprigs for garnish

Place pepper halves on paper towels and let drain and cool. In small bowl combine crab meat, 1oz (30g) of cheese and remaining ingredients except parsley, stirring to thoroughly combine. Let stand for 5 minutes. Preheat oven to 375°F, 190°C, Gas Mark 5. Spoon ¼ of crab mixture into each pepper half, sprinkle each with ½oz (15g) grated cheese. Place pepper halves in casserole and bake until stuffing is firm and cheese is browned, 25 to 30 minutes. Serve garnished with parsley sprigs.

Each serving provides: 4 Protein Exchanges, 1 Bread Exchange, 3 Vegetable Exchanges, 1 Fat Exchange, ½ Milk Exchange

•

— Chicken Hotpot —

SERVES 2

165 CALORIES PER SERVING

1 teaspoon margarine

1½oz (45g) onion, chopped

8oz (240g) chicken pieces, skinned

1 teaspoon Worcestershire sauce

¼ teaspoon dry mustard

pinch cayenne pepper

4oz (120g) canned tomatoes

4fl oz (120ml) hot water

3oz (90g) peeled cooked potatoes, cut into cubes

1oz (30g) cut green beans, fresh or frozen

pinch each salt and pepper

Heat margarine in saucepan, add onion and saute until soft. Add chicken and brown well on all sides. Sprinkle with Worcestershire sauce, mustard and cayenne pepper. Stir in tomatoes and water and bring to the boil. Reduce heat, cover and simmer for about 30 minutes. Add potatoes, green beans, salt and pepper and simmer uncovered, stirring occasionally, until chicken is tender, 10 to 15 minutes.

Each serving provides: 3 Protein Exchanges, ½ Bread Exchange, 1 Vegetable Exchange, ½ Fat Exchange

•

Quick Start 3 Menu Plan

	MONDAY		TUESDAY		WEDNESDAY	
BREAKFAST	4fl oz (120ml) orange juice	1	5oz (150g) strawberries	1	4fl oz (120ml) orange juice	1
	¾oz (20g) cereal	1	2½oz (75g) low-fat soft cheese	1	¾oz (20g) cereal	1
	¼ pint (150ml) skimmed milk	½	1 slice bread	1	¼ pint (150ml) skimmed milk	½
LUNCH	6oz (180g) baked beans	2	2oz (60g) canned salmon	2	2oz (60g) Cheddar cheese	2
	grilled tomatoes	2	mixed salad	2	mixed salad	2
	1 slice bread	1	1 slice bread	1	2 teaspoons salad dressing	1
	1 teaspoon margarine	1	1 teaspoon margarine	1	2 cream crackers	1
	1 medium apple	1	1 medium orange	1	1 teaspoon margarine	1
					1 medium apple	1
DINNER	4oz (120g) chicken	4	3oz (90g) lamb	3	4oz (120g) chicken	4
	2oz (60g) cooked pasta	1	3oz (90g) baked jacket potato	1	3oz (90g) broccoli	1
	3oz (90g) courgettes	1	2 teaspoons margarine	2	3oz (90g) peas	1
	3oz (90g) carrots	1	3oz (90g) green beans	1	1 teaspoon margarine	1
	2 teaspoons margarine	2	½ medium banana	1	3oz (90g) grapes	1
	1 medium peach	1	5fl oz (150ml) low-fat natural yogurt	1		
SNACKS OR DRINKS TO BE USED THROUGHOUT THE DAY	¾ pint (450ml) skimmed milk	1½	½ pint (300ml) skimmed milk	1	¾ pint (450ml) skimmed milk	1½

IMPORTANT NOTES

Refer to Quick Start 2 'Important Notes'. This plan introduces you to 'Optional Exchanges'. You may select up to 10 calories a day from this list to add variety and interest to your meals.

10 CALORIE FOODS

Anchovies, 2 fillets
Bacon bits, imitation, 1 tsp
Bran, 1 tbsp
Breadcrumbs, dried, 1 tsp
Chewing gum, 1 stick
Cocoa, unsweetened, 1 tsp
Coconut, desiccated, 1 tsp
Coffee whitener, 1 tsp
Curry paste, ½ tsp
Custard powder, 1 tsp
Egg white, ½
Flour, all types, 1 tsp

Gravy powder, 1 tsp
Honey/Syrup, ½ tsp
Ketchup, tomato, 2 tsps
Olives, all types, 2
Parmesan cheese, 1 tsp
Pickle/Relish, 1 tsp
Sauce, brown, 2 tsps
Seeds, ½ tsp
Sugar, ½ tsp
Tomato puree, 1 tbsp
Vegetable/Yeast extracts, 1 tsp
Wine for cooking, 2 tsps

Also, once a week only, you may choose one of the following:

	1 glass wine (4fl oz)
OR	½ pint bitter or light ale
OR	2oz ice cream (chocolate, vanilla or strawberry)
OR	2 extra pieces of fruit from the Fruit Exchange List.

FRUIT DAILY EXCHANGES

Women........................ 3
Men .... 4 to 6
Teenagers................ 4 to 6

One Exchange
Apple, 1 medium
Banana, ½ medium
Berries, 5oz Fruit salad, 4oz
★Gooseberries, 5oz
★Grapefruit, ½ medium or 4oz
★Grapefruit juice, 4fl oz
Grapes, 3oz
★Honeydew melon, 2″ wedge or 5oz chunks
★Orange, 1 medium
★Orange juice, 4fl oz
Peach, 1 medium
Pear, 1 medium
Pineapple, ¼ small
★Strawberries, 5oz
Watermelon, 5oz chunks

★Fruits marked with an asterisk are good sources of Vitamin C. Select at least one daily.
Rhubarb is low in calories and may be used freely at any time.

VEGETABLE DAILY EXCHANGES

Women............. 2 or more
Men .... 2 or more
Teenagers.......... 2 or more

One Exchange
of raw or cooked vegetables is 3oz. Do have at least 6oz daily, preferably more.
Asparagus   Aubergine
Bean Sprouts
★Beetroot and Peas
Broccoli
Brussels Sprouts
Cabbage   Carrots
Cauliflower   Celery
Courgettes   Cucumber
Green beans
Leeks
Lettuce
Mushrooms
Onions/Spring Onions
Peppers
Radishes
Spinach
Tomatoes

★Do not have more than 6oz weekly.

THURSDAY

½ medium banana	1
2½oz (75g) low-fat soft cheese	1
1 slice bread	1

2 hard-boiled eggs	2
mixed salad	2
2 teaspoons salad dressing	1
1 medium peach	1
1 digestive biscuit	1

3oz (90g) lemon sole	3
3oz (90g) poached mushrooms	1
3oz (90g) spinach	1
2 teaspoons margarine	2
5oz (150g) strawberries	1

5fl oz (150ml) low-fat natural yogurt	1
½ pint (300ml) skimmed milk	1

FRIDAY

½ medium grapefruit	1
¾oz (20g) cereal	1
¼ pint (150ml) skimmed milk	½

3oz (90g) chicken	3
mixed salad	2
2 teaspoons salad dressing	1
2 cream crackers	1
1 teaspoon margarine	1
1 medium apple	1

3oz (90g) liver	3
3oz (90g) onion	1
grilled tomato	1
3oz (90g) cauliflower	1
1 teaspoon margarine	1
3oz (90g) grapes	1

¾ pint (450ml) skimmed milk	1½

SATURDAY

4fl oz (120ml) orange juice	1
1 boiled egg	1
1 slice bread	1
1 teaspoon margarine	1

2oz (60g) tuna	2
mixed salad	2
2 teaspoons salad dressing	1
1 slice bread	1
1 teaspoon margarine	1
1 medium pear	1

3oz (90g) chicken	3
3oz (90g) beetroot	1
shredded lettuce	
sliced tomatoes and cucumber	2
5oz (150g) strawberries	1

5fl oz (150ml) low-fat natural yogurt	1
½ pint (300ml) skimmed milk	1

SUNDAY

½ medium grapefruit	1
¾oz (20g) cereal	1
¼ pint (150ml) skimmed milk	½

2-egg omelette	2
3oz (90g) poached mushrooms	1
1 grilled tomato	1
1 slice bread	1
2 teaspons margarine	2
1 medium orange	1

4oz (120g) luncheon meat	4
mixed salad	2
2 teaspoons salad dressing	1
3oz (90g) grapes	1
1 digestive biscuit	1

¾ pint (450ml) skimmed milk	1½

MILK DAILY EXCHANGES

Women........................ 2

Men.......................... 2

Teenagers.................... 3

One Exchange
Milk, skimmed, 10fl oz (½ pint)
Milk, low-fat dry, 1oz
Buttermilk, 10fl oz (½ pint)
Yogurt, low-fat natural, 5fl oz (¼ pint)

BREAD DAILY EXCHANGES

Women.................. 2 to 3

Men...................... 4 to 5

Teenagers.............. 4 to 5

One Exchange
Bagel, small, ½ (1oz)
Bread, any type, 1 slice (1oz)
Cereal, ready to eat, not sugar coated, ¾oz
Cereal, uncooked, ¾oz
Cream crackers, 2
Crispbreads, up to 80 calories
Digestive biscuit, 1
Melba toast, up to 80 calories
Pasta, cooked, 2oz
Potato, 3oz
Rice, cooked, 2oz

FAT DAILY EXCHANGES

Women......................... 3

Men.......................... 3

Teenagers.................... 3

One Exchange
Low-fat spread, 2 teaspoons
Margarine (high in polyunsaturates), 1 teaspoon
Mayonnaise, 1 teaspoon
Mayonnaise, low-calorie, 2 teaspoons
Salad Dressing, low-calorie, 4 teaspoons
Salad Dressing, any type, 2 teaspoons
Vegetable Oil, 1 teaspoon

■ = **Daily Exchanges**

PROTEIN DAILY EXCHANGES

Women................. 6 to 7

Men...................... 8 to 9

Teenagers.............. 8 to 9

One Exchange
★Beef, 1oz
Beans, canned and cooked, 3oz
Beans, lentils, peas, dried, 1oz
Cheese, low-fat soft, 2½oz
Cheese, hard, 1oz
Chicken, 1oz
Egg, 1
Fish, 1oz
★Ham, 1oz
★Lamb, 1oz
Liver, 1oz
★Luncheon Meat, 1oz
★Pork, 1oz
Turkey, 1oz
Veal, 1oz

★Limit these meats to a combined total of 8oz weekly.

— Lamb and Aubergine — Stew

SERVES 2

330 CALORIES PER SERVING

10oz (300g) boned leg of lamb, cut into 1-inch (2.5-cm) cubes

2 teaspoons vegetable oil

3oz (90g) onion, chopped

2 garlic cloves, crushed

8oz (240g) canned tomatoes, chopped

6fl oz (180ml) water

¼ teaspoon each salt and ground cumin

pinch pepper

8oz (240g) aubergine, cut into 1-inch (2.5-cm) cubes

2 teaspoons chopped parsley

Grill lamb cubes on rack, turning several times, until browned on all sides. Set aside. Heat oil in saucepan, add onion and garlic and saute until onion is lightly browned. Add lamb, tomatoes, water, salt, cumin and pepper and bring to the boil. Reduce heat, cover and simmer until meat is fork-tender, 50 minutes to 1 hour. Add aubergine to saucepan, cover and cook until aubergine is soft, about 20 minutes. Serve sprinkled with parsley.

Each serving provides: 4 Protein Exchanges, 3 Vegetable Exchanges, 1 Fat Exchange

•

— Three-Bean Soup —

SERVES 4

135 CALORIES PER SERVING

2 teaspoons olive or vegetable oil

1oz (30g) onion, chopped

1 garlic clove, crushed

5oz (150g) courgettes, thinly sliced

8oz (240g) canned tomatoes

9oz (270g) drained canned red kidney beans (reserve liquid)

3oz (90g) each drained canned chick-peas and small white beans (reserve liquid)

½ teaspoon basil

pinch each salt and pepper

Heat oil in a saucepan, add onion and garlic and saute until onion is softened, about 3 minutes. Add courgettes and cook, stirring constantly, until tender, about 5 minutes. Stir in tomatoes, beans, ½ pint (300ml) reserved liquid and the seasonings and bring to the boil. Reduce heat and simmer for 10 to 15 minutes.

Each serving provides: 1 Protein Exchange, 1 Vegetable Exchange, ½ Fat Exchange, 15 Calories Optional Exchange

•

— Sweet and Sour — Beetroot

SERVES 2

85 CALORIES PER SERVING

2 teaspoons margarine

1 tablespoon chopped onion

6oz (180g) drained canned small whole beetroot, cut into quarters

1 tablespoon each lemon juice and water

pinch each salt and pepper

artificial sweetener to equal ½ teaspoon sugar (optional)

Heat margarine in small non-stick frying pan, add onion and saute until softened, 1 to 2 minutes. Reduce heat to low and add remaining ingredients. Cover pan and cook, stirring once, for 5 minutes longer.

Each serving provides: 1 Vegetable Exchange, 1 Fat Exchange

•

— Honey Baked Apple —

SERVES 2

80 CALORIES PER SERVING

2 medium apples

2 teaspoons apricot jam

1 teaspoon honey

Remove core from each apple to ½ inch (1 cm) from bottom. Remove a thin strip of peel from round centre of each apple (this helps keep peel from bursting). Fill each apple with 1 teaspoon apricot jam and ½ teaspoon honey. Place each apple upright in individual ovenproof dish. Cover dishes with foil and bake at 400°F, 200°C, Gas Mark 6, until apples are tender, 25 to 30 minutes.

Each serving provides: 1 Fruit Exchange, 25 Calories Optional Exchange

— Lamb Chops in — Apricot Sauce

SERVES 2

335 CALORIES PER SERVING

2 lamb chump chops, each 6oz (180g)

2 teaspoons vegetable oil

2 tablespoons chopped onion

1 garlic clove, crushed

4 teaspoons apricot jam

1 teaspoon each chopped peeled ginger root and soy sauce

pinch each salt and pepper

4fl oz (120ml) water

Grill lamb chops on rack until rare, at least 3 minutes on each side. Set aside. Heat oil in a frying pan, add onion and garlic and saute until onion is softened. Add apricot jam, ginger and soy sauce and bring to the boil. Sprinkle lamb chops with salt and pepper and add chops and water to apricot sauce. Reduce heat, cover and simmer, turning once, until meat is fork-tender, about 30 minutes.

Each serving provides: 4 Protein Exchanges, ¼ Vegetable Exchange, 1 Fat Exchange, 30 Calories Optional Exchange

— Asparagus-Cheese — Bake

SERVES 4

405 CALORIES PER SERVING

4 teaspoons margarine, melted

24 asparagus spears, cooked

6oz (180g) strong Cheddar cheese, coarsely grated

4 slices white bread, lightly toasted and cut into 1-inch (2.5-cm) squares

1 pint (600ml) skimmed milk

2 eggs, lightly beaten

½ teaspoon salt

¼ teaspoon each white pepper and dry mustard

pinch cayenne pepper

Brush a shallow casserole with 1 teaspoon margarine. Arrange 8 asparagus spears in casserole, sprinkle with 2oz (60g) cheese and top cheese with ⅓ of the bread squares. Repeat layers of asparagus, cheese and bread twice more, ending with bread. Mix milk, eggs, seasonings and remaining 3 teaspoons margarine and pour over mixture in casserole. Cover and refrigerate for 1 hour. Preheat oven to 350°F, 180°C, Gas Mark 4. Set casserole in large baking tin and pour boiling water into tin to reach halfway up the sides of casserole. Bake for 1¼ hours or until a knife, inserted in centre, comes out clean. Remove cheese bake from water bath and let stand for 10 minutes before cutting.

Each serving provides: 2 Protein Exchanges, 1 Bread Exchange, 1 Vegetable Exchange, 1 Fat Exchange, ½ Milk Exchange

— Tuna Provencale —

SERVES 4

225 CALORIES PER SERVING

12oz (360g) aubergine, peeled and cut into small cubes

1 teaspoon salt

4 teaspoons olive oil

8oz (240g) onions, sliced

2 garlic cloves, crushed

2lbs (960g) canned tomatoes, crushed

6oz (180g) green peppers, seeded and sliced

16fl oz (480ml) water

1 teaspoon basil

½ teaspoon oregano

¼ teaspoon pepper

1lb (480g) drained canned tuna, flaked

1 tablespoon chopped parsley

Arrange aubergine on paper towel in single layer and sprinkle with salt. Let stand 30 minutes, then pat dry and set aside. Heat oil in a large saucepan, add onions and garlic and saute until onions are transparent. Add aubergine, tomatoes, green peppers, water, basil, oregano and pepper. Cover and simmer, stirring occasionally, for 35 minutes. Stir in tuna and cook for 5 minutes longer. Serve sprinkled with parsley.

Each serving provides: 4 Protein Exchanges, 5 Vegetable Exchanges, 1 Fat Exchange

Full Exchange Menu Plan

	MONDAY		TUESDAY		WEDNESDAY	
BREAKFAST	4oz (120g) orange sections	1	4fl oz (120ml) orange juice	1	½ medium grapefruit	1
	2½oz (75g) cottage cheese	1	¾oz (20g) cereal	1	1 boiled egg	1
	1 slice wholemeal bread	1	¼ pint (150ml) skimmed milk	½	1 slice bread	1
					1 teaspoon margarine	1
LUNCH	8fl oz (240ml) tomato juice	1	5oz (150g) low-fat soft cheese	2	8fl oz (240ml) tomato juice	1
	2oz (60g) canned salmon	2	mixed salad	2	2oz (60g) canned tuna	2
	mixed green salad with sliced tomato	2	2 teaspoons salad dressing	1	mixed green salad	2
	1 teaspoon mayonnaise	1	2 cream crackers	1	2 teaspoons salad dressing	1
	crispbreads up to 80 calories	1	2 teaspoons low-fat spread	1	1 slice bread	1
			4oz (120g) pineapple	1	1 teaspoon margarine	1
DINNER	3oz (90g) chicken	3	4oz (120g) fish	4	3oz (90g) chicken	3
	2oz (60g) cooked rice	1	3oz (90g) cauliflower	1	3oz (90g) mushrooms	1
	3oz (90g) spinach	1	3oz (90g) green beans	1	1 medium grilled tomato	1
	3oz (90g) carrots	1	3oz (90g) potatoes	1	3oz (90g) sweetcorn	1
	2 teaspoons margarine	2	2 teaspoons low-fat spread	1	3oz (90g) grapes	1
	1 medium pear	1	1 medium apple	1		
SNACKS OR DRINKS TO BE USED THROUGHOUT THE DAY	5fl oz (150ml) low-fat natural yogurt	1	¾ pint (450ml) skimmed milk	1½	5fl oz (150ml) low-fat natural yogurt	1
	½ pint (300ml) skimmed milk	1			½ pint (300ml) skimmed milk	1

This Menu Plan is based on the Full Exchange Plan which is your basic eating pattern for the rest of your journey to goal weight. The Full Exchange lists: Fruit, Vegetables, Milk, Fat,

THURSDAY	
2″ wedge honeydew melon	1
1 poached egg	1
1 slice bread	1
1 teaspoon margarine	1
5oz (150g) low-fat soft cheese	2
mixed green salad with lemon juice and herbs	2
melba toast up to 80 calories	1
2 teaspoons low-fat spread	1
1 medium orange	1
3oz (90g) grilled rump steak	3
3oz (90g) carrots	1
3oz (90g) green beans	1
3oz (90g) potatoes	1
2 teaspoons low-fat spread	1
4oz (120g) pineapple	1
5fl oz (150ml) low-fat natural yogurt	1
½ pint (300ml) skimmed milk	1

FRIDAY	
4fl oz (120ml) orange juice	1
1 scrambled egg	1
1 slice bread	1
1 teaspoon margarine	1
2oz (60g) Cheddar cheese, grated on mixed salad, with	2, 2
2 teaspoons salad dressing	1
1 slice bread	1
1 teaspoons margarine	1
1 medium apple	1
3oz (90g) fish	3
3oz (90g) carrots	1
3oz (90g) broccoli	1
1 medium apple	1
5fl oz (150ml) low-fat natural yogurt	1
½ pint (300ml) skimmed milk	1

SATURDAY	
1oz (30g) raisins	1
¾oz (20g) porridge oats, cooked with water	1
¼ pint (150ml) skimmed milk	½
2 tablespoons peanut butter (also uses fat exchanges)	2, 2
crispbreads up to 80 calories	1
tomato and lettuce salad with lemon juice	2
4oz (120g) pineapple	1
4oz (120g) grilled calf liver	4
3oz (90g) onion, cooked in	1
1 teaspoon vegetable oil	1
3oz (90g) Brussels sprouts	1
2oz (60g) cooked rice	1
1 medium orange	1
¾ pint (450ml) skimmed milk	1½

SUNDAY	
5oz (150g) strawberries	1
2½oz (75g) low-fat soft cheese	1
1 digestive biscuit	1
2oz (60g) ham	2
sliced celery and tomato with	2
2 teaspoons salad dressing	1
1 slice bread	1
1 teaspoon margarine	1
1 medium apple	1
3oz (90g) chicken	3
3oz (90g) broccoli	1
3oz (90g) carrots	1
mixed green salad with	
2 teaspoons salad dressing	1
4oz (120g) fruit salad	1
5fl oz (150ml) low-fat natural yogurt	1
½ pint (300ml) skimmed milk	1

Bread and Protein are on the following pages, together with the Optional Exchange list that you were introduced to in Quick Start 3 which has now been expanded.

■ = Daily Exchanges

FRUIT DAILY EXCHANGES

Women...................... 3
Men .... 4 to 6
Teenagers............... 4 to 6

One Exchange

Apple, 1 medium or 4oz
Apple juice, 2½fl oz
Apricots, dried, 1oz
Apricots, fresh, 2 medium or 4oz
Banana, ½ medium
Berries
Blackberries, 5oz
Blueberries, 5oz
Cranberries, 5oz
★Gooseberries, 5oz
Loganberries, 5oz
Raspberries, 5oz
★Strawberries, 5oz
Cantaloupe Melon, ½ medium
Cherries, 4oz
Currants, dried, 1oz
★Currants, 5oz
Dates, fresh or dried, 2
Dried Fruit, mixed, 1oz
Figs, fresh or dried, 1 large
Fruit Salad, 4oz
Grape juice, 2½fl oz
★Grapefruit, ½ medium or 4oz
★Grapefruit juice, 4fl oz
Grapes, 3oz
★Honeydew Melon, 2" wedge or 5oz chunks
★Kiwi fruit, 1 medium
Mandarin Orange, 1 large or 4oz
Nectarine, 1 medium
★Ogen Melon, ½ medium
★Orange, 1 medium or 4 oz
★Orange juice, 4fl oz
Peach, 1 medium or 4oz
Pear, 1 medium or 4oz
Pineapple, ¼ small or 4oz
Pineapple juice, 2½fl oz
Plums, 2 medium
Prunes, 3 medium, 2 large or 2oz
Raisins, 1oz
Sultanas, 1oz
Tangerine, 1 large or 2 small

★Tomato juice, 8fl oz
★Vegetable juice, mixed, 8fl oz
Watermelon, 5oz chunks

★Fruits marked with an asterisk are good sources of Vitamin C. Select at least one daily.
Rhubarb is low in calories and may be used freely at any time.
Amounts given for fruit are fresh, frozen or canned.

VEGETABLE DAILY EXCHANGES

Women............. 2 or more
Men .... 2 or more
Teenagers.......... 2 or more

One Exchange

of raw or cooked vegetables is 3oz. Do have at least 6oz daily, preferably more.
Artichokes
Asparagus
Aubergine
Bean Sprouts
★Beans, broad
Beans, green
★Beetroot
Broccoli
Brussels Sprouts
Cabbage
Carrots
Cauliflower
Celery
Courgettes
Cress
Cucumber
Leeks
Lettuce
Marrow
Mushrooms
Mange-tout
Onions
★Parsnips
★Peas
Peppers
Radishes
Sauerkraut
Spinach
Spring Onions
Swedes
Tomatoes
Turnips

★These vegetables are high in calories, so do not have more than 12oz weekly.

MILK DAILY EXCHANGES

Women...................... 2
Men 2
Teenagers............... 3 to 4

One Exchange

Milk, skimmed, 10fl oz (½ pint)
Milk, low-fat dry, 1oz
Buttermilk, 10fl oz (½ pint)
Yogurt, low-fat natural, 5fl oz (¼ pint)

Tea or coffee may be used in reasonable amounts with or without skimmed milk from the daily snacks or drinks on your Menu Plan.

BREAD DAILY EXCHANGES

Women...................2 to 3
Men ....4 to 5
Teenagers...............4 to 5

One Exchange
BREADS
Bagel, small, ½ (1oz)
Bread, any type, 1 slice (1oz)
Breadcrumbs, dried, 3 tablespoons
Bread rolls or baps, 1oz
Crispbreads, up to 80 calories
Crumpet, 1oz
Melba toast, up to 80 calories
Scone, plain, ¾oz
Scotch pancake, 1oz

BISCUITS
Cream Crackers, 2
Water, 2
Digestive, 1
Matzo, ¾oz

GRAINS
Barley, cooked, 2oz
Beans, canned or cooked, 3oz
Beans, lentils, peas, dried, 1oz
Cereal, not sugar coated, ¾oz
Cereal, uncooked, ¾oz
Corn on the cob, 1 medium
Corn, kernels, 3oz
Flour, ¾oz
Pasta, cooked (macaroni, noodles, spaghetti, etc.), 2oz
Potatoes, 3oz
Rice, cooked, 2oz

¾oz uncooked grains yields approximately 2oz when cooked.

FAT DAILY EXCHANGES

Women.......................3
Men 3
Teenagers....................3

One Exchange
Low-fat spread, 2 teaspoons
Margarine (high in polyunsaturates), 1 teaspoon
Mayonnaise, 1 teaspoon
Mayonnaise, low-calorie, 2 teaspoons
Salad Dressing, low-calorie, 4 teaspoons
Salad Dressing, any type, 2 teaspoons
Vegetable Oil, 1 teaspoon

PROTEIN DAILY EXCHANGES

Women..................6 to 8
Men ....8 to 10
Teenagers.............8 to 10

One Exchange
MEATS
★Beef, 1oz
Chicken, 1oz
★Corned Beef, 1oz
Fish, 1oz
★Frankfurter, 1oz
Game, 1oz
★Ham, 1oz
★Heart, 1oz
★Kidney, 1oz
★Lamb, 1oz
Liver, 1oz
★Liver Sausage, 1oz

★Luncheon Meat, 1oz
★Pork, 1oz
Rabbit, 1oz
★Sausage, beef/pork, 1oz
★Sweetbreads, 1oz
★Tongue, 1oz
Tripe, 1oz
Turkey, 1oz
Veal, 1oz

★Limit these meats to a combined total of 12oz weekly.

Liver is a good source of iron; have a main meal once a week.

FULL EXCHANGE LIST

One Exchange
DAIRY PRODUCTS
Cheese: low-fat soft, 2½oz
Hard, 1oz
Semisoft, 1oz

Do not have more than 4oz hard or semisoft cheese weekly.

OTHER PROTEINS
Beans, canned or cooked, 3oz
Beans, lentils, peas, dried, 1oz
Egg, 1
Peanut butter, 1 tablespoon
Tofu, 3oz

When Peanut butter is selected, because of its high fat content, for each tablespoon use one less Fat Exchange.

Do not have more than 7 eggs weekly.

PREPARED FOODS
These foods are built into the Full Exchange Plan to give variety. You may use one of them in place of your main course once a week. Each choice=4 Exchanges.

4 Fish Fingers (breadcrumbed), 1oz each
2 Fish Cakes (breadcrumbed), 2oz each
Lean back bacon (raw), 2oz
Boil-in-the-bag fish in sauce, 1 portion

OPTIONAL EXCHANGE LIST

DAILY:

You may select up to 50 calories from the foods listed below 5 days a week, and 150 calories on the other 2 days.

10 Calorie Foods

Anchovies	2 fillets
Bacon bits, imitation	1 teaspoon
Bran	1 tablespoon
Breadcrumbs, dried	1 teaspoon
Chewing gum	1 stick
Cocoa, unsweetened	1 teaspoon
Coconut, desiccated	1 teaspoon
Coffee whitener	1 teaspoon
Custard powder	1 teaspoon
Egg white	½
Flour, all types	1 teaspoon
Garlic puree	½ teaspoon
Gravy powder	1 teaspoon
Honey/syrup/treacle	½ teaspoon
Ketchup, tomato	2 teaspoons
Matzo meal	1 teaspoon
Olives, all types	2
Parmesan cheese, grated	1 teaspoon
Pickle, relish	1 teaspoon
Sauce: barbecue, chilli, brown	2 teaspoons
Seeds	½ teaspoon
Sugar, all varieties	½ teaspoon
Tomato puree	1 tablespoon
Vegetable, meat and yeast extract	1 teaspoon
Wheat germ	1 teaspoon
Wine for cooking	2 teaspoons

50 Calorie Foods

Chocolate sauce, spread or syrup	2 teaspoons
Chutney	1 tablespoon
Diet foods, e.g. drinks, jams, sauces, soups, and spreads	50 calories
Frozen whipped topping	3 tablespoons
Jams, jellies, marmalades	1 tablespoon
Sauces: cranberry, seafood, tartare, etc.	1 tablespoon

Exchanges

Bread	½ Exchange
Fat	1 Exchange
Fruit	1 Exchange
Milk	½ Exchange
Protein	1 Exchange

100 Calorie Foods

Avocado	¼ (2oz)
Bacon, lean, grilled	1oz raw
Beer, bitter or light ale	½ pint
Cider	½ pint
Cream, single	3 tablespoons
Coleslaw	2oz
Fruit	2 Exchanges
Ice cream, vanilla, chocolate or strawberry flavour	2oz
Jelly, fruit flavoured, prepared	¼ pint
Milk, whole	¼ pint
Sherry, dry/medium	3fl oz
Spirits	1½fl oz
Wine, red or white, or champagne	4fl oz
Whipped dessert topping	3 tablespoons

Seasonings, stock cubes, condiments, artificial sweeteners and gelatine may be used in reasonable amounts.

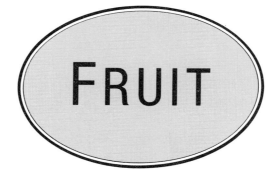

FRUIT

*C*olourful, delicious and naturally sweet, fruit adds variety to all our meals. Apples, pears and plums, for instance, make refreshing and satisfying desserts just as they are, but we've also given recipes for cooked puddings such as Pears with Blackcurrant Sauce and French Apple Pudding which are sure to become firm favourites. You will find ideas for using seasonal fruits such as melons and strawberries, and for those marvellously versatile dried fruits which will keep in the store cupboard all the year round.

— Meringue Pancakes —
with Fruit Custard Filling

SERVES 4

335 CALORIES PER SERVING

2oz (60g) low-fat dry milk, mixed with ½ pint (300ml) water

2 large eggs, separated

4 teaspoons sugar

2 teaspoons each cornflour and lemon juice

1lb 4oz (600g) bilberries or blackberries

8 pancakes (see 'Crepes Suzette' page 37)

Combine milk, egg yolks and 3 teaspoons sugar in medium saucepan and cook over very low heat, stirring constantly, until slightly thickened. Mix cornflour and lemon juice, gradually stir into milk mixture and cook, stirring constantly, until thick. Remove from heat and fold in bilberries or blackberries, reserving 8 berries for garnish. Cool. Spoon ⅛ of custard onto centre of each pancake and fold sides over filling to enclose. Arrange pancakes, seam-side down, in an 8 x 8 x 2-inch (20 x 20 x 5-cm) baking tin. Using electric mixer on high speed, beat egg whites until soft peaks form. Add remaining teaspoon sugar and continue beating until stiff but not dry. Pipe or spoon meringue over pancakes, dividing evenly. Top each with a reserved bilberry or blackberry and grill until meringue is lightly browned, 10 to 15 seconds. Serve immediately.

Each serving, including 'Crepes Suzette', provides: 1 Protein Exchange, 1 Bread Exchange, 2 Fat Exchanges, 1 Fruit Exchange, ¾ Milk Exchange, 40 Calories Optional Exchange

— Fruity Honey Loaf —

SERVES 16

136 CALORIES PER SERVING

8oz (240g) sultanas

4 fresh dates, stoned and chopped

6oz (180g) dried apricots, chopped

½ pint (300ml) strong cold tea

4 tablespoons clear honey

9oz (270g) wholemeal flour

1 teaspoon mixed spice

1 tablespoon baking powder

1 large egg

Soak fruit overnight in strong tea and honey. Add flour, mixed spice, baking powder and egg and mix thoroughly. Spoon into 2-lb (960-g) non-stick loaf tin and bake on centre shelf of oven at 300°F, 150°C, Gas Mark 2 for 1¼ hours. Leave for 5 minutes before turning out onto a wire rack and leaving to cool.

Each serving provides: ¾ Bread Exchange, 1 Fruit Exchange, 20 Calories Optional Exchange

— Pears with —
Blackcurrant Sauce

SERVES 4

100 CALORIES PER SERVING

4 medium pears, peeled (leave stems attached)

4 tablespoons water

2 tablespoons thawed frozen concentrated orange juice

2 teaspoons margarine, melted

2-inch (5-cm) cinnamon stick, broken in half

5oz (150g) blackcurrants

1 tablespoon water

1 teaspoon each sugar, cornflour and lemon juice

Preheat oven to 350°F, 180°C, Gas Mark 4. Arrange pears on their sides in shallow casserole. Mix water, orange juice and margarine and pour over fruit. Add cinnamon stick and bake until pears are tender, 20 to 30 minutes, basting occasionally and turning pears over once after 15 minutes. Using slotted spoon, transfer each pear, stem up, to a dessert dish. Strain cooking liquid and reserve. Mix cooking liquid with blackcurrants in small saucepan and bring to the boil. Mix water, cornflour and lemon juice in a cup, stirring well. Add to saucepan and, stirring constantly, bring to the boil. Reduce heat and cook, stirring frequently, until slightly thickened. To serve, pour ¼ of blackcurrant sauce over each pear.

Each serving provides: ½ Fat Exchange, 1½ Fruit Exchanges, 10 Calories Optional Exchange

— Strawberry Log —

SERVES 8

155 CALORIES PER SERVING

3oz (90g) flour

1 teaspoon baking powder

½ teaspoon salt

4 large eggs

8 teaspoons caster sugar

1lb 4oz (600g) strawberries, roughly chopped

½ teaspoon lemon juice

2 tablespoons strawberry jam, melted

12 tablespoons whipped dessert topping

Preheat oven to 400°F, 200°C, Gas Mark 6. Line a 12 x 9 x 1-inch (30 x 20 x 2.5-cm) swiss roll tin with greaseproof paper and set aside. Sift flour, baking powder and salt together twice and set aside. Using electric mixer on high speed, beat eggs with sugar until thick and light in colour, about 5 minutes. Very lightly fold in sifted ingredients. Spoon the mixture into paper-lined tin and bake towards the top of the oven until golden, 9 to 10 minutes (top should spring back when touched lightly with finger). Remove from oven and turn cake onto damp tea towel. Remove and discard paper. Take new sheet of greaseproof paper and lay over cake. Starting at narrow end, roll up with the tea towel. Cool on wire rack. Mix chopped strawberries with melted jam. Carefully unroll cooled cake, remove towel and spread strawberry mixture over cake surface. Roll cake up again and place, seam-side down, on serving dish. Swirl the whipped dessert topping over top and sides of log. To serve, cut into 8 equal slices.

Each serving provides: ½ Protein Exchange, ½ Bread Exchange, ½ Fruit Exchange, 65 Calories Optional Exchange

•

— Strawberries Marsala —

SERVES 1

75 CALORIES PER SERVING

5oz (150g) strawberries

1 teaspoon Marsala wine or sweet sherry

½ teaspoon sugar

dash lemon juice

1 tablespoon whipped dessert topping

Mix all ingredients except whipped dessert topping and toss to coat strawberries. Cover and refrigerate 3 to 4 hours before serving. To serve, transfer fruit mixture to dessert dish and top with whipped dessert topping.

Each serving provides: 1 Fruit Exchange, 35 Calories Optional Exchange

•

— Chocolate Figs with — Ice Cream

SERVES 2

140 CALORIES PER SERVING

2 large fresh figs, stems removed

2 tablespoons water

2 strips orange peel

1 teaspoon each unsweetened cocoa and icing sugar

4oz (120g) vanilla ice cream

Place figs in small shallow baking dish just large enough to hold them, add water and orange peel and bake at 375°F, 190°C, Gas Mark 5 until figs are soft to the touch but still hold their shape, about 15 minutes. Sift together cocoa and sugar, roll warm figs in cocoa mixture, then cut each fig in half. For each portion serve 2 fig halves with 2oz (60g) ice cream. Divide remaining cocoa mixture and cooking liquid from figs and spoon half over each serving.

Each serving provides: 1 Fruit Exchange, 115 Calories Optional Exchange

— Frozen Strawberry — Souffle

SERVES 4

140 CALORIES PER SERVING

10oz (300g) fresh strawberries or frozen strawberries, just thawed

8oz (240g) vanilla ice cream, softened

2 tablespoons thawed frozen concentrated orange juice

2 egg whites, at room temperature

pinch cream of tartar or salt

2 teaspoons sugar

Liquidise 7oz (210g) strawberries in blender or food processor with ice cream and thawed orange juice until smooth. Spoon into a bowl and set aside. Using electric mixer on high speed, beat egg whites with cream of tartar until soft peaks form, add sugar and continue beating until peaks form once again. Fold ⅓ of egg whites into strawberry mixture until combined, then gently fold in remaining egg whites. Spoon mixture into 4 freezer-proof dessert dishes, cover with cling film and freeze until firm. Remove from freezer 5 minutes before serving. To serve, decorate with remaining strawberries.

Each serving provides: ¾ Fruit Exchange, 120 Calories Optional Exchange

•

Top: Strawberry Log
Centre: Strawberries Marsala
Bottom: Frozen Strawberry Souffle

— Miniature Fruit — Crescents

SERVES 4

160 CALORIES PER SERVING

1½oz (45g) flour

pinch salt

4 teaspoons margarine

2 tablespoons low-fat natural yogurt

2 large prunes, stoned and finely chopped

3oz (90g) sultanas, finely chopped

2 teaspoons each sugar and apricot jam

1 teaspoon icing sugar, sifted

1 tablespoon flour for rolling out pastry

Mix flour and salt in mixing bowl and rub in margarine until mixture resembles breadcrumbs. Add yogurt and mix well. Form dough into a ball, wrap in cling film and refrigerate for at least 1 hour (may be kept in refrigerator for up to 3 days). Preheat oven to 400°F, 200°C, Gas Mark 6. Use extra tablespoon of flour to flour board and sprinkle on dough before rolling. Roll dough to form a circle about ⅛ inch (3 mm) thick. Cut into 12 equal wedges. Mix together all remaining ingredients except icing sugar. Spoon an equal amount of mixture (about ¼ teaspoon) onto each wedge near curved end. Roll each from curved end towards point and place on non-stick baking sheet, point-side down. Bake until golden brown, 18 to 20 minutes. Remove crescents to wire rack to cool. Just before serving, sprinkle each with an equal amount of icing sugar.

Each serving provides: ½ Bread Exchange, 1 Fat Exchange, 1 Fruit Exchange, 35 Calories Optional Exchange

— Orange-Pineapple — Delight

SERVES 2

190 CALORIES PER SERVING

1 tablespoon unflavoured gelatine

4fl oz (120ml) orange juice

4oz (120g) canned crushed pineapple, no sugar added

4fl oz (120ml) water

4 teaspoons orange marmalade

10fl oz (300ml) low-fat natural yogurt

2 teaspoons sugar

Sprinkle gelatine over orange juice in small saucepan and let stand to soften. Stir over very low heat until gelatine is completely dissolved. Remove from heat and add crushed pineapple, water and marmalade. Mix well. Add yogurt and sugar and mix quickly and thoroughly to disperse gelatine. Divide mixture between 2 small dessert dishes, cover and refrigerate 3 to 4 hours or until set.

Each serving provides: 1 Fruit Exchange, 1 Milk Exchange, 55 Calories Optional Exchange

— Cherry-Apple Crumble —

SERVES 4

115 CALORIES PER SERVING

2 slices currant bread, made into crumbs

2 teaspoons each sugar and margarine

pinch cinnamon

8oz (240g) cherries, stoned

2 medium apples, cored, peeled and sliced

4 tablespoons water

1-inch (2.5-cm) cinnamon stick

1 teaspoon cornflour

Combine crumbs, 1 teaspoon sugar, margarine and ground cinnamon. Set aside. Place fruit in small saucepan with 3 tablespoons water and the cinnamon stick. Cook over low heat for about 3 minutes. Mix remaining tablespoon water with cornflour, add to pan and cook, stirring constantly, until mixture thickens. Remove from heat. Remove and discard cinnamon stick and stir in remaining teaspoon sugar. Divide fruit mixture between 4 individual ovenproof dishes. Top each with ¼ of crumb mixture. Bake at 400°F, 200°C, Gas Mark 6 until topping is browned, about 15 minutes. Serve warm.

Each serving provides: ½ Bread Exchange, ½ Fat Exchange, 1 Fruit Exchange, 15 Calories Optional Exchange

— Banana-Orange — Cocktail

SERVES 2

70 CALORIES PER SERVING

1 medium banana, peeled

2 tablespoons thawed frozen concentrated orange juice

2 teaspoons fresh lime or lemon juice

1 teaspoon sugar

¼ teaspoon rum flavouring

4 ice cubes, crushed

Chill two large tumblers. Place all ingredients except ice in blender and process until smooth. With motor running, gradually add ice, blending until all ice is crushed and mixture is thick and frothy. Pour into chilled glasses and serve immediately.

Each serving provides: 1½ Fruit Exchanges, 10 Calories Optional Exchange

— Ice Cream with —
Sugar-Coated Bananas

SERVES 2

185 CALORIES PER SERVING

1 medium banana

1 tablespoon lemon juice

2 teaspoons margarine

1 teaspoon brown sugar

pinch cinnamon

dash rum flavouring

4oz (120g) vanilla ice cream

Peel banana and cut in half lengthwise, then cut each piece in half crosswise. Sprinkle banana quarters with lemon juice and set aside. Heat margarine in small frying pan, add brown sugar, cinnamon and flavouring and cook over low heat, stirring constantly, until sugar melts. Remove from heat. Using a wooden spoon, roll banana pieces in sugar mixture. Divide ice cream evenly between 2 champagne glasses. Top each portion with 2 banana quarters and half of any remaining sugar mixture.

Each serving provides: 1 Fat Exchange, ½ Fruit Exchange, 110 Calories Optional Exchange

●

— Cinnamon-Apricot —
Bananas

SERVES 2

255 CALORIES PER SERVING

4 digestive biscuits, made into crumbs

2 teaspoons desiccated coconut

¼ teaspoon cinnamon

4 teaspoons apricot jam

1 medium banana, peeled and cut in half lengthwise

Combine crumbs, coconut and cinnamon in small frying pan and toast lightly, being careful not to burn. Transfer to sheet of greaseproof paper and set aside. Warm apricot jam in the same pan and remove from heat. Roll each banana half in jam then quickly roll in crumb mixture, pressing crumbs so that they adhere to banana. Place coated halves on plate, cover and chill lightly in refrigerator before serving.

Each serving provides: 2 Bread Exchanges, ½ Fruit Exchange, 45 Calories Optional Exchange

●

— Melon Ice Cream —

SERVES 4

110 CALORIES PER SERVING

8oz (240g) vanilla ice cream

10oz (300g) chunks very ripe melon

Allow ice cream to soften slightly. Puree melon flesh in blender or food processor. Add softened ice cream and blend until smooth. Turn into freezer container, cover and freeze until firm. Break mixture into pieces and blend again until smooth. Divide between 4 freezer-proof dessert dishes, cover with cling film and freeze again until firm. Remove from freezer 5 minutes before serving.

Each serving provides: ½ Fruit Exchange, 100 Calories Optional Exchange

— Chilled Cherry Soup —

SERVES 2

105 CALORIES PER SERVING

8oz (240g) cherries, stoned

4fl oz (120ml) water

2 teaspoons sugar

2-inch (5-cm) cinnamon stick

1 strip lemon peel

2 tablespoons rose wine

1 teaspoon cornflour

2½fl oz (75ml) low-fat natural yogurt

Place cherries in small saucepan with the water, sugar, cinnamon stick and lemon peel and bring to the boil. Reduce heat, cover and simmer for 20 minutes. Remove and discard cinnamon stick and lemon peel from cherry mixture. Mix wine and cornflour, add to cherry mixture and bring to the boil, stirring constantly. Reduce heat and simmer until mixture thickens. Cool. Transfer cherry mixture to a bowl and stir in yogurt. Cover with cling film and refrigerate until well chilled.

Each serving provides: 1 Fruit Exchange, ¼ Milk Exchange, 40 Calories Optional Exchange

●

33

— Meringue Fruit Cups —

SERVES 4

55 CALORIES PER SERVING

2 medium oranges, cut crosswise into halves

5oz (150g) strawberries, sliced

3oz (90g) seedless green grapes, cut into halves

1 egg white, at room temperature

2 teaspoons sugar

½ teaspoon vanilla flavouring

Working over small bowl to catch juice and using a curved serrated knife, if available, remove orange sections, cut away skin and membrane and mix orange sections with the juice, reserving the skins to make 'cups'. Add strawberries and grapes to orange sections and toss lightly to combine. Spoon ¼ of fruit mixture into each 'cup' and set aside. Beat egg white using electric mixer on high speed, gradually adding sugar and vanilla, until stiff peaks form. Spoon ¼ of meringue onto each filled fruit cup. Transfer to grill pan and grill until meringue is golden, 10 to 15 seconds. Serve immediately.

Each serving provides: 1 Fruit Exchange, 15 Calories Optional Exchange

•

— Glazed Cinnamon — Grapefruit

SERVES 1

25 CALORIES PER SERVING

½ medium grapefruit

½ teaspoon honey

pinch cinnamon

Remove seeds from grapefruit, using the point of a sharp knife. Cut round each section to loosen and separate from membrane and skin. Place grapefruit half in small shallow fireproof dish. Spoon honey into centre of fruit, sprinkle lightly with cinnamon and grill 3 inches (8 cm) from heat for 8 to 10 minutes or until honey has melted and fruit is lightly browned.

Each serving provides: 1 Fruit Exchange, 10 Calories Optional Exchange

•

— Orange Baked Alaska —

SERVES 2

125 CALORIES PER SERVING

Orange Filling

1 medium orange, cut in half crosswise

2oz (60g) vanilla ice cream, softened

Meringue

4 teaspoons orange marmalade

1 egg white, at room temperature

2 teaspoons caster sugar

To Prepare Filling: Remove orange sections from skins, working over small bowl to catch juice and using a curved serrated knife if available. Cut away and discard skin and membrane and mix orange sections with juice. Reserve orange skins to make 'cups'. Stir softened ice cream into fruit and divide mixture into orange 'cups'. Cover with cling film and freeze until hard, about 1 hour.

To Prepare Meringue and Bake: Just before serving, warm marmalade in small cup standing in pan of boiling water. Preheat grill. In small mixing bowl, using electric mixer on high speed, beat egg white, gradually adding sugar, until stiff peaks form. Gently fold in marmalade. Remove filled orange halves from freezer and top each with half the meringue. Transfer to grill pan and grill until meringue is golden, 10 to 15 seconds. Serve immediately.

Each serving provides: ½ Fruit Exchange, 115 Calories Optional Exchange

•

— Iced Orange-Wine — Punch

SERVES 8

85 CALORIES PER SERVING

Ice Ring

soda water

1 lemon, sliced

1 lime, sliced

Punch

1 pint 12fl oz (960ml) each chilled orange juice, soda water and low-calorie ginger ale

16fl oz (480ml) dry white wine

lemon and lime slices, halved

sprigs of mint and ice cubes

To Prepare Ice Ring: Fill a large ring mould with soda water and top with lemon and lime slices in alternating pattern. Cover, transfer carefully to freezer and freeze until solid.

To Prepare Punch: Mix orange juice, soda water, low-calorie ginger ale and wine in a large punch bowl. Turn out ice mould and float in the punch. Decorate punch with halved lemon and lime slices and ice cubes. Garnish ice ring with mint sprigs.

Each serving provides: 1 Fruit Exchange, 55 Calories Optional Exchange

Iced Orange-Wine Punch

— Coconut-Topped Mixed — Fruit

SERVES 4

70 CALORIES PER SERVING

1 medium orange

5oz (150g) melon balls

1 medium banana, peeled and sliced

1 tablespoon lemon juice

½ teaspoon almond flavouring

4 teaspoons desiccated coconut, toasted

Working over a bowl to catch juice, remove skin and membrane from orange and section orange into bowl. Add melon balls, banana slices, lemon juice and flavouring. Toss gently to combine. Divide into 4 dessert dishes and sprinkle each portion with ¼ of toasted coconut.

Each serving provides: 1 Fruit Exchange, 10 Calories Optional Exchange

•

— Chocolate-Topped — Pears

SERVES 4

120 CALORIES PER SERVING

4 teaspoons each unsweetened cocoa and sugar

2 teaspoons cornflour

2oz (60g) low-fat dry milk, mixed with ½ pint (300ml) water

¼ teaspoon vanilla flavouring

8 canned pear halves, no sugar added

Mix cocoa, sugar and cornflour in small saucepan, gradually add 4 tablespoons milk and stir until sugar is completely dissolved. Add remaining milk and vanilla and cook over moderate heat, stirring constantly, until mixture comes to the boil. Continue to stir and cook until sauce thickens, about 2 minutes longer.

Remove from heat, pour into a small bowl and let cool. Cover with cling film and refrigerate until chilled. To serve, place 2 pear halves in each of 4 dessert dishes and top each portion with ¼ of the sauce.

Each serving provides: 1 Fruit Exchange, ½ Milk Exchange, 335 Calories Optional Exchange

•

— Pear Crumble —

SERVES 2

175 CALORIES PER SERVING

4 canned pear halves with 4 tablespoons juice, no sugar added

1 teaspoon cornflour

pinch ground cloves

2 slices currant bread, made into crumbs

1 teaspoon brown sugar

2 teaspoons margarine

Preheat oven to 400°F, 200°C, Gas Mark 6. Arrange pear halves, cut side down, in a casserole just large enough to hold them. Mix cornflour with the pear juice, pour over pears and sprinkle with cloves. Mix crumbs and sugar, add margarine and combine thoroughly. Sprinkle mixture over pears and bake until crumbs are golden, about 15 minutes.

Each serving provides: 1 Bread Exchange, 1 Fat Exchange, 1 Fruit Exchange, 15 Calories Optional Exchange

•

— Wine-Baked Plums —

SERVES 4

75 CALORIES PER SERVING

8 medium-sweet red plums, cut into halves and stoned

4 tablespoons dry red wine

1 tablespoon brown sugar

2 cinnamon sticks, broken into halves

3 tablespoons thawed, frozen whipped topping

Preheat oven to 350°F, 180°C, Gas Mark 4. Arrange plums in a casserole in a single layer, cut side down. Mix wine and sugar and stir until sugar is dissolved. Pour over fruit and add cinnamon sticks to casserole. Cover and bake until plums are soft, about 30 minutes. Remove and discard cinnamon sticks, peel plums and discard skin. Place 4 plum halves in each of 4 small dessert dishes, spoon ¼ of the cooking liquid over each portion and top with whipped topping, dividing topping evenly.

Each serving provides: 1 Fruit Exchange, 45 Calories Optional Exchange

•

— Fruit and Honey — Truffles

SERVES 2

140 CALORIES PER SERVING

2oz (60g) raisins, finely chopped

2 large dried figs, finely chopped

½ teaspoon mixed spice

1 teaspoon honey

½ teaspoon lemon juice

2 teaspoons sunflower seeds, finely crushed or ground in electric grinder

Mix raisins, figs and mixed spice and roll into 10 small balls, each about 1 inch (2.5 cm) in diameter. Place honey and lemon juice in a cup standing in pan of boiling water and stir until honey melts. Remove from heat and immediately roll each fruit ball in honey-lemon mixture, then in crushed sunflower seeds to coat. Arrange on plate, cover and refrigerate until chilled.

Each serving provides: 2 Fruit Exchanges, 30 Calories Optional Exchange

— Grape and Strawberry — Jelly

SERVES 4

115 CALORIES PER SERVING

1 tablespoon unflavoured gelatine

2 teaspoons caster sugar

4fl oz (120ml) water

8fl oz (240ml) dry white wine

1 tablespoon lemon juice

10oz (300g) strawberries, cut into small pieces

6oz (180g) small seedless green grapes

1 teaspoon vegetable oil

lemon and lime slices for garnish

Mix gelatine and sugar. Pour water into small saucepan, sprinkle in gelatine mixture and let stand for about 5 minutes to soften. Stir over low heat until gelatine is completely dissolved. Pour into bowl and stir in wine and lemon juice. Cover and refrigerate until syrupy. Lightly oil a jelly mould with the vegetable oil. Fold strawberries and grapes into syrupy gelatine mixture and pour into mould. Cover and refrigerate until firm. To serve, turn out onto serving dish and surround with lemon and lime slices.

Each serving provides: ¼ Fat Exchange, 1 Fruit Exchange, 120 Calories Optional Exchange

— Apple-Raisin Cake —

SERVES 12

185 CALORIES PER SERVING

9oz (270g) self-raising flour

1 teaspoon cinnamon

½ teaspoon ground cloves

4 tablespoons margarine

2 tablespoons sugar

1 teaspoon baking powder

12oz (360g) canned apple slices, no sugar added, pureed

2 medium eating apples, cored, peeled and grated

7oz (210g) raisins

Sift flour, cinnamon and cloves together in mixing bowl and set aside. Preheat oven to 350°F, 180°C, Gas Mark 4. Cream margarine in mixing bowl, using electric mixer. Add sugar and stir to combine. Stir baking powder into apple, then add to margarine mixture and stir to combine. Add sifted ingredients and, using electric mixer on medium speed, beat until thoroughly combined. Fold in grated apples and raisins, pour batter into 8 x 8 x 2-inch (20 x 20 x 5-cm) non-stick baking tin and bake for 45 to 50 minutes (until cake is browned and a metal skewer inserted in centre comes out clean). Remove cake from tin and cool on wire rack.

Each serving provides: 1 Bread Exchange, 1 Fat Exchange, 1 Fruit Exchange, 10 Calories Optional Exchange

— 'Crepes Suzette' —

SERVES 4

240 CALORIES PER SERVING

Pancakes

½ pint (300ml) skimmed milk

3oz (90g) flour

2 eggs

2 teaspoons vegetable oil

Sauce

2 tablespoons margarine

1 tablespoon sugar

8fl oz (240ml) orange juice

2fl oz (60ml) thawed frozen concentrated orange juice

1 teaspoon brandy flavouring

To Prepare Pancakes: Place milk, flour and eggs in blender container and blend until smooth. Let stand for 15 minutes. Transfer batter to measuring jug. Wipe 6-inch (15-cm) non-stick frying pan lightly with vegetable oil. Heat pan gently on moderate heat and pour in ⅛ of the batter, twisting pan so that batter spreads and covers the base. Cook over medium-high heat until edges and underside are dry. Using palette 'knife, carefully turn pancake over. Cook other side briefly just to dry, about 30 seconds. Slide pancakes on to a plate. Repeat procedure 7 times, using remaining vegetable oil and batter and making 7 more pancakes.

To Prepare Sauce: Melt margarine in large non-stick frying pan, add sugar and stir until dissolved. Stir in orange juice, concentrated orange juice and flavouring and bring mixture to the boil. Reduce heat to low.

To Prepare 'Crepes Suzette': Add 1 pancake to pan, coating both sides with sauce, fold in half, then fold again to create triangular shape. Slide to side of pan and repeat procedure with remaining pancakes. Serve immediately.

Each serving provides: ½ Protein Exchange, 1 Bread Exchange, 2 Fat Exchanges, 1 Fruit Exchange, ¼ Milk Exchange, 15 Calories Optional Exchange

— Orange-Iced — Carrot-Raisin Cake

SERVES 12

255 CALORIES PER SERVING

Cake

6 tablespoons margarine, softened

9oz (270g) flour

4 tablespoons caster sugar

1 tablespoon baking powder

6oz (180g) carrots, grated

4oz (120g) raisins, soaked in warm water until plumped, then drained

1 teaspoon cinnamon

4 eggs, separated

pinch salt or cream of tartar

2fl oz (60ml) thawed frozen concentrated orange juice

1 teaspoon vanilla flavouring

Icing

2 tablespoons sugar

1 tablespoon unflavoured gelatine

2fl oz (60ml) thawed frozen concentrated orange juice

10oz (300g) firm low-fat soft cheese

To Prepare Cake: Grease two 8-inch (20-cm) round sandwich tins with ½ teaspoon margarine each, sprinkle each with 1 teaspoon flour and set aside. Preheat oven to 325°F, 160°C, Gas Mark 3. Cream together margarine and sugar, beat in egg yolks, vanilla and orange juice. Stir in carrots and raisins. Sieve together flour, baking powder and cinnamon. Whisk egg whites with salt or cream of tartar until softly peaking. Fold half the flour into the margarine and egg yolk mixture, fold half the egg whites lightly into the mixture, repeat procedure with remaining flour and egg whites. Spoon mixture equally into sandwich tins. Level top and bake 35 to 40 minutes or until a skewer, inserted in centre, comes out clean. Let cakes cool in tins for 5 minutes, then remove to wire rack to cool.

To Prepare Icing: Sprinkle sugar and gelatine over juice in a small saucepan and let stand to soften. Stir over low heat until dissolved. Process cheese in blender container until smooth. Remove centre of blender cover and, with motor running, gradually add gelatine mixture, processing just until combined. Transfer icing to a bowl, cover, and refrigerate until mixture is thick but not firm. Immediately spread a thin layer of icing over top of one cake. Top with second cake and spread remaining icing over top and sides of entire cake. When beginning to set, roughen icing with prongs of fork. Cover lightly and refrigerate until icing is firm. To serve, cut into 12 equal slices.

Each serving provides: 1 Bread Exchange, ½ Vegetable Exchange, 1½ Fat Exchanges, 95 Calories Optional Exchange

— Poached Apples with — Honey and Lemon

SERVES 2

65 CALORIES PER SERVING

2 medium apples

2 teaspoons lemon juice

6fl oz (180ml) water

2-inch (5-cm) strip lemon peel

2 teaspoons honey

1 teaspoon vanilla flavouring

Core and peel apples, cut into thin wedges and place in bowl with water to cover. Add 1 teaspoon lemon juice and set aside. Bring water to the boil with the lemon peel in a small saucepan and cook for 5 minutes. Drain apples and add to saucepan with honey, vanilla and remaining teaspoon lemon juice. Cook until apples are tender, 8 to 10 minutes. Remove and discard lemon peel. Serve apple wedges warm or chilled in poaching liquid.

Each serving provides: 1 Fruit Exchange, 20 Calories Optional Exchange

— Apricot-Banana Muffin —

SERVES 2

170 CALORIES PER SERVING

1 medium banana

1 muffin (2oz/60g), split in half and toasted

2 teaspoons each margarine, melted, and apricot jam, warmed

cinnamon

Peel banana and cut in half crosswise, then cut each piece in half lengthwise. Place muffin halves on grill pan or on a sheet of foil. Top each with 2 banana quarters and dot with half the melted margarine. Brush each banana quarter with ½ teaspoon apricot jam and sprinkle with pinch of cinnamon. Grill until hot.

Each serving provides: 1 Bread Exchange, 1 Fat Exchange, 1 Fruit Exchange, 20 Calories Optional Exchange

Orange-Iced Carrot-Raisin Cake

—French Apple— Pudding

SERVES 4

280 CALORIES PER SERVING

4 eggs

¼ pint (150ml) skimmed milk

3 tablespoons thawed, frozen whipped topping

2 teaspoons vanilla flavouring

¼ teaspoon each cinnamon and nutmeg

3oz (90g) self raising flour

2 tablespoons sugar

1 teaspoon margarine

4 medium apples, cored, peeled and thinly sliced

1 tablespoon lemon juice

Preheat oven to 375°F, 190°C, Gas Mark 5. Combine eggs, milk, whipped topping, vanilla, cinnamon and nutmeg in mixing bowl. Beat until smooth using an electric mixer. Gradually beat in flour and sugar and continue beating until mixture is thick and smooth. Grease 10-inch (25-cm) pie plate with margarine. Arrange apple slices on plate in a single layer and sprinkle with lemon juice. Pour batter over fruit and bake until browned, 35 to 40 minutes.

Each serving provides: 1 Protein Exchange, 1 Bread Exchange, 1 Fruit Exchange, 60 Calories Optional Exchange

•

— Spiced Fruit Compote —

SERVES 2

225 CALORIES PER SERVING

Pastry Topping

¾oz (20g) flour

pinch salt

2 teaspoons margarine

1 tablespoon low-fat natural yogurt

1 tablespoon flour for rolling pastry

Fruit Mixture

1oz (30g) dried apricot halves, chopped

1oz (30g) raisins

1 large dried fig, chopped

1 teaspoon each brown sugar and lemon juice

¼ teaspoon mixed spice

1 medium apple, cored, peeled, chopped and sprinkled with lemon juice

To Prepare Pastry Topping: Mix flour and salt and rub in margarine until mixture resembles coarse bread-crumbs. Add yogurt and mix until thoroughly combined. Form dough into a ball, wrap in cling film and refrigerate for about 1 hour (may be kept in refrigerator for up to 3 days).

To Prepare Fruit Mixture: Place all ingredients except apple in small saucepan and cook over low heat, stirring constantly, until sugar begins to melt and glaze fruit mixture slightly. If necessary, add about 1 tablespoon water to keep fruit from burning. Simmer until fruit softens and raisins are plump, about 5 minutes. Add apple and stir to combine.

To Prepare Compote: Preheat oven to 400°F, 200°C, Gas Mark 6. Divide fruit mixture into 2 small ovenproof dishes. Use extra tablespoon flour to flour board and sprinkle on dough before rolling. Roll dough to about ⅛-inch (3-mm) thickness. Place one half on top of each portion of fruit mixture, moulding dough to inside edges of dish. Bake until topping is golden brown, about 20 minutes.

Each serving provides: ½ Bread Exchange, 1 Fat Exchange, 2 Fruit Exchanges, 40 Calories Optional Exchange

•

— Apple Pastry —

SERVES 1

320 CALORIES PER SERVING

¾oz (20g) flour

pinch salt

2 teaspoons margarine

1 tablespoon low-fat natural yogurt

1 tablespoon flour, for rolling out pastry

1 medium apple

pinch each nutmeg and cinnamon

2 teaspoons apricot jam

Combine flour and salt in mixing bowl and rub in margarine until mixture resembles coarse bread-crumbs. Add yogurt and mix thoroughly. Form dough into a ball, wrap in cling film and refrigerate for at least 1 hour (may be kept in refrigerator for up to 3 days). Use extra tablespoon flour to flour board and sprinkle on dough before rolling to form a 4½-inch (11-cm) circle about ⅛ inch (3 mm) thick. Place dough on foil or small baking sheet. Preheat oven to 350°F, 180°C, Gas Mark 4. Core, peel and thinly slice apple. Arrange slices decoratively over dough and sprinkle with nutmeg and cinnamon. Bake until crust is golden, 20 to 30 minutes. During last few minutes of cooking time, heat jam in a cup standing in saucepan of boiling water. When pastry is cooked, remove from oven and brush with warm jam.

Each serving provides: 1 Bread Exchange, 2 Fat Exchanges, 1 Fruit Exchange, 70 Calories Optional Exchange

•

— Baked Stuffed Apples — with Custard Sauce

SERVES 4

140 CALORIES PER SERVING

Stuffed Apples

5oz (150g) blackberries

1oz (30g) currants

2 teaspoons sugar

3 teaspoons lemon juice

pinch cinnamon

4 medium eating apples, cored

2fl oz water

Sauce

1oz (30g) low-fat dry milk, mixed with ¼ pint (150ml) water

1 egg

2 teaspoons sugar

¼ teaspoon vanilla flavouring

To Prepare Apples: Combine blackberries, currants, sugar, 1 teaspoon lemon juice and the cinnamon in small saucepan and bring to the boil. Cook, stirring occasionally, until blackberries are soft, about 3 minutes. Let cool. Preheat oven to 375°F, 190°C, Gas Mark 5. Starting at stem end of each apple, peel about ⅓ of the way down. Brush peeled section of each with ½ teaspoon lemon juice to prevent discoloration. Stuff each apple with ¼ of the blackberry mixture, heaping any mixture left over on top of apples. Set apples in baking tin just large enough to hold them upright. Add water. Cover with foil and bake until apples are tender, 45 to 50 minutes. Let cool to room temperature or cool slightly, cover and refrigerate until required.

To Prepare Sauce: Heat milk to simmering point. Beat egg with sugar until thoroughly combined and gradually beat in milk. Pour mixture into top half of double boiler and stir in vanilla. Cook over hot (not boiling) water, stirring constantly, until sauce is thick enough to coat the back of a spoon. Pour sauce into a bowl, cover with cling film and refrigerate until required. Serve ¼ of the sauce over each stuffed apple.

Each serving provides: 1½ Fruit Exchanges, ¼ Milk Exchange, 35 Calories Optional Exchange

•

VEGETABLES

Greengrocers' shops and supermarkets these days carry produce from all over the world as well as our own seasonal vegetables, so be adventurous. How about Braised Jerusalem Artichokes or Mushroom-Cheese Pate, for instance? Or delicious Ratatouille and Antipasto? Just stick to the golden rules: buy fresh, use as soon as possible or keep refrigerated, and never ill-treat vegetables by over-cooking.

— Olive-Stuffed — Tomatoes

SERVES 2

100 CALORIES PER SERVING

2 large tomatoes, each 6oz (180g)

2 teaspoons margarine

2 tablespoons each chopped onion and green pepper

4 large pimento-stuffed green olives, chopped

4 teaspoons breadcrumbs

pinch each salt and pepper

Cut thin slices from stem end of each tomato and scoop out pulp, reserving shells. Set shells upside-down on paper towels and let drain. Drain off excess liquid from pulp, chop and set aside. Heat margarine in non-stick frying pan, add onion and green pepper and saute until soft. Add reserved tomato pulp, cook until all moisture has evaporated and remove from heat. Preheat oven to 375°F, 190°C, Gas Mark 5. Add olives, breadcrumbs, salt and pepper to tomato pulp mixture and stir to combine. Spoon ¼ of mixture into each reserved tomato shell. Place stuffed tomatoes in shallow ovenproof dish just large enough to hold them upright and bake until tomatoes are soft, 25 to 30 minutes.

Each serving provides: 2½ Vegetable Exchanges, 1 Fat Exchange, 30 Calories Optional Exchange

•

— Asparagus Pancakes — 'Hollandaise'

SERVES 2

305 CALORIES PER SERVING

Pancakes

¼ pint (150ml) skimmed milk

1½oz (45g) flour

1 egg

1 teaspoon vegetable oil

12oz (360g) frozen, cooked or canned asparagus spears

'Hollandaise'

1 egg

1 tablespoon margarine, melted (warm)

1 tablespoon lemon juice

pinch each salt and cayenne pepper

To Prepare Pancakes: Place first 3 ingredients in blender and process until smooth, about 30 seconds. Let batter rest for about 15 minutes. Wipe 6-inch (15-cm) non-stick frying pan lightly with vegetable oil and heat pan briefly. Pour ¼ of batter into hot pan, quickly tilting pan to coat entire bottom with batter. Cook until underside of pancake is lightly browned and edges are dry. Turn carefully with palette knife and cook other side briefly, about 30 seconds. Slide pancake on to plate and repeat procedure 3 more times, using remaining oil and batter and making 3 more pancakes. Preheat oven to 350°F, 180°C, Gas Mark 4. Divide asparagus spears between pancakes and arrange so that some of the tips show at either end. Fold pancakes over to enclose asparagus and place seam-side down in casserole just large enough to hold them in 1 layer. Bake for 10 minutes.

To Prepare Sauce: Just before serving, process egg at high speed in blender until thick and lemon coloured. With motor running, slowly add margarine and continue processing until mixture is thickened. Add lemon juice and seasonings, processing briefly to blend. Pour sauce over hot pancakes and serve immediately.

Each serving provides: 1 Protein Exchange, 1 Bread Exchange, 2 Vegetable Exchanges, 2 Fat Exchanges, ¼ Milk Exchange

•

— Marinated Pepper — Salad

SERVES 2

65 CALORIES PER SERVING

2 teaspoons olive oil

2oz (60g) onion, thinly sliced

1 garlic clove, crushed

4oz (120g) each green and red peppers, seeded and thinly sliced

2 teaspoons wine vinegar

1½ teaspoons drained capers

½ teaspoon salt

pinch each oregano and pepper

artificial sweetener to equal ½ teaspoon sugar

Heat oil in non-stick frying pan, add onion and garlic and saute briefly (just until onion is tender-crisp). Add sliced peppers, toss lightly, cover and cook until peppers are tender-crisp, 3 to 5 minutes. Transfer vegetable mixture to salad bowl, add remaining ingredients and toss. Cover and chill lightly in refrigerator if not for immediate use.

Each serving provides: 2 Vegetable Exchanges, 1 Fat Exchange

•

— Cauliflower — Parmesan

SERVES 2

90 CALORIES PER SERVING

2 teaspoons margarine

1 teaspoon flour

2 tablespoons low-fat natural yogurt

2 teaspoons grated Parmesan cheese

pinch each salt, pepper and nutmeg

6oz (180g) cauliflower florets, blanched

1 teaspoon chopped parsley for garnish

Heat margarine in small saucepan and stir in flour. Remove from heat and, using a wire whisk, blend in yogurt, cheese, salt, pepper and nutmeg. Return to low heat and cook, stirring constantly until smooth. Do not boil. Add cauliflower and cook, stirring occasionally, until hot. Transfer mixture to small flameproof casserole and grill 6 inches (15 cm) from heat source until browned, about 1 minute. Serve sprinkled with parsley.

Each serving provides: 1 Vegetable Exchange, 1 Fat Exchange, 25 Calories Optional Exchange

•

— Oven-Braised Baby— Carrots

SERVES 4

60 CALORIES PER SERVING

12oz (360g) whole baby carrots, trimmed and scraped

4 tablespoons water

4 teaspoons margarine, melted

1 chicken stock cube, crumbled

¼ to ½ teaspoon dill weed

2 tablespoons chopped parsley

Preheat oven to 350°F, 180°C, Gas Mark 4. Arrange carrots in medium casserole. Mix all remaining ingredients except parsley, pour over carrots and toss well to coat. Cover casserole and bake until carrots are tender, 20 to 30 minutes. Just before serving, toss again and sprinkle with chopped parsley.

Each serving provides: 1 Vegetable Exchange, 1 Fat Exchange

•

— Chicory-Tomato Salad — with Sesame Dressing

SERVES 2

75 CALORIES PER SERVING

Salad

5 heads chicory, about 3oz (90g) each

4oz (120g) watercress leaves, chopped

6 small tomatoes, cut into quarters

Dressing

2 teaspoons each sesame seeds, toasted, lemon juice, wine vinegar and water

½ garlic clove, crushed

pinch salt

To Prepare Salad: Separate each chicory head into individual leaves. Line a glass salad bowl with the leaves with tips facing rim of bowl like petals. Fill centre with chopped watercress and top with tomato quarters, arranged in a circular pattern. Chill lightly in refrigerator before serving.

To Prepare Dressing: Crush sesame seeds, using pestle and mortar. Mix seeds with lemon juice, vinegar, water, garlic and salt and mix well. To serve, stir dressing and pour over salad.

Each serving provides: 4 Vegetable Exchanges, 20 Calories Optional Exchange

•

— Mixed Green Salad — with Buttermilk Dressing

SERVES 4

110 CALORIES PER SERVING

8oz (240g) lettuce leaves, chilled and torn into small pieces

4oz (120g) spinach leaves, washed well, chilled and torn into small pieces

Buttermilk Dressing (see page 79)

1 egg, hard-boiled and chopped

Mix lettuce and spinach in salad bowl, add dressing and toss to coat. Sprinkle with chopped egg and serve immediately.

Each serving, including Buttermilk Dressing, provides: ½ Protein Exchange, 1 Vegetable Exchange, 1 Fat Exchange, 10 Calories Optional Exchange

— Ratatouille —

SERVES 4

90 CALORIES PER SERVING

4 teaspoons olive oil

4oz (120g) onions, sliced

2oz (60g) green or red pepper, seeded and sliced

3 garlic cloves, chopped

15oz (450g) aubergine, cut in 1-inch (2.5-cm) cubes

12oz (360g) canned tomatoes, chopped

6oz (180g) courgettes, sliced

3 tablespoons chopped fresh basil or 2 teaspoons dried

1 teaspoon salt

pinch freshly ground pepper

Heat oil in large frying pan, add onions, pepper and garlic and saute until vegetables are tender-crisp. Add remaining ingredients and stir to combine. Reduce heat, cover and simmer until vegetables are tender, 20 to 25 minutes.

Each serving provides: 3½ Vegetable Exchanges, 1 Fat Exchange

Variations:

1. Use ratatouille as an omelette filling.

2. Place ratatouille in a baking dish, top with 4oz (120g) Cheddar cheese, grated, and bake at 350°F, 180°C, Gas Mark 4 until cheese is melted. Add 1 Protein Exchange to Exchange Information.

— French Bean Salad —

SERVES 2

135 CALORIES PER SERVING

1lb (480g) whole French beans

½ pint (300ml) water

2 tablespoons chopped onion

2 tablespoons each drained capers and fresh lemon juice

1 tablespoon each olive oil and wine vinegar

1 teaspoon oregano

¼ teaspoon each salt and dry mustard

1 egg, hard-boiled

Trim and discard ends of beans. Bring water to the boil in a saucepan, add beans and onion and cook until beans are tender-crisp, 5 to 8 minutes. Drain well. Mix all remaining ingredients except egg in a salad bowl, add warm beans and toss to coat. Cover bowl and chill lightly in refrigerator. Just before serving, chop hard-boiled egg, toss salad again and sprinkle with egg.

Each serving provides: ½ Protein Exchange, 3 Vegetable Exchanges, 1½ Fat Exchanges

— Cucumber-Orange — Salad

SERVES 2

50 CALORIES PER SERVING

6oz (180g) cucumber, scored and thinly sliced

1 medium orange, peeled and sectioned

2 tablespoons chopped onion

1 tablespoon lemon juice

½ teaspoon salt

¼ teaspoon pepper

1 teaspoon olive or vegetable oil

lettuce leaves

Mix cucumber, orange sections and onion in salad bowl. Combine all remaining ingredients except lettuce, pour over salad and toss to coat. Cover and chill lightly in refrigerator before serving on bed of lettuce leaves.

Each serving provides: 1½ Vegetable Exchanges, ½ Fat Exchange, ½ Fruit Exchange

— Parmesan-Stuffed — Artichokes

SERVES 2

135 CALORIES PER SERVING

2 small artichokes, each about 9oz (270g), thoroughly washed in cold water

lemon juice

3 tablespoons dried breadcrumbs

1 tablespoon chopped parsley

2 teaspoons each grated Parmesan cheese and olive oil

1 small garlic clove, finely chopped

½ teaspoon salt

freshly ground pepper

Using large stainless steel knife, cut off stem of each artichoke flush with base so that artichoke will stand upright and snap off any small or discoloured leaves at base. Cut off and discard about 1 inch (2.5 cm) of the top. Rub cut edges of each artichoke with lemon juice. Using stainless steel scissors, remove barbed tips of leaves by cutting about ½ inch (1 cm) off tip of each leaf. Rub cut edges of leaves with lemon juice. Mix breadcrumbs, parsley, cheese, oil and garlic. Sprinkle each artichoke with ¼ teaspoon salt and pinch pepper. Spread leaves open and stuff half the crumb mixture into each artichoke. Stand stuffed artichokes upright in deep ovenproof dish (not aluminium) just large enough to hold them. Pour about 1 inch (2.5 cm) water into pan and cover with foil. Bake at 375°F, 190°C, Gas Mark 5 until base of each artichoke is tender when pierced with a fork, about 45 minutes. Serve immediately.

Each serving provides: ½ Bread Exchange, 3 Vegetable Exchanges, 1 Fat Exchange, 10 Calories Optional Exchange

— Grape and Carrot — Salad

SERVES 2

115 CALORIES PER SERVING

8oz (240g) carrots, shredded or coarsely grated

6oz (180g) large seedless green grapes, cut into halves

2 teaspoons mayonnaise

½ teaspoon poppy seeds

¼ teaspoon salt

4 large lettuce leaves

Mix together all ingredients except lettuce leaves, cover and chill lightly in refrigerator. Serve on lettuce leaves.

Each serving provides: 2 Vegetable Exchanges, 1 Fat Exchange, 1 Fruit Exchange, 5 Calories Optional Exchange

— Orange Beetroot —

SERVES 2

115 CALORIES PER SERVING

6oz (180g) cooked beetroot, peeled and sliced

2 teaspoons margarine

1 teaspoon brown sugar

2fl oz (60ml) orange juice

1½ teaspoons lemon juice

1 teaspoon cornflour

pinch salt

1 teaspoon orange marmalade

Place beetroot, margarine and sugar in saucepan (not aluminium or cast iron). Cook over low heat, stirring constantly, until margarine and sugar are melted. Mix orange and lemon juice, cornflour and salt. Pour over beetroot mixture and, stirring constantly, bring to the boil. Continue cooking and stirring until combined. Remove from heat and serve at once. May also be refrigerated, covered, and reheated when needed. Keeps 3 to 4 days in refrigerator.

Each serving provides: 1 Vegetable Exchange, 1 Fat Exchange, 45 Calories Optional Exchange

— Coleslaw with — Buttermilk Dressing

SERVES 2

50 CALORIES PER SERVING

5fl oz (150ml) buttermilk

1 tablespoon lemon juice

1 teaspoon sugar

½ teaspoon salt

¼ teaspoon each celery seeds and pepper

pinch garlic powder

6oz (180g) cabbage, shredded

Combine all ingredients except cabbage in a salad bowl. Add cabbage and toss to coat. Cover and chill lightly in refrigerator. Toss again just before serving.

Each serving provides: 1 Vegetable Exchange, ¼ Milk Exchange, 15 Calories Optional Exchange

— Carrot and — Beansprout Salad

SERVES 2

75 CALORIES PER SERVING

★3oz (90g) beansprouts

4½oz (135g) carrots, shredded or coarsely grated

1½oz (45g) celery, chopped

2 tablespoons chopped spring onion

1 tablespoon thawed frozen concentrated orange juice

2 teaspoons each vegetable oil and lemon juice

pinch each garlic powder and salt

2 large lettuce leaves

Mix vegetables with the concentrated orange juice. Combine all remaining ingredients except lettuce and stir until well mixed. Pour over vegetables and toss until combined. Cover bowl and chill salad lightly in refrigerator. To serve, line salad bowl with lettuce, toss salad again and spoon onto lettuce leaves.

★This salad may be made with 2oz (60g) alfafa sprouts, if available, instead of the beansprouts.

Each serving provides: 2 Vegetable Exchanges, 1 Fat Exchange, 15 Calories Optional Exchange

— Cheesy Vegetable — Grill

SERVES 2

185 CALORIES PER SERVING

4oz (120g) aubergine, unpeeled and cut into 1-inch (2.5-cm) cubes

salt

1 teaspoon olive oil

3oz (180g) onion, chopped

½ garlic clove, crushed or pinch garlic powder

5oz (150g) courgettes, cut into ¼-inch (6-mm) slices

1½oz (45g) green pepper, seeded and cut into 1-inch (2.5-cm) squares

pinch each basil and pepper

8oz (240g) canned tomatoes

dash hot pepper sauce

1½ teaspoons chopped parsley and sprigs to garnish

2oz (60g) Cheddar cheese, grated

Spread aubergine on double layer of paper towels and sprinkle with salt. Let stand for 30 minutes, then rinse and pat dry. Heat oil in saucepan, add onion and crushed garlic and saute until onion is softened (if garlic powder is used, add later). Add aubergine, courgettes and green pepper and saute for 3 minutes. Sprinkle with basil, pepper, remaining pinch salt and garlic powder if used. Stir in tomatoes and hot sauce and bring to the boil. Reduce heat, cover and simmer for 15 minutes. Stir in parsley and simmer, uncovered, until liquid has evaporated slightly, about 5 minutes. Transfer mixture to a flameproof casserole, sprinkle with cheese and grill until cheese is melted and lightly browned. Garnish with parsley sprigs and serve.

Each serving provides: 1 Protein Exchange, 4 Vegetable Exchanges, ½ Fat Exchange

— Caraway-'Bacon' — Coleslaw

SERVES 2

55 CALORIES PER SERVING

6oz (180g) cabbage, finely shredded

2 tablespoons thinly sliced spring onion

¼ teaspoon caraway seeds

3 tablespoons white wine vinegar

2 tablespoons water

2 teaspoons imitation bacon bits

1 teaspoon olive oil

Toss cabbage in a salad bowl with spring onion and caraway seeds and set aside. Mix vinegar, water, 1 teaspoon bacon bits and the oil in a small saucepan and bring to the boil. Pour over cabbage mixture and toss to combine. Cover and chill lightly in refrigerator before serving. Just before serving, sprinkle coleslaw with remaining teaspoon bacon bits and toss to combine.

Each serving provides: 1½ Vegetable Exchanges, ½ Fat Exchange, 15 Calories Optional Exchange

— Vegetable-Cheese — Puffs

SERVES 4

255 CALORIES PER SERVING

Puff Shells

4 tablespoons margarine

4fl oz (120ml) water

1½oz (45g) flour

3 medium eggs

Filling

5oz (150g) low-fat soft cheese

3 tablespoons each chopped celery and carrot

2 tablespoons chopped spring onion

2 teaspoons French mustard

1 teaspoon horseradish relish

pinch each paprika and salt

To Prepare Puff Shells: Preheat oven to 400°F, 200°C, Gas Mark 6. Place margarine in saucepan, add water and bring to the boil. Add flour all at once and, using a wooden spoon, stir vigorously until mixture leaves sides of pan and forms a ball. Remove from heat. Add eggs, one at a time, beating very well after each addition until mixture is smooth. Dough should be smooth and shiny. Drop dough by rounded teaspoonsful onto non-stick baking sheet, making 24 mounds and leaving a 1-inch (2.5-cm) space between each, or divide dough equally between 24 small non-stick bun tins. Bake for 15 minutes. Reduce oven temperature to 350°F, 180°C, Gas Mark 4, and bake for 15 minutes longer. Turn oven off and remove baking sheet/bun tins. Using the point of a sharp knife, pierce side of each shell. Return to turned-off oven and let stand for 10 minutes, leaving oven door ajar. Carefully transfer shells to wire rack and stand away from draughts while cooling.
To Prepare Filling: Combine all ingredients and mix until well blended.
To Prepare Puffs: Shortly before serving, slice off top of each puff shell with a sharp knife. Spoon an equal amount of vegetable-cheese filling (about 1½ teaspoons) into each shell. Replace tops and serve.

Each serving provides: 1¼ Protein Exchanges, ½ Bread Exchange, ½ Vegetable Exchange, 3 Fat Exchanges, 5 Calories Optional Exchange

— Coleslaw with — Yogurt Dressing

SERVES 2

60 CALORIES PER SERVING

6oz (180g) cabbage, shredded

4oz (120g) carrots, shredded or coarsely grated

1 tablespoon each chopped green pepper and celery

1½ teaspoons chopped onion

1 tablespoon low-fat natural yogurt

1 teaspoon mayonnaise

½ teaspoon sugar

pinch each salt and white pepper

pinch celery seeds (optional)

Combine cabbage, carrots, green pepper, celery and onion in salad bowl. Combine remaining ingredients, pour over vegetables and toss until well coated. Cover and chill lightly in refrigerator.

Each serving provides: 2 Vegetable Exchanges, ½ Fat Exchange, 10 Calories Optional Exchange

— Carrot Soup —

SERVES 2

115 CALORIES PER SERVING

1 tablespoon margarine

2 tablespoons each chopped onion and celery

½ small garlic clove, crushed

¾ pint (450ml) water

4oz (120g) carrots, chopped

3oz (90g) peeled potato, chopped

1 chicken stock cube, crumbled

Heat margarine in saucepan, add onion, celery and garlic and saute, stirring constantly, until onion is soft. Add remaining ingredients and bring to the boil. Reduce heat, cover and simmer until vegetables are soft, about 20 minutes. Let mixture cool slightly, pour into blender container and puree at low speed until smooth. If too thick, add a little more water. Reheat if necessary.

Each serving provides: ½ Bread Exchange, 1½ Vegetable Exchanges, 1½ Fat Exchanges

•

— Glazed Carrots —

SERVES 2

40 CALORIES PER SERVING

1 teaspoon margarine

4oz (120g) carrots, coarsely grated and blanched

1 teaspoon brown sugar

pinch each salt and dry mustard

dash hot pepper sauce

Heat margarine in small frying pan, add remaining ingredients and saute, stirring occasionally, until carrots are tender-crisp, about 5 minutes.

Each serving provides: 1 Vegetable Exchange, ½ Fat Exchange, 10 Calories Optional Exchange

•

— Minted Carrots —

SERVES 4

35 CALORIES PER SERVING

8oz (240g) carrots, trimmed and scraped

4fl oz (120ml) water

½ chicken stock cube, crumbled

2 teaspoons margarine

½ teaspoon sugar

1 teaspoon chopped mint

Cut carrots into matchstick pieces and set aside. Bring water to the boil in a frying pan, add stock cube and stir to dissolve. Add carrots, cover, and cook for 5 minutes. Add margarine, sugar and mint and cook, uncovered, until most of liquid has evaporated and carrots are glazed, about 5 minutes.

Each serving provides: 1 Vegetable Exchange, ½ Fat Exchange, 5 Calories Optional Exchange

•

— Crunchy Cauliflower —

SERVES 2

170 CALORIES PER SERVING

1 egg

3 tablespoons dried breadcrumbs

6oz (180g) small cauliflower florets, blanched and cooled

1 tablespoon vegetable oil

pinch each salt and pepper (optional)

parsley sprigs for garnish

Beat egg lightly. Place breadcrumbs in a plastic or paper bag. Dip cauliflower into egg to coat, then place in bag with crumbs, seal or close bag and shake well. Heat oil in non-stick frying pan, add coated cauliflower and saute until browned on all sides. Season with salt and pepper, if desired, and serve garnished with parsley sprigs.

Each serving provides: ½ Protein Exchange, ½ Bread Exchange, 1 Vegetable Exchange, 1½ Fat Exchanges

•

— Courgettes Braised — in Wine

SERVES 2

90 CALORIES PER SERVING

2 teaspoons olive oil

9oz (270g) courgettes, thinly sliced

2 tablespoons chopped shallots

½ teaspoon basil

¼ teaspoon each salt and pepper

4 tablespoons dry white wine

1 teaspoon lemon juice

Heat oil in frying pan, add courgettes, shallots, basil, salt and pepper and saute for 3 minutes. Add wine and lemon juice, cover and simmer, stirring occasionally, for 10 minutes.

Each serving provides: 2 Vegetable Exchanges, 1 Fat Exchange, 25 Calories Optional Exchange

•

— Antipasto —

SERVES 8

250 CALORIES PER SERVING

Dressing

8 teaspoons olive or vegetable oil

1½oz (45g) onion, finely chopped

1 tablespoon each red wine vinegar, lemon juice and drained capers

1 garlic clove, crushed

¼ teaspoon each salt, pepper, oregano and basil

sprig of basil for garnish

Marinated Vegetable Mixture

6oz (180g) cauliflower florets, blanched and kept warm

9oz (270g) canned artichoke hearts, heated and kept warm

1½oz (45g) drained bottled cocktail onions

Salad

8 large lettuce leaves

4oz (120g) luncheon meat, sliced

8oz (240g) Mozzarella cheese, sliced

1lb 2oz (540g) asparagus spears, blanched and kept warm

8 drained anchovy fillets

8 capers for garnish

12oz (360g) drained canned chick peas

6oz (180g) tomatoes, each cut into eighths, or equivalent in cherry tomatoes, cut into quarters

16 small pimento-stuffed green olives

8 large black olives, stoned and sliced

To Prepare Dressing: Combine all ingredients for dressing and set aside. *To Prepare Marinated Vegetable Mixture:* Place cauliflower, artichoke hearts and cocktail onions in large bowl, pour dressing over vegetable mixture and toss to coat. Cover and refrigerate for at least 2 hours, tossing several times (may be refrigerated overnight). To serve, line a large serving dish with lettuce. Cut luncheon meat slices into halves and arrange round edge of dish with sliced cheese. Arrange asparagus spears on top. Toss marinated vegetable mixture, roll up anchovies and arrange on dish with a caper in the centre of each roll. Spoon vegetable mixture onto centre of dish. Sprinkle chick peas over the whole dish. Arrange tomatoes and olives decoratively over salad, alternating colours. Pour any remaining dressing over salad and serve.

Each serving provides: 2 Protein Exchanges, 2 Vegetable Exchanges, 1 Fat Exchange, 20 Calories Optional Exchange

•

— Aubergine with — 'Pesto' Topping

SERVES 2

160 CALORIES PER SERVING

1lb (480g) aubergine, cut into ¾-inch (2-cm) slices

pinch salt

2 tablespoons each chopped basil and grated Parmesan cheese

1 tablespoon olive oil

1 small garlic clove, crushed

pinch freshly ground pepper

Arrange aubergine slices in a single layer on non-stick baking sheet. Sprinkle with salt and bake at 425°F, 220°C, Gas Mark 7 until easily pierced with a fork, about 30 minutes. Combine remaining ingredients and spread an equal amount of mixture over each aubergine slice. Transfer slices to a casserole, return to oven, and bake until hot, about 10 minutes longer.

Each serving provides: 2½ Vegetable Exchanges, 1½ Fat Exchanges, 30 Calories Optional Exchange

•

— Aubergine Relish —

SERVES 4

85 CALORIES PER SERVING

9oz (270g) aubergine, cut in small cubes

1 teaspoon salt

4 teaspoons olive oil

4oz (120g) onions, thinly sliced

2 garlic cloves, crushed

4oz (120g) celery, chopped

8oz (240g) tomatoes, chopped

2 teaspoons wine vinegar

1 teaspoon sugar

8 black olives, stoned and cut into halves

1 tablespoon drained capers

Arrange aubergine cubes in a single layer on paper towels, sprinkle with salt and let stand for at least 1 hour. Pat dry and set aside. Heat oil in large frying pan, add onions and garlic and saute until onions are transparent, 3 to 5 minutes. Add aubergine and cook, stirring well, until aubergine begins to soften, about 5 minutes. Stir in celery and tomatoes, cover pan and simmer until celery is tender, about 15 minutes. Stir in vinegar and sugar and cook, uncovered, for 5 minutes longer. Remove from heat and add olives and capers, tossing to combine. Transfer to a small serving bowl, cover and chill lightly in refrigerator.

Each serving provides: 2 Vegetable Exchanges, 1 Fat Exchange, 15 Calories Optional Exchange

•

Antipasto

— Chicory Au Gratin —

SERVES 4

300 CALORIES PER SERVING

4 heads chicory, about 3oz (90g) each

6fl oz (180ml) water

½ teaspoon salt

2 tablespoons each margarine and chopped onion

3 tablespoons flour

16fl oz (480ml) skimmed milk, hot

pinch each white and cayenne pepper

4oz (120g) Emmenthal cheese, grated (reserve 2 tablespoons for topping)

4 slices ham, each 1oz (30g)

Place chicory in a frying pan with water and ¼ teaspoon salt. Bring to the boil, reduce heat and cover pan. Let chicory simmer, turning once, until tender, 20 to 25 minutes, adding a little more water if necessary to prevent burning. Using a slotted spoon, remove chicory from liquid and drain well. While chicory is draining, heat margarine in saucepan, add onion and saute until softened. Add flour and cook, stirring constantly, for 3 minutes. Remove from heat and gradually add milk, stirring until mixture is smooth. Add white and cayenne pepper and remaining ¼ teaspoon salt and cook over medium heat, stirring constantly, until sauce is thickened. Reduce heat to low and continue cooking and stirring for 10 minutes longer. Add all but reserved 2 tablespoons cheese and cook, continuing to stir, until cheese is melted and sauce is smooth. Remove from heat. Preheat oven to 350°F, 180°C, Gas Mark 4. Pour ¼ of the cheese sauce into shallow baking dish just large enough to hold chicory in one layer. Roll 1 slice ham round each head of chicory and place chicory in baking dish. Top with remaining sauce, then sprinkle with reserved 2 tablespoons cheese. Bake for 15 minutes.

Each serving provides: 2 Protein Exchanges, 1 Vegetable Exchange, 1½ Fat Exchanges, 65 Calories Optional Exchange

•

— Braised Fennel —

SERVES 2

50 CALORIES PER SERVING

1 teaspoon vegetable oil

2 garlic cloves, crushed

12oz (360g) fennel, sliced

4fl oz (120ml) water

½ chicken stock cube, crumbled

¼ teaspoon each basil and pepper

Heat oil in small frying pan, add garlic and saute until golden. Add fennel and saute over moderate heat, stirring occasionally, for 2 to 3 minutes. Add water, crumbled stock cube, basil and pepper and bring to the boil. Reduce heat and simmer until fennel is tender, about 15 minutes.

Each serving provides: 2 Vegetable Exchanges, ½ Fat Exchange

•

— Fennel Salad —

SERVES 2

75 CALORIES PER SERVING

8oz (240g) fennel, thinly sliced

2oz (60g) red pepper, seeded and chopped

4 black olives, stoned and chopped

2 tablespoons chopped spring onion

4 teaspoons wine vinegar

2 teaspoons olive oil

½ garlic clove, crushed

pinch each salt and pepper

Mix fennel, red pepper, olives and spring onion in salad bowl. Mix remaining ingredients well together, pour dressing over fennel mixture and toss to coat. Cover with cling film and chill lightly in refrigerator. Toss again just before serving.

Each serving provides: 2 Vegetable Exchanges, 1 Fat Exchange, 10 Calories Optional Exchange

•

— Braised Jerusalem — Artichokes

SERVES 2

115 CALORIES PER SERVING

2 teaspoons olive or vegetable oil

3oz (90g) onion, chopped

2 garlic cloves, crushed

12oz (360g) Jerusalem artichokes, peeled and cut into ⅛-inch (3-mm) slices

½ teaspoon salt

¼ teaspoon pepper

4fl oz (120ml) each dry white wine and water

1 teaspoon chopped parsley (optional)

Heat oil in frying pan, add onion and garlic and saute until onion is lightly browned. Add artichoke slices, salt and pepper and saute for 5 minutes. Add wine and cook until almost all liquid has evaporated. Add water, cover and simmer, stirring occasionally, until artichokes are tender, about 15 minutes. Serve sprinkled with parsley if desired.

Each serving provides: 2½ Vegetable Exchanges, 1 Fat Exchange, 50 Calories Optional Exchange

•

— Quick Caesar Salad —

SERVES 2

180 CALORIES PER SERVING

8oz (240g) lettuce leaves, chilled and torn into small pieces

2 slices white bread, toasted and cut into cubes

1 tablespoon each grated Parmesan cheese and lemon juice

4 teaspoons salad dressing

Toss lettuce in salad bowl with bread cubes and cheese, add lemon juice and dressing and toss to coat thoroughly. Let stand for 5 to 10 minutes and toss again just before serving.

Each serving provides: 1 Bread Exchange, 1½ Vegetable Exchanges, 1 Fat Exchange, 15 Calories Optional Exchange

— Okra Salad —

SERVES 6

50 CALORIES PER SERVING

3 teaspoons olive or vegetable oil

4 tablespoons each chopped onion, celery and red pepper

2 garlic cloves, crushed

6oz (180g) okra, sliced

3oz (90g) mushrooms, sliced

6oz (180g) courgettes, sliced

1lb (480g) canned tomatoes, chopped

4 tablespoons dry red wine

3 teaspoons drained capers

6 each black olives, stoned, and pimento-stuffed green olives, sliced

Heat oil in non-stick frying pan, add onion, celery, red pepper and garlic and saute, stirring constantly, until onion is transparent, about 3 minutes. Stir in okra, mushrooms and courgettes, stirring occasionally, until vegetables are lightly browned. Stir in tomatoes, wine and capers and cook until liquid has evaporated. Stir in olives and transfer mixture to serving bowl. Cover and chill lightly in refrigerator before serving.

Each serving provides: 2 Vegetable Exchanges, ½ Fat Exchange, 20 Calories Optional Exchange

— Mushroom-Cheese — Pate

SERVES 2

155 CALORIES PER SERVING

12oz (360g) mushrooms, sliced

2 tablespoons chopped spring onion

2 teaspoons dry red wine

½ vegetable stock cube, crumbled

5oz (150g) low-fat soft cheese

3 tablespoons dried breadcrumbs

½ teaspoon vegetable oil

2 large lettuce leaves

watercress sprigs and 4 sliced radishes for garnish

Mix mushrooms, spring onion, wine and stock cube in a non-stick frying pan and cook over moderate heat, stirring occasionally until all liquid has evaporated. Spoon mixture into blender container or food processor and process until smooth. Turn motor off, add cheese and breadcrumbs and process until combined. Grease 2 small moulds or bowls lightly with vegetable oil and spoon half the cheese mixture into each. Press down lightly and smooth tops. Cover with cling film and refrigerate for at least 2 hours. To turn out, run the point of a small knife round the edge of each mould. Place a lettuce leaf on each of 2 small plates and invert pates on to lettuce. Garnish with watercress and radish slices.

Each serving provides: 1 Protein Exchange, ½ Bread Exchange, 3 Vegetable Exchanges, 20 Calories Optional Exchange

— Onion Soup —

SERVES 4

200 CALORIES PER SERVING

2 tablespoons margarine

8oz (240g) onions, thinly sliced

1½ pints (900ml) water

2 beef stock cubes, crumbled

2 teaspoons Worcestershire sauce

½ bay leaf

pinch pepper

4 slices French bread

2oz (60g) Cheddar cheese, grated

Heat 4 teaspoons margarine in large saucepan, add onions and saute until transparent, 2 to 3 minutes. Add water, stock cubes and seasonings and bring to the boil. Reduce heat, partially cover pan and simmer for 30 minutes. Remove and discard bay leaf. While soup is simmering, spread each slice of bread with ½ teaspoon margarine and sprinkle each with ½oz (15g) Cheddar cheese. Transfer to baking sheet and bake at 350°F, 180°C, Gas Mark 4 until browned and crisp, 25 to 30 minutes. To serve, place 1 slice of baked bread in each of 4 soup bowls and pour ¼ of the soup into each bowl.

Each serving provides: ½ Protein Exchange, 1 Bread Exchange, 1 Vegetable Exchange, 1½ Fat Exchanges

— Grilled Tomatoes — with Crumb Topping

SERVES 2

135 CALORIES PER SERVING

2 large tomatoes, each 6oz (180g), cut crosswise into halves

2 teaspoons margarine

1 tablespoon chopped onion

3 tablespoons dried breadcrumbs

2 teaspoons grated Parmesan cheese

1½ teaspoons chopped fresh basil or ½ teaspoon dried

Preheat grill. Place tomatoes cut-side up on a non-stick baking sheet and grill 6 inches (15 cm) from heat source until lightly browned, about 5 minutes. While tomatoes are grilling, heat margarine in small frying pan, add onion and cook until transparent. Remove from heat, add remaining ingredients and stir to combine. Remove tomatoes from grill and spoon half the crumb mixture over each. Grill until topping is browned, 1 to 2 minutes.

Each serving provides: ½ Bread Exchange, 2 Vegetable Exchanges, 1 Fat Exchange, 10 Calories Optional Exchange

— Vegetable Borscht —

SERVES 2

105 CALORIES PER SERVING

1 teaspoon margarine

1½oz (45g) onion, chopped

6oz (180g) raw beetroot, coarsely grated

¾ pint (450ml) water

1 beef stock cube, crumbled

½ bay leaf

3oz (90g) cabbage, shredded

1½oz (45g) carrot, sliced

2 tablespoons tomato puree

1 tablespoon lemon juice

½ teaspoon sugar

pinch pepper

2½fl oz (75ml) low-fat natural yogurt

Heat margarine in saucepan. Add onion and saute until softened, 1 to 2 minutes. Add beetroot and toss to combine. Add water, crumbled stock cube and bay leaf and bring to the boil. Cover pan and cook over moderate heat for 10 minutes. Stir in all remaining ingredients except yogurt, cover and let simmer until vegetables are tender, about 25 minutes. Remove and discard bay leaf. Pour borscht into 2 soup bowls and top each portion with yogurt, dividing evenly. To serve cold, cover and refrigerate until required and add yogurt just before serving.

Each serving provides: 2 Vegetable Exchanges, ½ Fat Exchange, ¼ Milk Exchange, 15 Calories Optional Exchange

— Cabbage and Potato — Soup

SERVES 4

90 CALORIES PER SERVING

2 teaspoons vegetable oil

9oz (270g) cabbage, shredded

4oz (120g) onions, sliced

1 garlic clove, crushed

1¼ pints (750ml) water

6oz (180g) peeled potato, sliced

2oz (60g) carrots, sliced

4oz (120g) canned tomatoes, pureed

2 beef stock cubes, crumbled

1 each bay leaf and whole clove

Heat oil in large saucepan, add cabbage, onions and garlic and saute over medium heat, stirring frequently, until cabbage is soft, about 10 minutes. Reduce heat to low, add remaining ingredients and cook until vegetables are tender, about 30 minutes. Remove and discard bay leaf and clove before serving.

Each serving provides: ½ Bread Exchange, 2 Vegetable Exchanges, ½ Fat Exchange

Cabbage and Potato Soup

MILK

*S*kimmed milk features in lots of recipes throughout this book, but in this section we have put together some creamy soups and a variety of delicious milk drinks. Our yogurt-based desserts, too, are so satisfying that it's hard to believe they are helping you to keep in trim. Yogurt blends well with so many flavours, both sweet and savoury. As well as desserts such as Frozen Strawberry Yogurt and Mandarin Yogurt Dessert, try cutting crisp raw vegetables into fingers and serving them with tangy Yogurt-Mint Dip.

— Buttermilk Custard — Flan

SERVES 8

260 CALORIES PER SERVING

Crust

3oz (90g) flour

¼ teaspoon salt

8 teaspoons margarine

2fl oz (60ml) low–fat natural yogurt

1 teaspoon white vinegar

1 tablespoon flour for rolling out pastry

Filling

4 tablespoons each margarine and sugar

4 eggs, separated

3 tablespoons flour

1 teaspoon each grated orange peel, lemon juice and vanilla flavouring

10fl oz (300ml) buttermilk

To Prepare Crust: Mix flour and salt and rub in margarine until mixture resembles coarse breadcrumbs. Add yogurt and vinegar and mix well. Form dough into a ball, wrap in cling film and refrigerate for at least 1 hour (may be kept in refrigerator for up to 3 days). Use extra tablespoon flour to flour board and sprinkle on dough before rolling. Roll out dough to make a circle ⅛ inch (3 mm) thick. Use to line 9-inch (23-cm) flan dish. Wrap in cling film or plastic bag and return to refrigerator.

To Prepare Filling and Bake: Preheat oven to 450°F, 230°C, Gas Mark 8. Using electric mixer, cream margarine with sugar until light and fluffy. Beat in egg yolks. Add flour, orange peel, juice and vanilla and beat until well blended. Stir in buttermilk.

Using clean beaters, beat egg whites until stiff but not dry and fold into yolk mixture. Pour filling into prepared pie crust and bake for 15 minutes. Reduce oven temperature to 350°F, 180°C, Gas Mark 4 and continue baking for 45 to 50 minutes longer. Remove flan dish to wire rack and let cool. Serve hot or cold. May be refrigerated for several hours if not for immediate use.

Each serving provides: ½ Protein Exchange, ½ Bread Exchange, 2½ Fat Exchanges, 80 Calories Optional Exchange

•

— Strawberry-Pineapple — Sorbet

SERVES 4

95 CALORIES PER SERVING

10oz (300g) strawberries

8oz (240g) canned crushed pineapple, no sugar added

15fl oz (450ml) buttermilk

4 teaspoons sugar

2 teaspoons vanilla flavouring

Set aside 4 strawberries for garnish. Place remaining strawberries in blender with the pineapple and puree until smooth. Add all remaining ingredients except garnish and blend to combine. Pour mixture into two shallow freezer containers, cover and freeze until partially frozen, about 30 minutes. Chill a mixing bowl. Spoon sorbet into chilled bowl and, using electric mixer, beat until fluffy. Cover bowl with cling film and freeze until sorbet is almost firm. Spoon into 4 ice cream or dessert dishes, garnish each with a reserved strawberry, and serve immediately.

Each serving provides: 1 Fruit Exchange, ¼ Milk Exchange, 35 Calories Optional Exchange

•

— Carob Milk with — Cinnamon Stick

SERVES 1

70 CALORIES PER SERVING

1½ teaspoons unsweetened carob powder

½ teaspoon sugar

¼ pint (150ml) skimmed milk

dash vanilla flavouring

cinnamon stick, optional

Mix carob powder and sugar in small saucepan and gradually stir in milk, using a wire whisk. Add vanilla and bring mixture to the boil over moderate heat, beating with wire whisk until frothy. Pour into a mug, add cinnamon stick stirrer if desired and serve immediately.

Each serving provides: ½ Milk Exchange, 25 Calories Optional Exchange

•

— Frozen Strawberry — and Banana Yogurt

SERVES 4

120 CALORIES PER SERVING

2 teaspoons unflavoured gelatine

2 tablespoons water

10oz (300g) strawberries

1 medium banana, peeled and cut into chunks

15fl oz (450ml) low-fat natural yogurt

4 teaspoons sugar

¼ teaspoon vanilla flavouring

Sprinkle gelatine over water in small cup. Stand cup in pan of boiling water and stir gelatine until completely dissolved. Place strawberries, banana and dissolved gelatine in blender and puree until smooth. Add yogurt, sugar and vanilla and blend until combined. Pour mixture into shallow freezer container, cover and freeze, stirring every 30 minutes, until mixture is the consistency of ice cream.

Each serving provides: 1 Fruit Exchange, ¾ Milk Exchange, 20 Calories Optional Exchange

— Frozen Strawberry — Yogurt

SERVES 4

140 CALORIES PER SERVING

15oz (450g) strawberries

15fl oz (450ml) low-fat natural yogurt

2 tablespoons thawed frozen concentrated orange juice

4 teaspoons sugar

2 large egg whites, at room temperature

4 teaspoons icing sugar

1 teaspoon vanilla flavouring

Set aside 4 strawberries for garnish. Crush remaining strawberries in mixing bowl with a fork and stir in yogurt, orange juice and sugar. In another bowl, using electric mixer on high speed, beat egg whites until soft peaks form. Add icing sugar and flavouring and continue beating until stiff but not dry. Fold beaten whites into strawberry mixture, transfer mixture to 2 freezer trays or a shallow baking tin, cover and freeze until almost firm, about 45 minutes. Chill mixing bowl with cold water or ice cubes. Turn strawberry yogurt into chilled bowl and, using electric mixer on high speed, beat until thick and creamy. Cover with cling film and freeze until just firm. To serve, let yogurt mixture soften slightly, spoon into 4 ice cream or dessert dishes and garnish each with a reserved strawberry.

Each serving provides: 1 Fruit Exchange, ¾ Milk Exchange, 50 Calories Optional Exchange

— Mandarin-Yogurt — Dessert

SERVES 6

105 CALORIES PER SERVING

4 teaspoons sugar

8fl oz (240ml) boiling water

2 tablespoons unflavoured gelatine

4 tablespoons thawed frozen concentrated orange juice

1 pint (600ml) low-fat natural yogurt

8oz (240g) canned mandarin orange sections, drained, no sugar added (reserve some for decoration)

Dissolve sugar in boiling water and add gelatine. Leave to dissolve, add orange juice. Mix yogurt and remaining orange sections and gently fold in gelatine mixture. Rinse a 2 pint (1 litre 200ml) mould with cold water and pour in the fruit mixture. Cover and refrigerate until firm, about 4 hours. To serve, turn out onto serving plate and decorate with reserved orange sections.

Each serving provides: ½ Fruit Exchange, ½ Milk Exchange, 40 Calories Optional Exchange

— Chocolate Shake —

SERVES 1

170 CALORIES PER SERVING

¼ pint (150ml) skimmed milk, chilled

2oz (60g) chocolate ice cream

1 teaspoon chocolate syrup

¼ teaspoon vanilla flavouring

Place all ingredients in blender and blend until smooth, about 1 minute. Serve immediately.

Each serving provides: ½ Milk Exchange, 125 Calories Optional Exchange

— Honey 'Eggnog' —

SERVES 2

130 CALORIES PER SERVING

½ pint (300ml) skimmed milk

2oz (60g) vanilla ice cream

2 tablespoons thawed frozen whipped topping

1 teaspoon honey

¼ teaspoon each rum and brandy flavouring

pinch nutmeg

Place all ingredients except nutmeg in blender and blend until smooth. Pour into 2 champagne glasses and sprinkle each with pinch of nutmeg.

Each serving provides: ½ Milk Exchange, 85 Calories Optional Exchange

— Honey Shake —

SERVES 1

155 CALORIES PER SERVING

¼ pint (150ml) skimmed milk

2oz (60g) vanilla ice cream

½ teaspoon honey

¼ teaspoon vanilla flavouring

Place all ingredients in blender and blend until smooth, about 1 minute. Serve immediately.

Each serving provides: ½ Milk Exchange, 110 Calories Optional Exchange

— Honeyed Pear — Parfait

SERVES 2

205 CALORIES PER SERVING

2 ripe medium pears, cored, peeled and diced

1 teaspoon each lemon juice and honey

pinch cinnamon

10fl oz (300ml) low-fat natural yogurt

1 teaspoon vanilla flavouring

2 digestive biscuits, crushed

Chill 2 ice cream glasses. Mix pears, lemon juice, honey and cinnamon, cover and refrigerate until chilled. Mix yogurt and vanilla in another container, cover and refrigerate until chilled. To serve, spoon ¼ of fruit mixture into each glass, top with ¼ of yogurt mixture and repeat layers with remaining fruit and yogurt mixture. Sprinkle each parfait with half the biscuit crumbs.

Each serving provides: 1 Bread Exchange, 1 Fruit Exchange, 1 Milk Exchange, 10 Calories Optional Exchange

— Mango Shake —

SERVES 2

50 CALORIES PER SERVING

½ very ripe small mango, peeled and stoned

¼ pint (150ml) skimmed milk

1 tablespoon lemon juice

2 ice cubes

mint sprigs for garnish

Chill two large glasses. Place mango, milk and lemon juice in blender and blend until smooth. With motor running, add ice cubes, one at a time, blending after each addition until all ice is crushed. Pour half the mixture into each glass, garnish and serve immediately.

Each serving provides: ½ Fruit Exchange, ¼ Milk Exchange

— Yogurt-Fruit Pie —

SERVES 8

270 CALORIES PER SERVING

Crust

16 digestive biscuits, made into crumbs

8 teaspoons margarine, softened

Filling

4 tablespoons thawed frozen concentrated orange juice

8 teaspoons sugar

1 tablespoon unflavoured gelatine

15fl oz (450ml) low-fat natural yogurt

4oz (120g) canned crushed pineapple, no sugar added

1 teaspoon vanilla flavouring

Topping

3oz (90g) small seedless black grapes

3oz (90g) small seedless green grapes

5oz (150g) strawberries, halved

To Prepare Crust: Preheat oven to 350°F, 180°C, Gas Mark 4. Combine crumbs and margarine, mixing thoroughly. Using the back of a spoon, press crumb mixture over base and sides of 9-inch (23-cm) flan dish. Bake about 10 minutes or until crust is crisp and brown. Remove from oven and cool.

To Prepare Filling: Pour orange juice into small cup and sprinkle with sugar and gelatine. Stand cup in pan of boiling water and stir until gelatine is dissolved. Set aside. Gently stir yogurt and pineapple together, add gelatine mixture and vanilla and stir until completely blended. Pour mixture into cooled pie crust, cover and refrigerate for 4 hours or until firm. Use within 8 hours. To serve, arrange fruit decoratively over filling and serve immediately.

Each serving provides: 2 Bread Exchanges, 2 Fat Exchanges, ½ Fruit Exchange, 75 Calories Optional Exchange

— Creamy Chicken- — Mushroom Soup

SERVES 2

130 CALORIES PER SERVING

2 teaspoons margarine

2 tablespoons chopped onion

6oz (180g) mushrooms, sliced

1 tablespoon flour

12fl oz (360ml) water

1 chicken stock cube, crumbled

pinch thyme

1oz (30g) low-fat dry milk, mixed with ¼ pint (150ml) water

2 teaspoons dry sherry

pinch each salt and white pepper

1 teaspoon chopped parsley

Heat margarine in saucepan, add onion and saute, stirring occasionally, until softened. Add mushrooms and saute for 5 minutes longer. Remove and reserve 2 tablespoons mushroom mixture. Sprinkle flour over vegetables in saucepan and stir quickly to combine. Cook, stirring constantly, for 2 minutes. Gradually add water, stock cube and thyme and stirring constantly, bring mixture to the boil. Reduce heat, cover and simmer for 15 minutes. Puree soup in blender, in 2 batches if necessary. Pour soup back into saucepan. Stir in milk, sherry and reserved mushroom mixture and simmer for 5 minutes. Season with salt and pepper and serve garnished with parsley.

Each serving provides: 1½ Vegetable Exchanges, 1 Fat Exchange, ½ Milk Exchange, 20 Calories Optional Exchange

— Creamy Celery Soup —

SERVES 2

110 CALORIES PER SERVING

2 teaspoons margarine

3oz (90g) onion, chopped

8oz (240g) celery, chopped

1 teaspoon flour

1 chicken stock cube, crumbled

8fl oz (240ml) skimmed milk

pinch each nutmeg and white pepper

Heat margarine in non-stick frying pan, add onion and saute until transparent. Add celery and stir to combine. Reduce heat, cover and cook until celery is soft. Sprinkle flour and crumbled stock cube over vegetables and stir quickly to combine. Cook, stirring constantly, for 1 minute. Gradually add milk, still stirring, and bring to the boil. Reduce heat, season with nutmeg and pepper and simmer, stirring, until mixture thickens. Transfer soup to blender and puree at low speed until smooth. Reheat if necessary, but do not boil.

Each serving provides: 2 Vegetable Exchanges, 1 Fat Exchange, 45 Calories Optional Exchange

— Creamy Broccoli — Soup

SERVES 4

90 CALORIES PER SERVING

2 teaspoons margarine

3oz (90g) onion, chopped

10oz (300g) thawed frozen chopped broccoli

½ teaspoon salt

1 bay leaf

1 teaspoon flour

2oz (60g) low-fat dry milk, mixed with ½ pint (300ml) water

4fl oz (120ml) chicken stock, prepared according to package directions

Heat margarine in non-stick frying pan, add onion and saute until transparent. Add broccoli, salt and bay leaf and stir to combine. Sprinkle vegetables with flour and stir well. Cook, stirring constantly, for 1 minute. Gradually add milk, then stock, stirring constantly, and bring just to the boil. Reduce heat and simmer, stirring, until mixture thickens slightly. Remove and discard bay leaf. Transfer soup to blender container and puree at low speed until smooth. Reheat if necessary, but do not boil.

Each serving provides: 1½ Vegetable Exchanges, ½ Fat Exchange, ½ Milk Exchange, 5 Calories Optional Exchange

Yogurt-Fruit Pie (P61)

BREAD

In this section you will find recipes using both bread and the foods which play a similar role in the Food Plan, including potatoes, rice, pasta and sweetcorn. Flour comes under this heading, too, and we have included baking-day treats such as Cinnamon Crumb Coffee Cake and Orange Sponge Cake which are bound to win compliments all round!

— Sugar-Glazed — Cinnamon Wedges

SERVES 4

125 CALORIES PER SERVING

1½oz (45g) flour

pinch salt

4 teaspoons margarine

2 tablespoons low-fat natural yogurt

1 tablespoon flour for rolling out pastry

2 teaspoons thawed frozen whipped topping

1 tablespoon light brown sugar

pinch cinnamon

Mix flour and salt and rub in margarine until mixture resembles coarse breadcrumbs. Add yogurt and mix well. Form dough into a ball, wrap in cling film and refrigerate for at least 1 hour (may be kept in refrigerator for up to 3 days). Preheat oven to 425°F, 220°C, Gas Mark 7. Use extra tablespoon flour to flour board and sprinkle on dough before rolling out to form a round about ¼ inch (5 mm) thick. Use to line a 7-inch (18-cm) pie plate. Prick pastry well with a fork. Spread whipped topping over pastry and sprinkle entire surface with sugar and cinnamon. Bake until sugar is melted and no longer bubbles, 10 to 15 minutes. To serve, cut into 12 equal wedges.

Each serving provides: ½ Bread Exchange, 1 Fat Exchange, 40 Calories Optional Exchange

— Semolina-Date — Dessert

SERVES 1

255 CALORIES PER SERVING

½ pint (300ml) skimmed milk

2 dates, stoned and chopped

pinch salt

¾oz (20g) semolina

½ teaspoon sugar

¼ teaspoon vanilla flavouring

1 teaspoon margarine

pinch cinnamon

Place milk, dates and salt in small saucepan, bring to the boil and gradually stir in semolina. Add sugar and vanilla and cook, stirring frequently, for 7 to 8 minutes. Spoon into a bowl, stir in margarine and sprinkle with cinnamon.

Each serving provides: 1 Bread Exchange, 1 Fat Exchange, 1 Fruit Exchange, 1 Milk Exchange, 10 Calories Optional Exchange

— Strawberry-Topped — Crunchy Cereal

SERVES 2

130 CALORIES PER SERVING

5oz (150g) strawberries

2 teaspoons sugar

½ teaspoon grated orange peel

2fl oz (60ml) low-fat natural yogurt

1½oz (45g) crisped rice cereal

Place strawberries, sugar and orange peel in blender and puree. Stir in yogurt, but do not blend again as this thins the yogurt. Pour ¾oz (20g) cereal into each of 2 bowls and top each portion with half the strawberry puree.

Each serving provides: 1 Bread Exchange, ½ Fruit Exchange, 40 Calories Optional Exchange

— Plain Cake —

SERVES 8

135 CALORIES PER SERVING

3oz (90g) flour

1½ teaspoons baking powder

4 tablespoons margarine

2 tablespoons sugar

2 eggs

2 teaspoons vanilla flavouring

Grease a small loaf tin lightly with ½ teaspoon margarine. Sift the flour with the baking powder and set aside. Preheat oven to 350°F, 180°C, Gas Mark 4. Using electric mixer, cream remaining margarine, gradually add sugar and beat until light and fluffy. Beat in eggs, one at a time, beating after each addition until well mixed. Beat in vanilla, then gradually add flour, beating just until blended. Pour batter into loaf tin and bake 20 to 30 minutes or until cake is golden brown and a skewer, inserted in centre, comes out clean. Transfer tin to wire rack and let cake cool in tin. To serve, cut into 8 equal slices.

Each serving provides: ½ Bread Exchange, 1½ Fat Exchanges, 30 Calories Optional Exchange

Serving Suggestion: Toast 1 slice cake, place on serving plate and top with a 2oz (60g) scoop of vanilla ice cream and ½ teaspoon chocolate syrup. Increase Optional Exchange to 140 Calories.

— Hot Cross Buns —

SERVES 10

240 CALORIES PER SERVING

6fl oz (180ml) skimmed milk

4 tablespoons sugar

1 tablespoon dried yeast

12oz (360g) strong flour

1 teaspoon mixed spice

1 teaspoon salt

4 tablespoons margarine

3oz (90g) currants, soaked in warm water until plumped, then drained

Crosses

¾oz (20g) flour

2 teaspoons margarine

1 tablespoon low-fat natural yogurt

1 tablespoon flour for rolling pastry

2 tablespoons granulated sugar and 2 tablespoons water to glaze

Reserve 1 tablespoon skimmed milk, heat the remainder until hand hot. Whisk in 1 tablespoon sugar and all the dried yeast until dissolved, add 4oz (120g) flour. Cover and leave in a warm place 15 to 20 minutes until frothy. Sieve together the remaining flour, spice and salt. Rub in margarine. Stir in the currants and remaining sugar. Mix to form a soft dough with the frothy yeast batter. Either knead well by hand for about 10 minutes or use an electric mixer for 2 to 3 minutes. Cover with a damp cloth and leave in a warm place until risen to about double the size, 1½ to 2 hours. Knead the dough once again. Divide the dough into 10 even-sized pieces, shape to form buns. Place on non-stick baking sheets and cover with damp cloth. Return to the warm place until well risen.
To Make Pastry Crosses: Sieve the flour and rub in the margarine, mix to form a dough with the yogurt. Roll out as thinly as possible with the extra tablespoon flour. Cut into 20 strips.

Preheat oven to 400°F, 200°C, Gas Mark 6. Brush the buns with the reserved milk, lay over the pastry strips to form crosses. Bake for 15 to 20 minutes. While the buns are cooking, make the sugar glaze. Heat the sugar and water together until the sugar has dissolved. Boil uncovered for 1 minute. Brush the hot buns with the hot glaze. Transfer to a cooling rack.

Each serving provides: 1½ Bread Exchanges, 1 Fat Exchange, ¼ Fruit Exchange, 90 Calories Optional Exchange

•

— Spanish Rice —

SERVES 2

160 CALORIES PER SERVING

2 teaspoons olive or vegetable oil

4oz (120g) green pepper, seeded and chopped

6oz (180g) onions, chopped

1 small garlic clove, crushed

1½oz (45g) uncooked long grain rice

6fl oz (180ml) water

4oz (120g) canned tomatoes, pureed

1 chicken stock cube, crumbled

1 tablespoon chopped parsley

Heat oil in saucepan, add peppers, onions and garlic and saute until vegetables are soft, 3 to 4 minutes. Stir in all remaining ingredients except parsley and bring to the boil. Reduce heat, cover and let simmer, stirring occasionally, until rice is tender and liquid is absorbed, 20 to 25 minutes. Serve sprinkled with parsley.

Each serving provides: 1 Bread Exchange, 3 Vegetable Exchanges, 1 Fat Exchange

•

— Pasta Salad with — Herb Dressing

SERVES 4

205 CALORIES PER SERVING

1 garlic clove

pinch each salt and pepper

8 teaspoons olive oil

2 tablespoons chopped basil

1 tablespoon chopped parsley

2 drained canned anchovy fillets, mashed (optional)

8oz (240g) cooked pasta spirals (or any other type)

3oz (90g) red pepper, seeded and chopped

8 teaspoons grated Parmesan cheese

8 black olives, stoned and sliced

basil or parsley sprig to garnish

Crush garlic with salt and pepper. Combine garlic mixture with oil, basil, parsley and anchovies, if used. Set aside. Place remaining ingredients in salad bowl, add garlic mixture and toss well to coat. Cover and refrigerate until chilled. Serve garnished with sprig of basil or parsley.

Each serving provides: 1 Bread Exchange, ¼ Vegetable Exchange, 2 Fat Exchanges, 35 Calories Optional Exchange

•

Top: Spanish Rice
Bottom: Pasta Salad with Herb Dressing

— Hot Potato Salad —
with Vinegar Dressing

SERVES 2

140 CALORIES PER SERVING

2 teaspoons vegetable oil

1oz (30g) onion, thinly sliced

2 teaspoons imitation bacon bits

2 tablespoons cider vinegar

1 teaspoon sugar

pinch each salt and pepper

6oz (180g) peeled cooked potatoes, thinly sliced

Heat oil in small frying pan, add onion slices and bacon bits and saute until onion is transparent. Add vinegar, sugar, salt and pepper and cook, stirring occasionally, until mixture starts to boil. Add potatoes and cook, stirring gently, until well heated through. Serve hot.

Each serving provides: 1 Bread Exchange, ¼ Vegetable Exchange, 1 Fat Exchange, 20 Calories Optional Exchange

•

— Potato and Pea —
Curry

SERVES 2

125 CALORIES PER SERVING

1 teaspoon margarine

6oz (180g) peeled potatoes, cut into ½-inch (1-cm) cubes

6oz (180g) canned tomatoes, crushed

3oz (90g) fresh or frozen peas

1 teaspoon curry powder

pinch salt

4fl oz (120ml) water

Heat margarine in frying pan, add potatoes and tomatoes and saute for 5 minutes. Add peas, curry powder and salt, then stir in water. Cover and simmer, stirring occasionally, until potatoes and peas are tender, about 25 minutes. Add more water if necessary to prevent sticking.

Each serving provides: 1 Bread Exchange, 1½ Vegetable Exchanges, ½ Fat Exchange

•

— Potato Rosettes —

SERVES 4

115 CALORIES PER SERVING

9oz (270g) potatoes, peeled, cooked and drained

2 tablespoons buttermilk

4 teaspoons each grated Parmesan cheese and margarine

1½ teaspoons each chopped parsley and chives

¼ teaspoon salt

pinch white pepper

Sieve the potatoes into a mixing bowl. Add milk, 3 teaspoons cheese and the margarine and seasonings and mix well. Fit an icing bag with large rosette nozzle and pipe potato mixture on to non-stick baking sheet to form 8 spiral cones, each about 2 inches (5 cm) in diameter. Alternatively, spoon mixture onto baking sheet in 8 mounds and fork up surface decoratively. Sprinkle each potato cone with remainder of cheese and grill about 6 inches (15 cm) from heat, until golden brown.

Each serving provides: ¾ Bread Exchange, 1 Fat Exchange, 25 Calories Optional Exchange

•

— Spaghetti Pie —

SERVES 4

360 CALORIES PER SERVING

Crust

4 teaspoons margarine, softened

8oz (240g) cooked thin spaghetti

2 tablespoons grated Parmesan cheese

1 egg, beaten

Filling

5oz (150g) low-fat soft cheese

2 teaspoons margarine

3oz (90g) onion, chopped

2oz (60g) red or green pepper, seeded and chopped

1 garlic clove, crushed

7oz (210g) cooked minced beef, crumbled

8oz (240g) canned tomatoes, drained and chopped (reserve liquid)

2 teaspoons tomato puree

2oz (60g) mozzarella or Emmenthal cheese, grated

To Prepare Crust: Grease 9-inch (23-cm) flan dish with ½ teaspoon margarine. Combine remaining margarine with spaghetti, cheese and egg. Spread mixture over base and sides of flan dish to form a crust.

To Prepare Filling and Pie: Preheat oven to 350°F, 180°C, Gas Mark 4. Carefully spread soft cheese over bottom of crust and set aside. Heat margarine in frying pan, add onion, pepper and garlic and saute until onion is transparent. Add beef, tomatoes, reserved liquid and tomato puree and cook, stirring constantly, until mixture is hot and slightly thickened. Spoon beef mixture over soft cheese and bake for 20 to 25 minutes. Sprinkle pie with mozzarella or Emmenthal cheese and bake until cheese is melted and beginning to brown, about 5 minutes. Remove from oven and let stand for 5 minutes before cutting.

Each serving provides: 3 Protein Exchanges, 1 Bread Exchange, 1 Vegetable Exchange, 1½ Fat Exchanges, 20 Calories Optional Exchange

●

— Lasagne Rolls —

SERVES 2

395 CALORIES PER SERVING

½ teaspoon vegetable oil

5oz (150g) low-fat soft cheese

1 egg, beaten

1oz (30g) mozzarella cheese, grated

2 tablespoons grated Parmesan cheese

pinch each oregano, basil and garlic powder

4 sheets lasagne pasta (uncooked weight about 3oz/90g), cooked according to package directions and drained

4oz (120g) canned tomatoes, pureed

parsley sprigs for garnish

Preheat oven to 350°F, 180°C, Gas Mark 4. Grease 2 individual casseroles lightly with oil. Combine cheese, egg, mozzarella cheese, 1 tablespoon Parmesan cheese and the seasonings, mixing well. Place cooked lasagne on a damp towel, spoon ¼ of the cheese mixture lengthwise along the centre of each piece and roll carefully to enclose filling. Place 2 rolls in each casserole and divide pureed tomatoes between them. Sprinkle each roll with ¾ teaspoon Parmesan cheese and bake until well heated, 35 to 40 minutes. Serve garnished with parsley.

Each serving provides: 2 Protein Exchanges, 2 Bread Exchanges, 1 Vegetable Exchange, 45 Calories Optional Exchange

●

— Spiced Sweet — Potatoes

SERVES 2, ½ POTATO EACH

90 CALORIES PER SERVING

1 sweet potato, 6oz (180g)

1 teaspoon honey

pinch each cinnamon and nutmeg

Preheat oven to 400°F, 200°C, Gas Mark 6. Scrub sweet potato well and pierce the skin all over with a fork. Wrap potato in foil, using a piece big enough to leave airspace inside, and place on baking sheet. Bake for 35 to 40 minutes or until cooked through. Remove foil and let potato cool slightly. Reduce oven heat to 350°F, 180°C, Gas Mark 4. When cool enough to handle, cut in half lengthwise and scoop pulp out into a bowl, reserving shells. Add honey and spices to potato pulp and beat with electric mixer until smooth and fluffy. Divide mixture between reserved shells and bake until heated through, about 15 to 20 minutes.

Each serving provides: 1 Bread Exchange, 10 Calories Optional Exchange

●

— Baked Macaroni — Cheese

SERVES 2

455 CALORIES PER SERVING

2 teaspoons margarine

3oz (90g) onion, chopped

6oz (180g) cooked elbow macaroni

3oz (90g) Cheddar cheese, grated

2oz (60g) low-fat dry milk, mixed with ½ pint (300ml) water

1 large egg

¼ teaspoon salt

pinch cayenne pepper

¼ teaspoon paprika

Preheat oven to 350°F, 180°C, Gas Mark 4. Heat 1 teaspoon margarine in small non-stick frying pan, add onion and saute until transparent. Do not brown. Spoon half the macaroni into a casserole, top with half the cheese and half the cooked onion. Repeat layers. Mix milk, egg, salt and pepper, pour over macaroni mixture and sprinkle with paprika. Dot with remaining teaspoon margarine and bake until set, 20 to 25 minutes.

Each serving provides: 2 Protein Exchanges, 1½ Bread Exchanges, ½ Vegetable Exchange, 1 Fat Exchange, 1 Milk Exchange

●

— Rice and Onion — Soup

SERVES 4

140 CALORIES PER SERVING

4 teaspoons margarine

3oz (90g) onion, chopped

4 teaspoons flour

1 pint (600ml) water

2fl oz (60ml) dry sherry

2 chicken stock cubes, crumbled

4oz (120g) cooked long grain rice

1oz (30g) low-fat dry milk, mixed with ¼ pint (150ml) water

4 teaspoons chopped parsley

Heat margarine in saucepan. Add onion and saute, stirring constantly, until transparent. Add flour, stir quickly to combine and gradually stir in water. Add sherry and stock cubes and, stirring constantly, bring to the boil. Reduce heat to low and cook, stirring, until mixture thickens. Remove pan from heat, add rice and milk and stir to combine. Return to low heat and cook until soup is heated through. Do not boil. Serve each portion garnished with 1 teaspoon chopped parsley.

Each serving provides: ¼ Vegetable Exchange, ½ Bread Exchange, 1 Fat Exchange, ¼ Milk Exchange, 30 Calories Optional Exchange

— Pasta and — Vegetables in Cheese Sauce

SERVES 2

400 CALORIES PER SERVING

4 teaspoons margarine

2 tablespoons flour

½ pint (300ml) skimmed milk

pinch each salt, paprika and dry mustard

pinch each nutmeg (optional) and white pepper

2oz (60g) Emmenthal cheese, grated

8oz (240g) cooked broccoli florets

4oz (120g) cooked pearl onions

6oz (180g) cooked small mushroom caps

4oz (120g) cooked small macaroni

Heat margarine in saucepan, add flour and cook over low heat, stirring constantly, for 3 minutes. Remove pan from heat and gradually stir in milk. Continue stirring until mixture is smooth, add seasonings and cook over moderate heat, stirring constantly, until thickened. Reduce heat to low and cook for 10 minutes longer, stirring occasionally. Add cheese and cook, stirring constantly, until cheese is melted. Add vegetables and macaroni and cook, stirring gently, until vegetables and macaroni are well coated with sauce and heated through.

Each serving provides: 1 Protein Exchange, 1 Bread Exchange, 3 Vegetable Exchanges, 2 Fat Exchanges, ½ Milk Exchange, 30 Calories Optional Exchange

— Raisin-Rice Custard —

SERVES 2

225 CALORIES PER SERVING

½ pint (300ml) skimmed milk

1 tablespoon custard powder

2 teaspoons sugar

4oz (120g) cooked pudding rice

2oz (60g) raisins

½ teaspoon vanilla flavouring

cinnamon or nutmeg for garnish

Make up custard with milk, custard powder and sugar according to package directions. Allow to cool for 3 to 5 minutes. Mix rice, raisins and vanilla and stir into cooled custard. Divide mixture evenly between 2 small dessert dishes and sprinkle each with cinnamon or nutmeg. Cover and refrigerate until set.

Each serving provides: 1 Bread Exchange, 1 Fruit Exchange, ½ Milk Exchange, 35 Calories Optional Exchange

— Quick Corn — Chowder

SERVES 2

210 CALORIES PER SERVING

2 teaspoons margarine

3oz (90g) onion, chopped

2oz (60g) celery, chopped

1 tablespoon flour

½ pint (300ml) skimmed milk

6oz (180g) drained canned sweetcorn

1 teaspoon imitation bacon bits, crushed

pinch each salt, pepper and dry mustard

nutmeg for garnish

Heat margarine in saucepan, add onion and celery and saute until onion is transparent. Add flour and cook, stirring constantly, for 1 minute.

Gradually stir in milk and, stirring constantly, bring to the boil. Reduce heat and cook, stirring, until mixture is smooth and thickened, 2 to 3 minutes. Add all remaining ingredients except nutmeg and, stirring constantly, cook until well mixed and hot. Pour into 2 bowls and sprinkle each portion with pinch of nutmeg. (For a thicker and sweeter soup, canned cream-style corn may be used instead of sweetcorn.)

Each serving provides: 1 Bread Exchange, 1 Vegetable Exchange, 1 Fat Exchange, ½ Milk Exchange, 20 Calories Optional Exchange

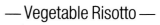

— Vegetable Risotto —

SERVES 2

150 CALORIES PER SERVING

2 teaspoons peanut oil

1½oz (45g) onions, chopped

1oz (30g) celery, chopped

2 tablespoons diced carrot

2 tablespoons chopped green pepper

1 garlic clove, crushed

8fl oz (240ml) water

1½oz (45g) uncooked long grain rice

½ chicken stock cube, crumbled

1½ teaspoons sesame seeds, toasted

Heat oil in small saucepan, add onion, celery, carrot, green pepper and garlic and saute until vegetables are tender-crisp. Stir in water, rice and stock cube and bring to the boil. Reduce heat, cover and simmer, stirring occasionally, until rice is tender and liquid is absorbed, 15 to 20 minutes. Stir in sesame seeds and serve hot.

Each serving provides: 1 Bread Exchange, ¾ Vegetable Exchange, 1 Fat Exchange, 10 Calories Optional Exchange

— Cheese Polenta —

SERVES 6

155 CALORIES PER SERVING

4½oz (135g) uncooked cornmeal

4fl oz (120ml) cold water

1¼ pints (750ml) boiling water

1 tablespoon margarine

1oz (30g) Parmesan cheese, grated

2oz (60g) Emmenthal cheese, grated

Mix cornmeal and cold water in saucepan, add boiling water and cook over high heat, stirring constantly, until mixture comes to the boil and thickens. Reduce heat, cover and cook, stirring occasionally, until mixture is smooth, 8 to 10 minutes. Preheat oven to 350°F, 180°C, Gas Mark 4. Grease a flameproof casserole lightly with margarine. Spoon in half the cooked cornmeal and smooth the top. Dot with half remaining margarine and sprinkle with ½oz (15g) Parmesan cheese. Repeat with remaining cornmeal, margarine and Parmesan cheese, top with Emmenthal cheese and bake until cheese is hot and bubbly, 20 to 25 minutes. Place casserole under hot grill until cheese is browned, about 1 minute.

Each serving provides: ½ Protein Exchange, 1 Bread Exchange, ½ Fat Exchange

— Couscous Salad —

SERVES 4

230 CALORIES PER SERVING

2 tablespoons olive or vegetable oil

½ chicken stock cube, crumbled

¼ teaspoon each cinnamon and ginger

12fl oz (360ml) water

3oz (90g) uncooked couscous

4oz (120g) raisins

6oz (180g) tomatoes, chopped

3oz (90g) courgettes, shredded or coarsely grated

2oz (60g) carrot, shredded or coarsely grated

1½oz (45g) onion, chopped

1 tablespoon lemon juice

¼ teaspoon salt

8 large lettuce leaves

parsley sprigs for garnish

Pour 1 tablespoon oil in a saucepan and mix in the crumbled stock cube, cinnamon and ginger. Add water and bring to the boil. Stir in couscous, bring back to the boil and cook until liquid is absorbed. Transfer to large bowl and let cool. Add raisins, tomatoes, courgettes, carrot, onion, lemon juice, salt and remaining tablespoon oil to cooled couscous mixture and toss to combine. Cover and refrigerate for several hours to allow flavours to blend (may be refrigerated overnight). Toss salad again just before serving on bed of lettuce leaves. Garnish with parsley sprigs. Serve couscous salad with cheese or cold cooked meat or poultry.

Each serving provides: 1 Bread Exchange, 1½ Vegetable Exchanges, 1½ Fat Exchanges, 1 Fruit Exchange

— Roasted Chestnuts —

SERVES 6

75 CALORIES PER SERVING

36 small chestnuts

To Roast: Using a sharp vegetable knife, cut a cross through the flat side of each chestnut, partially penetrating top portion of nutmeat. Place in shallow baking tin and add just enough water to cover the bottom of tin. Roast at 350°F, 180°C, Gas Mark 4, until peel on cut side begins to separate, 30 to 40 minutes. Serve hot as a snack, or peel and freeze for future use in stuffings and desserts.

To Peel: Place roasted chestnuts in bowl of warm water. Peel off outer shell and brown inner skin, keeping chestnuts whole if possible.

To Freeze: Place peeled chestnuts in plastic freezer bags, seal securely, pressing out as much air as possible, and freeze.

Each serving provides: 1 Bread Exchange

— Chestnut Stuffing —

SERVES 6

165 CALORIES PER SERVING

2 tablespoons vegetable oil

6oz (180g) onions, chopped

2oz (60g) celery, chopped

2oz (60g) red or green pepper, seeded and chopped

1 chicken stock cube, crumbled

2 garlic cloves, crushed

6oz (180g) mushrooms, sliced

18 peeled Roasted Chestnuts (see page 71), chopped

6oz (180g) cooked long grain rice

3oz (90g) raisins

2 tablespoons chopped parsley

¼ teaspoon allspice

pinch freshly ground pepper

Heat oil in frying pan, add onions, celery, pepper, crumbled stock cube and garlic and saute over medium heat until vegetables are tender-crisp, about 5 minutes. Add mushrooms and continue sauteing for 5 minutes longer. Transfer vegetable mixture to a bowl, add remaining ingredients and toss well to combine. Transfer to shallow casserole and bake at 325°F, 160°C, Gas Mark 3, for 20 minutes. This stuffing may also be frozen, uncooked, for future use.

Each serving provides: 1 Bread Exchange, 1 Vegetable Exchange, 1 Fat Exchange, ½ Fruit Exchange

•

— Broad Bean and — Pepper Saute

SERVES 2

100 CALORIES PER SERVING

1 teaspoon each olive oil and margarine

½ garlic clove, crushed

3oz (90g) onion, chopped

2oz (60g) red pepper, seeded and chopped

6oz (180g) broad beans or frozen broad beans, thawed to room temperature

1½ teaspoons chopped fresh basil or ½ teaspoon dried

1 teaspoon dry white wine

pinch each salt and pepper

Heat oil and margarine in non-stick frying pan, add garlic and saute for 1 minute, being careful not to burn. Add onion and red pepper and saute until onion is transparent. Add remaining ingredients, stirring to combine. Reduce heat, cover and cook, stirring occasionally, for about 15 minutes or until vegetables are done to taste.

Each serving provides: 2 Vegetable Exchanges, 1 Fat Exchange, 5 Calories Optional Exchange

•

— Almond Biscuits —

SERVES 4

150 CALORIES PER SERVING

1½oz (45g) flour

¼ teaspoon baking powder

pinch bicarbonate of soda

2 tablespoons each margarine, softened, and sugar

1 egg

½ teaspoon almond flavouring

¼ teaspoon vanilla flavouring

Preheat oven to 375°F, 190°C, Gas Mark 5. Sift together flour, baking powder and bicarbonate of soda and set aside. Using electric mixer, cream margarine with sugar until light and fluffy, add dry ingredients and beat until combined. Add egg and flavourings and continue beating until batter is smooth. Drop batter by heaping tablespoons onto 2 non-stick baking sheets, forming 6 biscuits on each sheet and leaving 4-inch (10-cm) spaces between them to allow for spreading. Bake until edges of biscuits are dark brown, 8 to 10 minutes. Lift off carefully with a palette knife and cool on wire rack.

Each serving provides: ½ Bread Exchange, 1½ Fat Exchanges, 45 Calories Optional Exchange

— Lemon Biscuits —

SERVES 8

100 CALORIES PER SERVING

10 teaspoons margarine

5 teaspoons sugar

1 tablespoon lemon juice

½ teaspoon grated lemon peel

3oz (90g) flour

Preheat oven to 300°F, 150°C, Gas Mark 2. Using electric mixer, combine all ingredients except flour, beating until light and smooth. Add flour and beat until flour has been incorporated and mixture forms sticky batter. Using wet hands, roll batter into 16 small balls, about 1 tablespoon batter each. Arrange on non-stick baking sheet, leaving 2-inch (5-cm) spaces between them. Lightly press each ball down with a fork to flatten, then press down lightly in opposite direction to make a checkerboard pattern. Bake until edges of biscuits are lightly browned, about 15 minutes. Remove carefully with a palette knife and cool on wire rack.

Each serving provides: ½ Bread Exchange, 1¼ Fat Exchanges, 15 Calories Optional Exchange

— Apple Crumb Muffins —

SERVES 12

185 CALORIES PER SERVING

8oz (240g) flour

4 tablespoons sugar

1 tablespoon baking powder

1 teaspoon mixed spice

8fl oz (240ml) skimmed milk

1 medium eating apple, cored, peeled and grated

4 tablespoons margarine, melted

1 egg

Crumb Topping

1oz (30g) flour

7 teaspoons sugar

2 tablespoons margarine, melted

pinch cinnamon

To Prepare Batter: Place 12 paper cake cases (2½-inch/6-cm diameter) inside 12 deep bun tins. Preheat oven to 400°F, 200°C, Gas Mark 6. Combine first 4 ingredients in mixing bowl. Mix milk, apple, margarine and egg in separate bowl. Pour into dry ingredients and stir until combined. Do not beat or over-mix. Batter should be lumpy. Fill each cake case with an equal amount of batter, each should be about ⅔ full.

To Prepare Topping and Bake: Mix all ingredients for topping, stirring until thoroughly combined. Sprinkle an equal amount of topping over each muffin and bake for 15 to 20 minutes or until muffins are golden brown and a skewer inserted in centre comes out dry. Remove carefully from tins and cool on wire rack.

Each serving provides: 1 Bread Exchange, 1½ Fat Exchanges, 50 Calories Optional Exchange

•

— Rice-Crisp Biscuits —

SERVES 4

95 CALORIES PER SERVING

1 tablespoon sugar

2 teaspoons margarine, softened

½ teaspoon vanilla flavouring

1 egg, beaten

¾oz (20g) self raising flour

¾oz (20g) crisped rice cereal

Preheat oven to 350°F, 180°C, Gas Mark 4. Cream sugar well with the margarine and vanilla. Add egg and beat well. Work in the flour, then lightly fold in cereal. Do not overmix or beat. Drop batter in heaped teaspoons on to non-stick baking sheet, making 12 biscuits and leaving 2-inch (5-cm) spaces between them. Flatten each biscuit slightly with a moistened fork. Bake until golden brown, 8 to 10 minutes. Remove biscuits carefully with a palette knife and cool on wire rack.

Each serving provides: ½ Bread Exchange, ½ Fat Exchange, 30 Calories Optional Exchange

Variations:

1. Lemon-Crisp Biscuits – Add 2 teaspoons each grated lemon peel and lemon juice to batter before adding cereal.

95 CALORIES PER SERVING

2. Raisin Biscuits – Add 2oz (60g) raisins to batter before adding cereal; add ½ Fruit Exchange to Exchange Information.

130 CALORIES PER SERVING

3. Spiced Raisin Biscuits – When preparing Raisin Biscuits, add ½ teaspoon cinnamon and pinch ginger to sifted flour.

130 CALORIES PER SERVING

4. Chocolate Biscuits – Decrease sugar to 2 teaspoons. Add 1 teaspoon chocolate syrup to batter before adding cereal.

95 CALORIES PER SERVING

•

— Sugar Muffins —

SERVES 4

260 CALORIES PER SERVING

3oz (90g) flour

3 tablespoons sugar

1½ teaspoons baking powder

8 teaspoons margarine, softened

2 eggs, beaten

½oz (15g) low-fat dry milk, mixed with 2½fl oz (75ml) water

1 teaspoon vanilla flavouring

Preheat oven to 425°F, 220°C, Gas Mark 7. Mix flour, 2 tablespoons sugar and the baking powder and rub in 6 teaspoons margarine until mixture resembles coarse bread-crumbs. Mix eggs, milk and vanilla, add to flour mixture and mix well to make a thin batter. Using 1 teaspoon margarine, lightly grease 8 deep bun tins (2½-inch/6-cm diameter). Divide batter between tins; each should be about half full. Bake until muffins are golden brown, about 10 minutes. While muffins are baking, melt remaining teaspoon margarine. Remove cooked muffins from oven and brush each with ⅛ of the melted margarine. Sprinkle each with ⅛ of the remaining tablespoon sugar and return to oven for 2 minutes longer. Remove carefully from tins and cool on wire rack.

Each serving provides: ½ Protein Exchange, 1 Bread Exchange, 2 Fat Exchanges, 60 Calories Optional Exchange

•

— Orange Sponge Cake —

SERVES 12

110 CALORIES PER SERVING

4½oz (135g) flour

½ teaspoon salt

3fl oz (90ml) thawed frozen concentrated orange juice

2 teaspoons grated orange peel

6 large eggs, separated, at room temperature

¼ teaspoon cream of tartar

4 tablespoons sugar

Sift flour with salt and set aside. Mix juice with enough water to make 4fl oz (120ml) liquid, add orange peel and set aside. Preheat oven to 350°F, 180°C, Gas Mark 4. Using electric mixer on high speed, beat egg yolks until thick and pale yellow. Reduce mixer to low speed and beat in flour and juice mixture alternately. Mix egg whites and cream of tartar and, using clean beaters, beat at high speed until soft peaks form. Gradually add sugar, beating until stiff peaks form. Fold ¼ of beaten whites into yolk mixture, pour yolk mixture into remaining beaten whites and fold in gently until just blended. Turn batter into 10-inch (25-cm) ring cake tin and run a knife through batter to release air bubbles. Bake 35 to 40 minutes or until cake is golden brown and springs back when touched with tip of finger. Cool in tin until completely cold, then run knife round edges of cake to loosen before turning out. Cut into 12 equal slices.

Each serving provides: ½ Protein Exchange, ½ Bread Exchange, 35 Calories Optional Exchange

●

— Apple-Orange Spice — Buns

SERVES 4

295 CALORIES PER SERVING

3oz (90g) flour

1½ teaspoons baking powder

½ teaspoon cinnamon

¼ teaspoon bicarbonate of soda

pinch each salt, nutmeg and ground cloves

1oz (30g) low-fat dry milk

8 teaspoons margarine

4 teaspoons brown sugar

1 large egg, separated

2 medium apples, cored, peeled and grated

2oz (60g) raisins

4 teaspoons concentrated apple juice

1 teaspoon grated orange peel

pinch cream of tartar

1 teaspoon vegetable oil

Preheat oven to 375°F, 190°C, Gas Mark 5. Sift together flour, baking powder, cinnamon, bicarbonate of soda, salt, nutmeg and cloves, stir in low-fat dry milk and set aside. Cream margarine with sugar, add egg yolk and, using electric mixer on medium speed, beat until thick and creamy. Add apples, raisins, juice and orange peel and stir to combine. Add flour mixture and beat until well blended. In separate bowl, using clean beaters and mixer on high speed, beat egg white with cream of tartar until stiff but not dry and fold into batter. Using the vegetable oil, lightly grease 8 non-stick deep bun tins (2½-inch/6-cm diameter) or 16 small non-stick bun tins. Divide batter between tins. Tins should be about ⅔ full. Bake 20 to 25 minutes or until skewer, inserted in centre, comes out clean. Remove carefully from tins and cool on wire rack.

Each serving provides: 1 Bread Exchange, 2 Fat Exchanges, 1 Fruit Exchange, ¼ Milk Exchange, 60 Calories Optional Exchange

— Vanilla Chocolate — Sandwich Biscuits

SERVES 6

65 CALORIES PER SERVING

1½oz (45g) flour

¼ teaspoon baking powder

4 teaspoons margarine

1 tablespoon sugar

½ teaspoon vanilla flavouring

¼ teaspoon grated lemon peel

2 teaspoons iced water

1 teaspoon chocolate spread or lemon curd

1 tablespoon flour for rolling out pastry

½ teaspoon icing sugar

Sift together flour and baking powder and set aside. Cream margarine with sugar, add vanilla and lemon peel and stir to combine. Add sifted flour and iced water and mix to form a dough. Preheat oven to 375°F, 190°C, Gas Mark 5. Use extra tablespoon flour to flour board and sprinkle on dough before rolling to about ⅛-inch (3-mm) thickness. Cut out 6 biscuits with 2-inch (5-cm) diameter round cutter, cut out centre with 1-inch (2.5-cm) fluted cutter. Gather up scraps and re-roll dough to cut 6 x 2-inch (5-cm) fluted bases. Place on a non-stick baking sheet and bake for 10 to 12 minutes. Remove biscuits carefully with spatula and cool on wire rack. Spread 6 biscuits with chocolate spread or lemon curd and top with remaining 6 biscuits.

Each serving provides: ¼ Bread Exchange, ½ Fat Exchange, 30 Calories Optional Exchange

●

Top: Coconut Custard Tarts (P77)
Bottom: Vanilla Chocolate Sandwich Biscuits

— Baked Alaska —

SERVES 4

270 CALORIES PER SERVING

8oz (240g) vanilla ice cream, slightly softened

2 egg whites, at room temperature

pinch cream of tartar

2 tablespoons icing sugar, sifted

8 digestive biscuits, broken into pieces

Line a small loaf tin with sheet of foil large enough to overhang edges. Pack softened ice cream into tin and bring edges of foil up to cover top. Freeze until firm. Using electric mixer, beat egg whites with cream of tartar until soft peaks form, gradually add sugar and continue beating until egg whites are stiff but not dry. Preheat grill. Transfer ice cream to a flameproof serving dish and peel off foil. Arrange digestive biscuits along sides and over top of ice cream and spread with meringue, covering ice cream and biscuits completely. Grill until meringue is lightly browned, 1 to 2 minutes. Serve immediately.

Each serving provides: 2 Bread Exchanges, 140 Calories Optional Exchange

— Cinnamon Crumb — Coffee Cake

SERVES 8

255 CALORIES PER SERVING

9oz (270g) flour

3 tablespoons sugar

2 teaspoons baking powder

1 teaspoon bicarbonate of soda

¼ teaspoon salt

1 teaspoon vegetable oil

5 tablespoons margarine

2 eggs

8fl oz (240ml) buttermilk

1 teaspoon vanilla flavouring

½ teaspoon grated lemon peel

1 tablespoon brown sugar

½ teaspoon cinnamon

Preheat oven to 400°F, 200°C, Gas Mark 6. Set aside 2 tablespoons flour and 4 teaspoons margarine. Sift remaining flour with the sugar, baking powder, bicarbonate of soda and salt. Grease an 8-inch (20-cm) square or round non-stick cake tin with the oil and rub the remainder of the margarine into the remaining dry ingredients until mixture resembles coarse breadcrumbs. Add eggs, buttermilk, vanilla and lemon peel and, using electric mixer, beat just until smooth. Pour into cake tin. Mix remaining 4 teaspoons margarine with the brown sugar. Add remaining 2 tablespoons flour and the cinnamon and mix until crumbly. Sprinkle crumbs evenly over batter and bake for 25 to 30 minutes or until cake pulls away slightly from sides of tin. Transfer to wire rack and let cake cool in tin. To serve, cut into 8 equal pieces.

Each serving provides: 1½ Bread Exchanges, 2 Fat Exchanges, 55 Calories Optional Exchange

— Oatmeal- — Blackcurrant Buns

SERVES 12

180 CALORIES PER SERVING

4½oz (135g) flour

4½oz (135g) porridge oats

6 tablespoons sugar

1 tablespoon baking powder

½ teaspoon salt

5fl oz (150ml) skimmed milk

2 eggs

4 tablespoons vegetable oil

10oz (300g) blackcurrants, fresh or frozen (thawed before using)

1 teaspoon cinnamon

Preheat oven to 425°F, 220°C, Gas Mark 7. Place 12 paper cake cases (2½-inch/6-cm diameter) inside 12 deep bun tins, or 24 small paper cake cases inside 24 small bun tins. Mix flour, porridge oats, 5 tablespoons sugar and the baking powder and salt. Mix milk, eggs and oil, add to the flour mixture and beat until all ingredients are blended. Fold in blackcurrants. Pour an equal amount of batter into each cake case. Each will be about ⅔ full. Combine remaining tablespoon of sugar with the cinnamon and sprinkle evenly over buns. Bake for 20 to 25 minutes or until buns are lightly browned and a skewer, inserted in centre, comes out dry. Remove carefully from tins and cool on wire rack.

Each serving provides: 1 Bread Exchange, 1 Fat Exchange, 50 Calories Optional Exchange

— Coconut Custard — Tarts

SERVES 12

85 CALORIES PER SERVING

3oz (90g) flour

¼ teaspoon salt

8 teaspoons margarine

2fl oz (60ml) low-fat natural yogurt

1 tablespoon flour for rolling out pastry

½ pint (300ml) skimmed milk

2 tablespoons custard powder

2 tablespoons sugar

8 teaspoons shredded coconut, toasted

To Prepare Crust: Mix flour and salt and rub in margarine until mixture resembles coarse breadcrumbs. Add yogurt and mix thoroughly to form dough. Form dough into a ball, wrap in cling film and refrigerate for at least 1 hour (may be kept in refrigerator for up to 3 days). Preheat oven to 400°F, 200°C, Gas Mark 6. Use extra tablespoon flour to flour board and sprinkle on dough before rolling. Roll dough out and divide between 12 patty tins. Prick well with a fork and bake 10 to 12 minutes or until lightly browned.

To Prepare Filling: Using milk, custard powder and sugar, make up custard according to package directions. Remove from heat. Let cool slightly, then pour into cooled tart cases. Sprinkle each with a little shredded coconut and serve.

Each serving provides: ¼ Bread Exchange, ½ Fat Exchange, 45 Calories Optional Exchange

•

— Potato Torte —

SERVES 8

245 CALORIES PER SERVING

3oz (90g) flour

3 tablespoons warm water

4 teaspoons vegetable oil

pinch salt

8 teaspoons margarine

6oz (180g) spring onions, chopped

1 tablespoon flour for rolling out pastry

12oz (360g) cooked potatoes, mashed

10oz (300g) low-fat soft cheese

4 eggs

1 teaspoon salt

¼ teaspoon freshly ground pepper

4 teaspoons grated Parmesan cheese

Mix flour, water, oil and salt in a mixing bowl and knead together to form a smooth ball. The dough should cling together without being sticky – up to 1 tablespoon more warm water may be added if necessary. Wrap in cling film and set aside while preparing filling. Heat margarine in small frying pan, add spring onions and saute over low heat until soft. Set aside. Mix mashed potatoes, soft cheese, 3 eggs, 1 teaspoon salt and the pepper. Beat until smooth with electric mixer or in food processor. Stir in sauteed spring onions. Use extra tablespoon flour to flour board and sprinkle on dough before rolling. Roll dough out to make a rectangle about ⅛ inch (3 mm) thick. Use dough to line a baking tin about 10 x 6 x 2 inches (25 x 15 x 5 cm), leaving edges overlapping the sides slightly. Spoon potato mixture into the tin and turn edges of pastry in over the filling, leaving centre uncovered. Preheat oven to 350°F, 180°C, Gas Mark 4. Beat remaining egg with Parmesan cheese and pour over entire surface of torte. Bake until browned, 35 to 40 minutes. Remove from oven and let stand until set, about 15 minutes, before serving.

Each serving provides: 1 Protein Exchange, 1 Bread Exchange, ¼ Vegetable Exchange, 1½ Fat Exchanges, 15 Calories Optional Exchange

•

— Bran Muffins —

SERVES 12

160 CALORIES PER SERVING

3oz (90g) bran flakes, or bran flakes with sultanas, crumbled

6oz (180g) wholemeal flour

4 tablespoons sugar

1 tablespoon baking powder

8fl oz (240ml) skimmed milk

6 tablespoons margarine, melted

1 egg, beaten

Preheat oven to 400°F, 200°C, Gas Mark 6. Mix cereal, flour, sugar and baking powder. Mix milk, margarine and egg in separate bowl. Add milk mixture to dry ingredients and, using a fork, stir to combine. Do not overmix or beat. Divide mixture between 12 deep non-stick bun tins (2½-inch/6-cm diameter). Bake for 15 to 20 minutes or until muffins are browned and a skewer inserted in centre of muffin comes out dry. Remove carefully from tins and eat warm.

Each serving provides: 1 Bread Exchange, 1½ Fat Exchanges, 35 Calories Optional Exchange

•

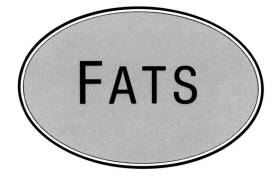

FATS

*T*he secret of using fats is to use just a little at a time, and the
Food Plan makes the most of margarine, vegetable oil and
low-fat spreads. You can get plenty of flavour and texture with
a modest spoonful of salad dressing, and just to prove it, try our
Buttermilk Dressing! Make marinades, too, and turn meat or
poultry in them for several hours before cooking – particularly
good for barbecues, tangy kebabs and lots of oriental meat dishes.

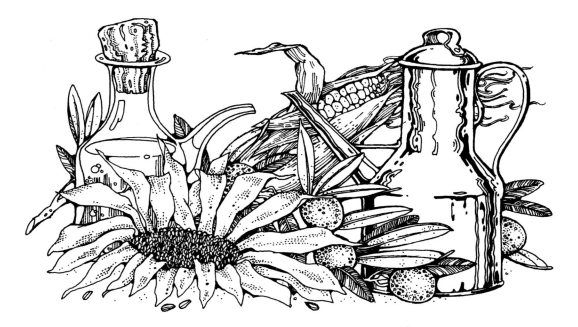

— Creole Sauce —

SERVES 4

40 CALORIES PER SERVING

2 teaspoons vegetable oil

3oz (90g) onion, chopped

1 garlic clove, crushed

4oz (120g) green pepper, chopped

3oz (90g) mushrooms, sliced

2oz (60g) celery, chopped

8oz (240g) canned tomatoes, drained and chopped (reserve liquid)

6fl oz (180ml) beef stock, prepared according to package directions

1 bay leaf

1 tablespoon chopped parsley

¼ teaspoon salt

pinch pepper

Heat oil in a saucepan, add onion and garlic and saute until onion is softened. Add green pepper, mushrooms and celery and saute for 5 minutes. Add tomatoes, reserved liquid, stock and bay leaf. Cover and simmer for 20 minutes, stirring occasionally. Stir in parsley, salt and pepper. Remove bay leaf before serving.

Each serving provides: 2 Vegetable Exchanges, ½ Fat Exchange

— Curry Sauce —

SERVES 4

55 CALORIES PER SERVING

2 teaspoons margarine

1 tablespoon each chopped onion and flour

1 teaspoon curry powder

8fl oz (240ml) skimmed milk, hot

pinch each salt and pepper

Heat margarine in small saucepan, add onion and saute until softened. Add flour and cook over low heat, stirring constantly, for 3 minutes. Add curry powder and continue to stir and cook for 1 minute longer. Remove from heat. Gradually add hot milk, stirring, until mixture is smooth. Add salt and pepper and cook over low heat, stirring frequently, for 10 minutes.

Each serving provides: ½ Fat Exchange, 30 Calories Optional Exchange

— Buttermilk Dressing —

SERVES 4

75 CALORIES PER SERVING

1 egg, well beaten

4 teaspoons mayonnaise

1 tablespoon wine vinegar, warmed

2 teaspoons French mustard

5fl oz (150ml) buttermilk

½ teaspoon Worcestershire sauce

pinch white pepper

Combine egg, mayonnaise, vinegar and mustard, mixing well. Gradually beat in buttermilk and seasonings.

Each serving provides: 1 Fat Exchange, 25 Calories Optional Exchange

— Lemon Marinade —

SERVES 2

45 CALORIES PER SERVING

3 tablespoons lemon juice

2 teaspoons olive oil

2 garlic cloves, crushed

½ teaspoon oregano or marjoram

¼ teaspoon salt

pinch pepper

Combine all ingredients and mix well. Use as a marinade for fish.

Each serving provides: 1 Fat Exchange

—Lemon-Mustard— Vinaigrette

SERVES 4

50 CALORIES PER SERVING

4 teaspoons olive or vegetable oil

1 tablespoon each wine vinegar and lemon juice

2 teaspoons French mustard

pinch white pepper

Mix all ingredients in screw-topped jar and shake well to combine.

Each serving provides: 1 Fat Exchange

— 'Hollandaise' — Sauce

SERVES 4

25 CALORIES PER SERVING

4fl oz (120ml) chicken stock, prepared according to package directions

1 tablespoon cornflour

2 tablespoons each margarine and mayonnaise

1½ teaspoons lemon juice

pinch each salt, white pepper and cayenne pepper

Mix stock and cornflour and cook over medium heat, stirring constantly, until mixture comes to the boil. Continue cooking and stirring until thickened, about 1 minute longer. Remove sauce from heat and add margarine, stirring until margarine is melted. Add remaining ingredients and stir to combine.

Each serving provides: 3 Fat Exchanges, 10 Calories Optional Exchange

•

— Anchovy Vinaigrette —

SERVES 2

100 CALORIES PER SERVING

7 teaspoons wine vinegar

4 drained canned anchovy fillets, mashed

4 teaspoons olive oil

pinch basil

¼ garlic clove, crushed

Gradually stir vinegar into anchovies, mixing well to combine. Add oil in a thin stream, beating constantly. Stir in basil and garlic and mix well.

Each serving provides: 2 Fat Exchanges, 10 Calories Optional Exchange

•

— Parsley Vinaigrette —

SERVES 1

90 CALORIES PER SERVING

1 teaspoon each olive oil, vegetable oil, wine vinegar and water

1 teaspoon chopped parsley

½ teaspoon Worcestershire sauce

pinch each salt and pepper

artificial sweetener to equal ¼ teaspoon sugar

Place all ingredients in a small bowl and beat together until well mixed.

Variations:
1. Substitute chopped fresh mint for the parsley.
2. Substitute lemon juice for the vinegar.

Each serving provides: 2 Fat Exchanges

•

— Chicken Gravy —

SERVES 4

35 CALORIES PER SERVING

2 teaspoons margarine

3oz (90g) carrot, chopped

2oz (60g) celery, including leaves, chopped

12fl oz (360ml) water

2 teaspoons cornflour

1 chicken stock cube, crumbled

Heat margarine in small frying pan, add vegetables and saute until softened. Mix 1 tablespoon water with the cornflour and add to vegetable mixture with remaining water and stock cube. Reduce heat and simmer for 5 minutes. Let cool slightly. Pour vegetable mixture into blender and process at low speed until smooth. Return to the pan and reheat.

Each serving provides: ½ Vegetable Exchange, ½ Fat Exchange, 10 Calories Optional Exchange

— Orange-Honey — Vinaigrette

SERVES 1

75 CALORIES PER SERVING

1 tablespoon thawed frozen concentrated orange juice

2 teaspoons wine vinegar

1 teaspoon each basil, chopped chives and vegetable oil

½ teaspoon honey

pinch each salt and pepper

Mix all ingredients in screw-topped jar and shake well to combine.

Each serving provides: 1 Fat Exchange, ½ Fruit Exchange, 10 Calories Optional Exchange

•

— Sesame Vinaigrette —

SERVES 2

110 CALORIES PER SERVING

4 teaspoons vegetable oil

1 teaspoon sesame seeds

½ garlic clove, crushed

4 tablespoons wine vinegar

1 teaspoon sugar

¼ teaspoon salt

pinch pepper

Pour oil into frying pan, add sesame seeds and cook over low heat, stirring constantly, until seeds are lightly browned. Stir in garlic and remove from heat. Combine vinegar, sugar, salt and pepper, add sesame seed mixture and mix well.

Each serving provides: 2 Fat Exchanges, 20 Calories Optional Exchange

•

— Brown Gravy —

SERVES 4

50 CALORIES PER SERVING

**1 tablespoon each margarine and
flour**

**2 tablespoons each chopped
carrot, celery and onion**

8 fl oz (240ml) water

**1 tablespoon tomato puree mixed
with 1 tablespoon water**

½ beef stock cube, crumbled

1 bay leaf

½ garlic clove

pinch each pepper and thyme

Heat margarine in small saucepan,
add flour and cook, stirring
constantly, for 3 minutes. Add carrot,
celery and onion and continue to stir
and cook until vegetables are lightly
browned, about 5 minutes. Remove
from heat and gradually stir in water.
Add remaining ingredients, stirring
to combine. Return pan to heat and,
stirring constantly, bring mixture to
the boil. Reduce heat and simmer,
stirring occasionally, for 30 minutes.
Let mixture cool slightly, then
remove and discard bay leaf. Transfer
gravy to blender container and puree
until smooth.

Each serving provides: ¼ Vegetable Exchange, ½ Fat
Exchange, 25 Calories Optional Exchange

•

— Barbecue Marinade —

SERVES 2

70 CALORIES PER SERVING

2 teaspoons vegetable oil

2 tablespoons chopped onion

8 teaspoons tomato ketchup

2 tablespoons water

**1 teaspoon each Worcestershire
sauce and wine vinegar**

½ teaspoon dry mustard

¼ to ½ teaspoon hot pepper sauce

Heat oil in small saucepan, add onion
and saute until softened. Stir in
remaining ingredients and simmer,
stirring constantly, for 3 minutes.
Cool. Use as a marinade for poultry.

Each serving provides: ¼ Vegetable Exchange, 1 Fat
Exchange, 20 Calories Optional Exchange

•

— Chinese-Style — Marinade

SERVES 2

60 CALORIES PER SERVING

2 tablespoons soy sauce

1 tablespoon lemon juice

2 teaspoons vegetable oil

**1 teaspoon each chopped peeled
ginger root and honey**

1 medium garlic clove, crushed

Combine all ingredients and mix
well. Use as a marinade for poultry or
fish.

Each serving provides: 1 Fat Exchange, 10 Calories
Optional Exchange

Variation:
Substitute 2 tablespoons dry sherry
for the lemon juice and proceed as
directed. Increase Optional Exchange
to 25 calories.

•

— Swiss Cheese Sauce —

SERVES 4

160 CALORIES PER SERVING

**2 tablespoons each margarine and
flour**

8 fl oz (240ml) skimmed milk

**2oz (60g) Emmenthal cheese,
grated**

¼ teaspoon salt

**pinch each white pepper and
cayenne pepper**

Heat margarine in small saucepan,
add flour and cook, stirring
constantly, for 2 minutes. Set aside.
Heat milk just to boiling point and
remove from heat. Stir milk into flour
mixture a little at a time, mixing well
with wooden spoon to avoid lumps.
Cook over moderate heat, stirring
constantly, until thickened, add
cheese, salt and peppers and continue
cooking and stirring until cheese is
melted. Reduce heat as low as possible
and cook, stirring occasionally, for 10
minutes. Pour over cooked
vegetables, such as cauliflower,
broccoli, asparagus or potato and
brown lightly under the grill.

Each serving provides: ½ Protein Exchange, 1½ Fat
Exchanges, 35 Calories Optional Exchange

•

— Veloute Sauce —

SERVES 4

55 CALORIES PER SERVING

4 teaspoons each margarine and flour

8fl oz (240ml) chicken stock, prepared according to package directions

pinch each salt and pepper

Heat margarine in small saucepan, add flour and cook over low heat, stirring constantly, for 2 minutes. Set aside. Bring stock to the boil in another saucepan and remove from heat. Add stock gradually to margarine mixture, stirring well after each addition to avoid lumps. Cook over medium heat, stirring constantly until thickened, and season with salt and pepper. Reduce heat to as low as possible and continue cooking for 15 minutes longer, stirring occasionally. Serve with fish, poultry or meat.

Each serving provides: 1 Fat Exchange, 10 Calories Optional Exchange

— Parmesan Pesto —

SERVES 2

155 CALORIES PER SERVING

4oz (120g) fresh basil leaves, chopped

4 teaspoons olive oil

½ teaspoon salt

pinch pepper

1 garlic clove, crushed

1oz (30g) grated Parmesan cheese

Place all ingredients except cheese in blender and puree until smooth, stopping motor when necessary to scrape down sides of container. Transfer sauce to small bowl and stir in cheese. Serve immediately or cover and refrigerate. When ready to use, bring to room temperature. Serve with cooked vegetables.

Each serving provides: ½ Protein Exchange, 2 Fat Exchanges

— White Sauce —

SERVES 4

140 CALORIES PER SERVING

2 tablespoons margarine

3 tablespoons flour

¾ pint (450 ml) skimmed milk, hot

pinch each salt and pepper

pinch nutmeg (optional)

Heat margarine in saucepan, add flour and cook over low heat, stirring constantly, for 3 minutes. Remove pan from heat. Gradually add milk, stirring well until mixture is smooth. Add remaining ingredients and cook over medium heat, stirring constantly, until sauce is thickened. Reduce heat to low and cook for 10 minutes longer, stirring occasionally. White sauce may be frozen for future use.

Each serving provides: 1½ Fat Exchanges, ¼ Milk Exchange, 30 Calories Optional Exchange

— Tomato-Chive — Dressing

SERVES 4

35 CALORIES PER SERVING

8fl oz (240ml) tomato juice

1 tablespoon chopped chives

1 tablespoon wine vinegar

2 teaspoons olive oil

1 garlic clove, crushed

¼ teaspoon salt

pinch pepper

Combine all ingredients in blender and process at high speed until blended.

Each serving provides: ½ Fat Exchange, 15 Calories Optional Exchange

— Sauce Tartare —

SERVES 4

50 CALORIES PER SERVING

4 tablespoons low-calorie mayonnaise

1 teaspoon French mustard

dash each Worcestershire sauce and lemon juice

1 tablespoon chopped pickled gherkins

1 teaspoon chopped drained capers

½ teaspoon chopped parsley

Mix mayonnaise with mustard, Worcestershire sauce and lemon juice. Stir in chopped gherkins, capers and parsley. Serve immediately or cover and refrigerate until ready to use. Serve with fish.

Each serving provides: 1½ Fat Exchanges

**Top: Tomato-Chive Dressing
Centre: Parmesan Pesto
Bottom: Sauce Tartare**

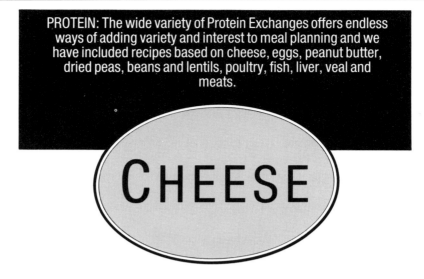

PROTEIN: The wide variety of Protein Exchanges offers endless ways of adding variety and interest to meal planning and we have included recipes based on cheese, eggs, peanut butter, dried peas, beans and lentils, poultry, fish, liver, veal and meats.

CHEESE

*F*rom soups through to desserts, there is no course where you cannot use cheese. The stronger flavoured hard cheeses such as Parmesan and Cheddar are ideal for soups and pasta – just a spoonful can make all the difference to a dish. Hard cheeses also go well with all sorts of vegetable bakes and hors d'oeuvres. Try Cheese-Stuffed Celery Appetiser to hand round at a party, or Asparagus-Cheese Bake for a satisfying supper dish. Low-fat soft cheese is even more versatile as it blends so well with other flavours. From Vegetable Cheese Burgers to Pineapple-Strawberry Cheese Parfait, you can use it in a tremendous variety of cooked dishes, salads and desserts.

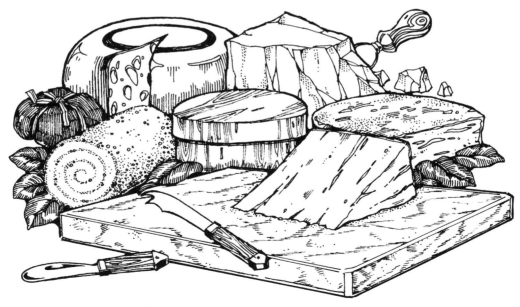

Vegetable-Cheese Loaf

SERVES 4

440 CALORIES PER SERVING

2 tablespoons margarine

4oz (120g) carrots, grated

6oz (180g) spring onions, chopped

6oz (180g) peeled potatoes, grated

2 garlic cloves, crushed

6oz (180g) cooked chopped broccoli

1½oz (45g) flour

1 packet low-calorie chicken soup powder

4fl oz (120ml) skimmed milk

4oz (120g) Cheddar cheese, grated

5oz (150g) low-fat soft cheese

6 tablespoons dried breadcrumbs

2 eggs

pinch each salt and pepper

2 teaspoons sesame seeds

Heat 4 teaspoons margarine in non-stick frying pan. Add carrots, spring onions, potatoes and garlic and saute, stirring occasionally, for about 3 minutes. Reduce heat to lowest setting, cover pan and cook until vegetables are tender, 10 to 15 minutes. Add broccoli, flour and soup powder, stir to combine and gradually stir in milk. Add cheeses and cook, stirring constantly, until mixture thickens. Remove from heat. Preheat oven to 350°F, 180°C, Gas Mark 4. Combine cheese mixture with all remaining ingredients except sesame seeds. Grease a 2lb (960g) loaf tin with remaining 2 teaspoons margarine. Turn cheese mixture into tin and smooth top. Sprinkle with sesame seeds and bake until golden brown, 50 minutes to 1 hour. Remove from oven and let loaf cool in tin for about 10 minutes before serving.

Each serving provides: 2 Protein Exchanges, 1½ Bread Exchanges, 1½ Vegetable Exchanges, 1½ Fat Exchanges, 30 Calories Optional Exchange

Welsh Rarebit

SERVES 2

385 CALORIES PER SERVING

4oz (120g) Cheddar cheese, grated

4 teaspoons flour

4 tablespoons beer

2 teaspoons margarine

½ teaspoon Worcestershire sauce

¼ teaspoon dry mustard

pinch cayenne pepper

1 x 2-oz (60-g) muffin, split and toasted

1 medium tomato, sliced

Place cheese in a saucepan with the flour and gradually stir in beer. Add margarine and seasonings and cook over low heat, stirring constantly, until cheese is melted and mixture is smooth and thick. Place each muffin half in a shallow individual flameproof casserole. Top each half with half the tomato slices, then half the cheese mixture. Grill 3 inches (8 cm) from heat until cheese is browned, about 1 minute.

Each serving provides: 2 Protein Exchanges, 1 Bread Exchange, ½ Vegetable Exchange, 1 Fat Exchange, 30 Calories Optional Exchange

Cheese and Broccoli Soup

SERVES 4

175 CALORIES PER SERVING

2 teaspoons margarine

3oz (90g) onion, chopped

10oz (300g) frozen chopped broccoli, thawed

8fl oz (240ml) skimmed milk

4fl oz (120ml) chicken stock, prepared according to package directions

10oz (300g) low-fat soft cheese

4 teaspoons Parmesan cheese, grated

Heat margarine in a saucepan, add onion and saute until transparent. Add broccoli and cook until hot, 2 to 3 minutes. Add milk and stock and stir to combine. Stirring occasionally, bring just to the boil. Transfer mixture to blender container and puree at low speed until smooth. Add soft cheese and blend until combined. Reheat if necessary but do not boil. Serve each portion sprinkled with 1 teaspoon Parmesan cheese.

Each serving provides: 1 Protein Exchange, 1 Vegetable Exchange, ½ Fat Exchange, 30 Calories Optional Exchange

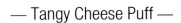

Tangy Cheese Puff

SERVES 2

215 CALORIES PER SERVING

½ teaspoon vegetable oil

2½oz (75g) low-fat soft cheese

1oz (30g) Cheddar cheese, grated

2 eggs, separated

2 teaspoons grated onion

1 teaspoon French mustard

dash Worcestershire sauce

Preheat oven to 375°F, 190°C, Gas Mark 5. Grease 2 individual casseroles or ramekins with vegetable oil and set aside. Place cheeses, egg yolks, grated onion, mustard and Worcestershire sauce in blender and puree until smooth, scraping down sides of container as necessary. Set aside. Beat egg whites until firm but not dry. Fold ⅓ of cheese mixture into beaten whites, then fold in the remainder. Spoon half the mixture into each casserole, place on baking sheet and bake until puffs are golden brown, about 25 minutes.

Each serving provides: 2 Protein Exchanges, ¼ Fat Exchange

— Macaroni Supreme —

SERVES 4

235 CALORIES PER SERVING

5oz (150g) low-fat soft cheese

2fl oz (60ml) skimmed milk

4 teaspoons margarine

3oz (90g) ham, chopped

1 garlic clove, crushed

5oz (150g) cooked broccoli, chopped

8oz (240g) cooked macaroni

1oz (30g) Parmesan cheese, grated

pinch white pepper

2 tablespoons chopped parsley for garnish

Place soft cheese and milk in blender and puree until smooth. Set aside. Heat margarine in frying pan, add ham and garlic and saute until garlic is golden, about 1 minute. Add broccoli and cheese mixture and cook over moderate heat until sauce begins to bubble. Reduce heat and add all remaining ingredients except parsley. Cook, stirring and tossing gently, until macaroni is well coated with sauce. Serve sprinkled with parsley.

Each serving provides: 1½ Protein Exchanges, 1 Bread Exchange, ½ Vegetable Exchange, 1 Fat Exchange, 5 Calories Optional Exchange

— Greek Salad —

SERVES 4

155 CALORIES PER SERVING

Salad

1 garlic clove, cut in half

1lb (480g) salad greens e.g. round and cos lettuce, endive, etc, torn into small pieces

2 medium tomatoes, each cut into 8 wedges

3oz (90g) green pepper, seeded and sliced

5oz (150g) cucumber, sliced

2oz (60g) radishes, sliced

1oz (30g) onion, sliced

1oz (30g) spring onion, including green tops, sliced

4 each black olives, stoned, and pimento-stuffed green olives, sliced

6oz (180g) feta cheese, cubed or crumbled

8 drained canned anchovy fillets, chopped

Dressing

1 to 2 tablespoons lemon juice

4 teaspoons olive oil

1 tablespoon red wine vinegar

½ teaspoon oregano

pinch each salt and pepper

Rub inside of a large wooden salad bowl with cut garlic. Crush garlic and reserve. Add all salad ingredients except garlic, cheese and anchovies to bowl, cover and chill lightly in refrigerator. Mix all ingredients for dressing, add crushed garlic and stir to combine. To serve, pour dressing over salad and toss well, add cheese and anchovies and toss again gently.

Each serving provides: 1½ Protein Exchanges, 3 Vegetable Exchanges, 1 Fat Exchange, 15 Calories Optional Exchange

— Courgettes with — Cheese Topping

SERVES 2

285 CALORIES PER SERVING

4 medium courgettes, each about 5oz (150g), cut lengthwise into ½-inch (1-cm) thick strips

½ teaspoon salt

½ teaspoon vegetable oil

4oz (120g) Edam cheese, grated

5fl oz (150ml) low-fat natural yogurt

1 teaspoon each chopped onion and French mustard

Pour water into a large frying pan to a depth of about 1 inch (2.5 cm) and bring to the boil. Add courgettes and salt, cover and cook until tender-crisp, about 3 minutes. Grease a flameproof casserole with the vegetable oil. Drain courgettes and transfer to casserole. Mix remaining ingredients well together, spread over courgettes and grill until cheese melts and begins to brown, 4 to 5 minutes.

Each serving provides: 2 Protein Exchanges, 3½ Vegetable Exchanges, ¼ Fat Exchange, ½ Milk Exchange

— Cheese-Stuffed — Celery Appetiser

SERVES 4

155 CALORIES PER SERVING

1 teaspoon vegetable oil

1oz (30g) celery, chopped

1oz (30g) spring onions, chopped

4oz (120g) strong Cheddar cheese, grated

1 teaspoon French Mustard

pinch garlic powder

dash Worcestershire sauce

5fl oz (150ml) low-fat natural yogurt

8 medium celery sticks

Grease top section of double boiler with vegetable oil. Add celery and spring onions and cook directly over low heat until celery is tender, stirring occasionally to prevent sticking or burning. Place over lower section of double boiler containing hot water and add cheese, mustard, garlic powder and Worcestershire sauce to vegetable mixture. Cook, stirring constantly until cheese is melted. Spoon yogurt into a bowl and gradually stir in cheese mixture, stirring until thoroughly blended. Cover and refrigerate until firm. To serve, fill each celery stick with 1/8 of the cheese mixture.

Each serving provides: 1 Protein Exchange, 1 Vegetable Exchange, 1/4 Fat Exchange, 1/4 Milk Exchange

— Pumpkin-Cheese — Pie

SERVES 8

190 CALORIES PER SERVING

Crust

8 digestive biscuits, made into crumbs

4 teaspoons margarine, melted

Filling

2 eggs, separated

4 tablespoons light brown sugar

5oz (150g) low-fat soft cheese

8oz (240g) cooked pumpkin

2 tablespoons lemon juice

1 teaspoon grated lemon peel

1/2 teaspoon cinnamon

pinch each ginger and nutmeg

1oz (30g) low-fat dry milk, mixed with 1/4 pint (150ml) water

2 tablespoons cornflour

pinch salt

To Prepare Crust: Preheat oven to 350°F, 180°C, Gas Mark 4. Mix biscuit crumbs with the melted margarine. Press crumb mixture over base and sides of 9-inch (23-cm) pie plate. Bake until crisp and brown, 8 to 10 minutes. Remove pie plate from oven to wire rack to cool.

To Prepare Filling and Bake: Beat egg yolks with 8 teaspoons brown sugar until well combined, add cheese, pumpkin, lemon juice, lemon peel and spices and stir to combine. Add milk gradually to the cornflour, stirring to blend, and stir into pumpkin mixture. Using electric mixer on high speed, beat egg whites with salt until soft peaks form. Beat in remaining 4 teaspoons sugar and continue beating until stiff. Gently fold whites into pumpkin mixture, pour filling into cooled crust and bake at 350°F, 180°C, Gas Mark 4 for 35 to 40 minutes or until a knife, inserted in centre, comes out clean. Set on wire rack and allow to cool completely before cutting.

Each serving provides: 1/2 Protein Exchange, 1/3 Vegetable Exchange, 1/2 Fat Exchange, 1/4 Milk Exchange, 1 Bread Exchange, 40 Calories Optional Exchange

— Macaroni and — Asparagus in Parmesan Sauce

SERVES 4

230 CALORIES PER SERVING

4 teaspoons margarine

3oz (90g) mushrooms, sliced

1 garlic clove, crushed

6oz (180g) asparagus spears, steamed and sliced

1 egg

2 1/2oz (75g) low-fat soft cheese

4fl oz (120ml) skimmed milk

2oz (60g) Parmesan cheese, grated

pinch each salt and freshly ground pepper

8oz (240g) cooked macaroni, hot

2 tablespoons chopped parsley for garnish

Heat margarine in large frying pan, add mushrooms and garlic and saute briefly, about 2 minutes. Stir in asparagus and set aside. Mix egg and soft cheese together until smooth, add milk and Parmesan cheese and stir to combine. Sprinkle with salt and pepper and add to pan. Bring to a slow simmer, stirring constantly, and cook for about 2 minutes. Add macaroni and toss to combine. Serve sprinkled with parsley.

Each serving provides: 1 Protein Exchange, 1 Bread Exchange, 1 Vegetable Exchange, 1 Fat Exchange, 10 Calories Optional Exchange

— Cheese and — Aubergine Pie

SERVES 2

265 CALORIES PER SERVING

1 large aubergine, about 1lb 8oz/ 720g, peeled and cut lengthwise into ¼-inch (5-mm) slices

2oz (60g) each mozzarella cheese and strong Cheddar cheese, grated

6oz (180g) tomato, chopped

2oz (60g) green pepper, seeded and chopped

2oz (60g) onion, chopped

2oz (60g) mushrooms, sliced

pinch each oregano and garlic powder

2 teaspoons grated Parmesan cheese

Arrange aubergine slices on baking sheet in a single layer and grill, turning once, for 3 to 5 minutes on each side (slices should be crisp and brown). Remove aubergine from grill and set oven temperature at 350°F, 180°C, Gas Mark 4. Combine mozzarella and Cheddar cheeses. Arrange overlapping aubergine slices in a 9-inch (23-cm) non-stick pie plate and press edges together to resemble a pie crust. Spread vegetables evenly over aubergine and sprinkle with oregano and garlic powder. Top evenly with the mixed cheeses, then sprinkle with Parmesan cheese. Bake until cheese is melted and browned, 20 to 25 minutes. Cut into 4 equal wedges.

Each serving provides: 2 Protein Exchanges, 6 Vegetable Exchanges, 10 Calories Optional Exchange

— Aubergine — Parmigiana

SERVES 2

285 CALORIES PER SERVING

1 aubergine (about 1lb/480g), cut into 8 rounds, each about ¾ inch (2 cm) thick

4 teaspoons olive oil

salt and pepper

2 tablespoons chopped onion

1 garlic clove, crushed

4oz (120g) canned tomatoes, pureed

pinch oregano

4oz (120g) cheese, grated (mozzarella, Cheddar or Emmenthal)

2 teaspoons grated Parmesan cheese

1 tablespoon chopped parsley for garnish

Brush one side of each aubergine slice with ¼ teaspoon oil. Transfer slices to non-stick baking sheet, oiled side up, and sprinkle each with salt and pepper. Bake at 400°F, 200°C, Gas Mark 6, until browned, about 10 minutes. Turn slices, brush each with ¼ teaspoon oil, and bake 10 minutes longer. While aubergine is baking, cook onion and garlic together in a small frying pan until onion is tender. Spread 3 tablespoons of the pureed tomatoes in a shallow casserole and sprinkle with oregano. Arrange aubergine in casserole, overlapping slices, and pour remaining sauce over aubergine. Top with onion mixture, then grated cheeses. Reduce oven temperature to 350°F, 180°C, Gas Mark 4 and bake until cheese is melted and browned, 25 to 30 minutes. Serve garnished with parsley.

Each serving provides: 2 Protein Exchanges, 3½ Vegetable Exchanges, 2 Fat Exchanges, 10 Calories Optional Exchange

— Mixed Vegetable- — Cheese Bake

SERVES 4

195 CALORIES PER SERVING

1 small aubergine, about 12oz/ 360g, cut into cubes

9oz (270g) canned or frozen artichoke hearts

2 medium tomatoes, each cut into 8 wedges

6oz (180g) onions, chopped

2 garlic cloves, crushed

½ teaspoon each oregano, basil and salt

¼ teaspoon pepper

4 teaspoons olive oil

4oz (120g) Cheddar cheese, grated

Preheat oven to 425°F, 220°C, Gas Mark 7. Mix all vegetables in a shallow casserole. Sprinkle with seasonings, then drizzle oil over the top. Cover casserole and bake until vegetables are tender, about 45 minutes. Remove lid and sprinkle vegetables with cheese. Return to oven and bake, uncovered, until cheese is melted, 8 to 10 minutes. If crisper topping is desired, grill for about 1 minute. If dish is to be grilled, be sure to use a flameproof casserole.

Each serving provides: 1 Protein Exchange, 3 Vegetable Exchanges, 1 Fat Exchange

— Vegetable-Cheese — Burgers

SERVES 2

340 CALORIES PER SERVING

1 teaspoon margarine

1½oz (45g) onion, chopped

1½ oz (45g) green pepper, seeded and chopped

5oz (150g) low-fat soft cheese

6 tablespoons dried breadcrumbs

1oz (30g) strong Cheddar cheese, grated

1 egg

pinch each salt, pepper and paprika

4 teaspoons tomato ketchup

Preheat oven to 350°F, 180°C, Gas Mark 4. Heat margarine in small frying pan, add onion and green pepper and saute until soft. Combine sauteed vegetables, soft cheese, 2 tablespoons breadcrumbs and the Cheddar cheese, egg and seasonings, mixing well (mixture will be soft). Divide cheese mixture into 4 equal portions and roll each into a ball. Roll balls in remaining 4 tablespoons breadcrumbs and transfer to non-stick baking sheet, leaving 2-inch (5-cm) spaces between them. Flatten each ball slightly. Bake until golden brown and slightly puffed, about 15 minutes. Turn burgers over and bake 3 to 5 minutes longer. Serve each burger with 1 teaspoon ketchup and a mixed green salad.

Each serving provides: 2 Protein Exchanges, 1 Bread Exchange, ½ Vegetable Exchange, ½ Fat Exchange, 10 Calories Optional Exchange

— Quick Creamy — Cheese Sauce

SERVES 2

165 CALORIES PER SERVING

1oz (30g) low-fat dry milk, mixed with ¼ pint (150ml) water

2oz (60g) strong Cheddar cheese, grated

dash each Worcestershire sauce and hot pepper sauce

pinch each salt and pepper

Heat milk in small saucepan to just below boiling. Remove pan from heat and stir in remaining ingredients. Cook over low heat, stirring constantly, until cheese is melted. Serve with cooked vegetables.

Each serving provides: 1 Protein Exchange, ½ Milk Exchange

— Soft Cheese Torte —

SERVES 8

240 CALORIES PER SERVING

Dough

4½oz (135g) flour

¼ teaspoon salt

6 teaspoons margarine

3 tablespoons low-fat natural yogurt

1 tablespoon flour for rolling out pastry

Filling

4 teaspoons margarine

4oz (120g) spring onions, chopped

6oz (180g) courgettes, grated

2oz (60g) carrot, grated

2 garlic cloves, crushed

8oz (240g) cooked long grain rice

10oz (300g) low-fat soft cheese

4 eggs

3 tablespoons grated Parmesan cheese

pinch each salt and freshly ground pepper

2 small tomatoes, sliced, to garnish

To Prepare Dough: Mix flour and salt and rub in margarine until mixture resembles coarse breadcrumbs. Add yogurt and mix thoroughly to form dough. Form dough into a ball, wrap in cling film and refrigerate for at least 1 hour (may be kept in refrigerator for up to 3 days).

To Prepare Filling: Heat margarine in a frying pan, add vegetables and garlic and saute over medium-low heat, stirring occasionally, until vegetables are soft, about 3 minutes. Set aside and let cool. Mix rice, soft cheese, 3 eggs, 2 tablespoons Parmesan cheese and the salt and pepper and beat until smooth. Add cooled vegetables and stir to combine.

To Prepare Torte: Preheat oven to 350°F, 180°C, Gas Mark 4. Roll out dough to make a rectangle about ⅛ inch (3 mm) thick, dusting worktop, pastry dough and rolling pin lightly with the remaining tablespoon flour. Line a 10 x 6 x 2-inch (25 x 15 x 5-cm) baking tin. Spoon cheese mixture over dough and bring up edges, leaving centre of filling uncovered. Beat remaining egg with remaining tablespoon Parmesan cheese and pour over entire surface of torte. Bake until browned, about 1 hour. Remove from oven and let stand until set, about 15 minutes. Garnish with sliced tomatoes and serve warm or at room temperature.

Each serving provides: 1 Protein Exchange, 1¼ Bread Exchanges, ½ Vegetable Exchange, 1¼ Fat Exchanges, 20 Calories Optional Exchange

Soft Cheese Torte

— Pineapple-Strawberry —
Cheese Parfait

SERVES 4

165 CALORIES PER SERVING

**8oz (240g) canned crushed
pineapple, no sugar added
(drain and reserve juice)**

10oz (300g) strawberries, sliced

10oz (300g) low-fat soft cheese

4 teaspoons sugar

½ teaspoon vanilla flavouring

Set aside 2 tablespoons crushed pineapple and 12 strawberry slices for garnish. Combine cheese, reserved pineapple juice, 3 teaspoons sugar and the vanilla, mixing well. Mix strawberry slices (except those required for garnish) with remaining teaspoon sugar. Spoon 2 tablespoons pineapple into each of 4 sundae glasses and top with 2 tablespoons cheese mixture, then 2 tablespoons sliced strawberries. Repeat layers, using ¼ of the remaining pineapple, 2 tablespoons cheese mixture and ¼ of the remaining strawberries for each portion. Top strawberries in each glass with ¼ of remaining cheese mixture and garnish each with 1½ teaspoons reserved pineapple and 3 strawberry slices.

Each serving provides: 1 Protein Exchange, 1 Fruit Exchange, 20 Calories Optional Exchange

•

— Cheese Buns —

SERVES 6

240 CALORIES PER SERVING

4½oz (135g) flour

1 tablespoon sugar

2 teaspoons baking powder

5oz (150g) Cheddar cheese, grated

4fl oz (120ml) skimmed milk

1 egg

2 tablespoons margarine, melted

Preheat oven to 400°F, 200°C, Gas Mark 6. Line 6 deep bun tins (2½ inch/6 cm diameter) with paper cake cases and set aside. Mix flour, sugar and baking powder and stir in cheese until coated with flour mixture. Mix milk, egg and margarine. Pour into dry ingredients and stir with a fork until all ingredients are moist. Mixture will be thick and lumpy. Divide batter into paper cake cases (each will be about ⅔ full). Bake for 15 minutes or until buns are golden brown. Transfer to wire rack to cool.

Each serving provides: 1 Protein Exchange, 1 Bread Exchange, 1 Fat Exchange, 20 Calories Optional Exchange

•

— Cheese Pancakes —

SERVES 2

320 CALORIES PER SERVING

1½oz (45g) flour

½ teaspoon baking powder

¼ teaspoon salt

pinch paprika

2 eggs

2oz (60g) Cheddar cheese, grated

**2 tablespoons finely chopped
spring onion**

2 teaspoons margarine

Sift together flour, baking powder, salt and paprika. Beat eggs slightly and gradually add flour mixture, stirring until smooth. Stir in cheese and spring onion. Heat 1 teaspoon margarine in a frying pan and drop in 4 heaped tablespoons batter, making 4 pancakes. Cook until bubbles appear on surface and edges are browned. Turn pancakes over and brown other side. Set aside and keep warm. Repeat procedure, using remaining margarine and batter and making 4 more pancakes.

Each serving provides: 2 Protein Exchanges, 1 Bread Exchange, ½ Vegetable Exchange, 1 Fat Exchange

•

— Spicy Cheese and —
Caper Dip

SERVES 8

65 CALORIES PER SERVING

10oz (300g) low-fat soft cheese

5fl oz (150ml) buttermilk

8 teaspoons tomato ketchup

**2 tablespoons each chopped spring
onion and chopped drained capers**

2 teaspoons prepared mustard

dash Worcestershire sauce

Place all ingredients in blender and puree at low speed, scraping down sides of container as necessary, until mixture is smooth, about 30 seconds. Pour into a serving bowl, cover and refrigerate for at least 30 minutes. Serve with raw vegetables.

Each serving provides: ½ Protein Exchange, 25 Calories Optional Exchange

•

— Soft Cheese and — Vegetable Salad

SERVES 1

270 CALORIES PER SERVING

6 small tomatoes

5oz (150g) low-fat soft cheese

2 tablespoons chopped spring onion

2 pimento-stuffed green olives, sliced

1 tablespoon chopped parsley (optional)

lettuce leaves

Cut 5 tomatoes into quarters and reserve remaining tomato for garnish. Combine all ingredients except lettuce and garnish and mix well. Line a salad plate with lettuce leaves, top with cheese mixture and garnish with reserved tomato.

Each serving provides: 2 Protein Exchanges, 1 Vegetable Exchange, 10 Calories Optional Exchange

•

— Easy Cheese Sauce —

SERVES 2

195 CALORIES PER SERVING

2 teaspoons each margarine and flour

¼ pint (150ml) skimmed milk

2oz (60g) Cheddar cheese, grated

½ teaspoon Worcestershire sauce

¼ teaspoon dry mustard

Heat margarine in small non-stick saucepan, add flour and stir quickly to combine. Remove from heat and gradually stir in milk, stirring until well mixed. Set over low heat and add remaining ingredients. Cook, stirring constantly, until cheese is melted and sauce thickens, about 2 minutes.

Each serving provides: 1 Protein Exchange, 1 Fat Exchange, ¼ Milk Exchange, 10 Calories Optional Exchange

•

— Blue Cheese — Dressing

SERVES 4

90 CALORIES PER SERVING

2oz (60g) Danish blue cheese, crumbled

2 tablespoons wine vinegar

2 teaspoons olive oil

½ teaspoon French mustard

pinch pepper

5fl oz (150ml) buttermilk

Using a fork, mix blue cheese with vinegar, oil, mustard and pepper. Stir in buttermilk gradually.

Each serving provides: ½ Protein Exchange, ½ Fat Exchange, 15 Calories Optional Exchange

•

— Cheese Pancakes — with Fruit Sauce

SERVES 4

390 CALORIES PER SERVING

Pancakes

½ pint (300ml) skimmed milk

3oz (90g) flour

2 eggs

1 teaspoon margarine, melted

Filling

12½oz (375g) low-fat soft cheese

1 egg, beaten

2 tablespoons sugar

2½oz (75g) blackcurrants or blackberries

pinch cinnamon

1 tablespoon margarine

Sauce

5fl oz (150ml) low-fat natural yogurt

1 teaspoon vanilla flavouring

2½oz (75g) blackcurrants or blackberries

To Prepare Pancakes: Place milk, flour and eggs in blender and process until smooth, scraping down sides of container as necessary. Refrigerate, covered, for 1 hour. Heat an 8-inch (20-cm) non-stick frying pan and brush with a little of the melted margarine. Pour in ⅛ of batter (about 4 tablespoons), quickly swirling batter so that it covers pan. Cook until bottom of pancake is lightly browned. Turn carefully with palette knife and brown other side. Slide onto a plate and repeat procedure 7 times, using remaining batter and melted margarine and making 7 more pancakes.

To Prepare Filling: Force soft cheese through a sieve into a small bowl, add egg and sugar and stir until well blended. Fold in blackcurrants or blackberries and cinnamon. Spoon ⅛ of filling onto centre of each pancake. Fold sides in and roll to enclose filling. Melt margarine in large frying pan, place pancake seam-side down in the pan and cook until golden on all sides.

To Prepare Sauce: Mix yogurt and vanilla and stir until smooth. Fold in blackcurrants or blackberries and spoon sauce over pancakes.

Each serving provides: 2 Protein Exchanges, 1 Bread Exchange, 1 Fat Exchange, ½ Milk Exchange, 45 Calories Optional Exchange

•

— Mexican-Style — Aubergine

SERVES 4

290 CALORIES PER SERVING

1 large aubergine (about 1lb 8oz/ 720g), cut into rounds each about ½ inch (1 cm) thick

8oz (240g) canned tomatoes, pureed

8oz (240g) canned tomatoes, chopped

1oz (30g) spring onions, sliced

½oz (15g) green chillies, seeded and finely chopped

8 black olives, stoned and sliced

2 garlic cloves, crushed

½ teaspoon ground cumin

8oz (240g) strong Cheddar cheese, grated

5fl oz (150ml) low-fat natural yogurt

parsley sprigs for garnish

Arrange aubergine slices in a single layer on a non-stick baking sheet and bake at 450°F, 230°C, Gas Mark 8, for about 20 minutes or until soft. While aubergine is baking, mix the pureed and chopped tomatoes in a saucepan with the spring onions, chillies, olives, garlic and cumin and simmer for 10 minutes. Line the bottom of a shallow casserole with half the aubergine slices in a single layer. Spread half the tomato mixture over aubergine and sprinkle with 4oz (120g) cheese. Repeat layers, ending with cheese. Bake at 350°F, 180°C, Gas Mark 4, until bubbly and hot, about 25 minutes. Serve each portion topped with yogurt and garnished with parsley. Serve with a mixed green salad.

Each serving provides: 2 Protein Exchanges, 3½ Vegetable Exchanges, ¼ Milk Exchange, 10 Calories Optional Exchange

— Broccoli-Cheese — Pancakes

SERVES 4

465 CALORIES PER SERVING

Pancakes

4 eggs

3oz (90g) flour

4fl oz (120ml) water

pinch salt

4 teaspoons vegetable oil

Cheese Sauce

8 teaspoons margarine

1oz (30g) shallots or onion, chopped

3 tablespoons flour

½ pint (300ml) skimmed milk

4oz (120g) Cheddar cheese, grated

2 teaspoons Worcestershire sauce

½ teaspoon prepared mustard

Filling

1lb (480g) cooked chopped broccoli

pinch each salt and pepper

To Prepare Pancakes: Place first 4 ingredients in blender and process until smooth. Let stand about 15 minutes. Lightly oil a 9-inch (23-cm) non-stick frying pan with ½ teaspoon oil and heat over moderate flame. Pour ⅛ of batter (about 4 tablespoons) into pan and quickly swirl batter so that it covers entire pan. Cook over medium-high heat until edges and underside of pancake are dry. Turn pancake carefully with palette knife and cook other side briefly just to dry, about 30 seconds. Slide onto a plate and repeat procedure 7 times, using remaining batter and oil and making 7 more pancakes. Set aside.

To Prepare Sauce: Heat margarine in non-stick saucepan, add shallots or onion and saute briefly (do not brown). Add flour and stir quickly to combine, remove from heat and gradually stir in milk, stirring until mixture is smooth. Set over low heat

and add cheese, Worcestershire sauce and mustard. Cook, stirring briskly, until cheese is melted and sauce thickens, about 2 minutes.

To Prepare Filled Pancakes: Preheat oven to 400°F, 200°C, Gas Mark 6. Mix broccoli with seasonings and half the cheese sauce. Spoon ⅛ of filling onto centre of each pancake and roll pancakes to enclose filling. Place seam-side down in shallow flameproof casserole. Top with remaining cheese sauce and bake until cheese begins to bubble. Place under hot grill until lightly browned.

Each serving provides: 2 Protein Exchanges, 1 Bread Exchange, 1½ Vegetable Exchanges, 3 Fat Exchanges, ¼ Milk Exchange, 35 Calories Optional Exchange

Mexican-Style Aubergine

— Spinach-Cheese —
Turnovers

SERVES 2

270 CALORIES PER SERVING

Pastry

1½oz (45g) flour

4 teaspoons margarine

pinch salt

1 tablespoon low-fat natural yogurt

1 tablespoon flour for rolling out pastry

Filling

2oz (60g) well drained cooked spinach, chopped

1oz (30g) Parmesan cheese, grated

pinch each onion powder, salt and freshly ground pepper

To Prepare Pastry: Mix flour and salt and rub in margarine until mixture resembles coarse breadcrumbs. Add yogurt and mix well. Form dough into a ball, wrap in cling film and chill for about 1 hour (may be kept in the refrigerator for up to 3 days).

To Prepare Filling and Bake: Mix spinach, cheese and seasonings. Preheat oven to 400°F, 200°C, Gas Mark 6. Roll out dough to about ⅛ inch (3 mm) thick, dusting worktop, pastry dough and rolling pin with the remaining tablespoon flour. Cut into rounds with 2½-inch (6-cm) cutter, re-rolling scraps until all dough has been used. Spoon an equal amount of spinach mixture onto each round and fold in half to enclose filling. Press edges together with a fork to seal. Transfer turnovers to non-stick baking sheet and bake until lightly browned, 15 to 20 minutes.

Each serving provides: ½ Protein Exchange, 1 Bread Exchange, ½ Vegetable Exchange, 2 Fat Exchanges, 40 Calories Optional Exchange

●

— Cheese and 'Bacon' —
Pinwheel Appetisers

SERVES 4

275 CALORIES PER SERVING

3oz (90g) flour

2oz (60g) Cheddar cheese, grated

2 teaspoons each imitation bacon bits, crushed, and grated onion

pinch each salt and cayenne pepper

8 teaspoons margarine

2fl oz (60ml) low-fat natural yogurt

1 tablespoon flour for rolling out pastry

2 tablespoons each French mustard and chopped parsley or chives

4 teaspoons grated Parmesan cheese

Mix flour, Cheddar cheese, bacon bits, onion, salt and pepper and rub in margarine until mixture resembles coarse breadcrumbs. Add yogurt and mix well. Form dough into a ball, wrap in cling film and refrigerate for at least 1 hour. Roll out dough to make a rectangle about ⅛ inch (3 mm) thick, dusting worktop, pastry dough and rolling pin lightly with the remaining tablespoon flour. Spread mustard over dough and sprinkle with parsley or chives, then roll up like a Swiss roll. Wrap in cling film and freeze until dough slices easily, about 30 minutes. Preheat oven to 400°F, 200°C, Gas Mark 6. Cut rolled dough into pinwheels about ¼ inch (5 mm) thick and place on non-stick baking sheet. Sprinkle each pinwheel with an equal amount of Parmesan cheese and bake until lightly browned, about 15 minutes.

Each serving provides: ½ Protein Exchange, 1 Bread Exchange, 2 Fat Exchanges, 25 Calories Optional Exchange

●

— Swiss-Style —
Pinwheel Rolls

SERVES 4

155 CALORIES PER SERVING

4 slices white bread, lightly toasted

4 teaspoons low-fat spread

2oz (60g) Emmenthal cheese, grated

4 teaspoons imitation bacon bits, crushed

Using a rolling pin, lightly roll each slice of toast as flat as possible without breaking the bread. Spread 1 teaspoon low-fat spread on each slice. Mix cheese and bacon bits and sprinkle ¼ of the mixture over each slice of toast, covering entire surface. Roll each slice up like a Swiss roll, wrap tightly in cling film and freeze for 30 minutes. Preheat oven to 350°F, 180°C, Gas Mark 4. Unwrap bread rolls and cut each into 5 equal pinwheels, securing them with cocktail sticks. Transfer pinwheels, cut-side down, to non-stick baking sheet and bake for 10 minutes.

Each serving provides: ½ Protein Exchange, 1 Bread Exchange, ½ Fat Exchange, 10 Calories Optional Exchange

●

— Broccoli-Cheese —
Canapes

SERVES 4

250 CALORIES PER SERVING

4oz (120g) cooked broccoli florets, pureed

½oz (15g) low-fat dry milk, mixed with 2½fl oz (75ml) water

4 teaspoons mayonnaise

½ teaspoon salt

pinch each garlic powder and freshly ground pepper

4 slices white bread, toasted

4oz (120g) Emmenthal cheese, thinly sliced

4 teaspoons grated Parmesan cheese

3oz (90g) pimentos, cut into strips for garnish

Mix broccoli, milk, mayonnaise and seasonings. Arrange toast slices on non-stick baking sheet and top each slice with 1oz (30g) Emmenthal cheese and ¼ of the broccoli mixture. Sprinkle each with 1 teaspoon Parmesan cheese and bake at 400°F, 200°C, Gas Mark 6, until cheese is melted, about 10 minutes. Cut each slice into 4 triangles and garnish each with pimento strips.

Each serving provides: 1 Protein Exchange, 1 Bread Exchange, ½ Vegetable Exchange, 1 Fat Exchange, 20 Calories Optional Exchange

— Aubergine —
Appetisers

SERVES 4

200 CALORIES PER SERVING

4 small aubergines, each about 4oz (120g)

2 teaspoons olive oil

2 tablespoons each chopped onion and red pepper

1 garlic clove, crushed

5oz (150g) low-fat soft cheese

1 egg, beaten

3 tablespoons dried breadcrumbs

¼ teaspoon each basil, oregano and salt

pinch pepper

3oz (90g) mozzarella cheese, grated

1 teaspoon vegetable oil

Cut each aubergine in half lengthwise and scoop out pulp, leaving ¼-inch (5-mm) thick shells. Reserve shells, chop pulp and reserve. Preheat oven to 350°F, 180°C, Gas Mark 4. Heat oil in small frying pan, add onion, pepper, aubergine pulp and garlic and saute until vegetables are tender. Remove from heat and stir in soft cheese, then egg, breadcrumbs and seasonings. Grease a flameproof baking dish with the vegetable oil. Divide aubergine mixture between the reserved shells and place them in the dish. Bake until mixture is hot and shells are tender, about 25 minutes. Remove from oven and sprinkle each aubergine half with an equal amount of mozzarella cheese. Grill until cheese is melted.

Each serving provides: 1½ Protein Exchanges, 1½ Vegetable Exchanges, ½ Fat Exchange, 35 Calories Optional Exchange

— Cheese Soup —

SERVES 2

355 CALORIES PER SERVING

1 tablespoon margarine

1½oz (45g) onion, chopped

2 tablespoons each chopped celery and carrot

2 teaspoons flour

½ chicken stock cube, dissolved in 6fl oz (180ml) hot water

8fl oz (240ml) skimmed milk

4oz (120g) strong Cheddar cheese, grated

pinch pepper

Heat margarine in small saucepan, add vegetables and saute, stirring frequently, until tender. Sprinkle flour over vegetables and stir quickly to combine. Gradually stir in dissolved stock cube and cook, stirring constantly, until mixture is smooth and thickened. Stir in milk and cook, stirring occasionally, until hot. Do not boil. Add cheese and cook over low heat, stirring constantly, until cheese is melted. Season with pepper and serve immediately.

Each serving provides: 2 Protein Exchanges, ½ Vegetable Exchange, 1½ Fat Exchanges, 50 Calories Optional Exchange

EGGS

With eggs in the fridge you need never be stuck for an easy, tasty meal. They are astonishingly versatile – as well as boiling, poaching or scrambling them for breakfast, you can whip up tasty omelettes and pancakes, use them in baking and make delicious custard-based dishes, both sweet and savoury. Hard-boil them for Garden Salad or Devilled Eggs, and if you follow our recipe for Broccoli-Cheese Souffle, you can prove that souffle-making is simple after all – an elegant result for very little effort!

— Egg Foo Yung — (Chinese Omelette)

SERVES 2

210 CALORIES PER SERVING

Egg Mixture

4oz (120g) shelled prawns or skinned and boned cooked chicken or boned cooked pork, chopped

2 large eggs, beaten with 2 teaspoons water

3oz (90g) bean sprouts

2 tablespoons chopped spring onions

pinch each salt, pepper and garlic powder

2 teaspoons peanut or vegetable oil

Sauce

1½ teaspoons soy sauce

1 teaspoon each cornflour and wine vinegar

pinch ginger

4fl oz (120ml) water

To Prepare Egg Mixture: Mix prawns, chicken or pork with the beaten eggs, bean sprouts, spring onion and seasonings, mixing well. Heat oil in non-stick frying pan. Spoon in ⅛ of the egg mixture to form a patty and cook until mixture is set and underside lightly browned. Turn patty over, brown other side, remove to a warm serving dish and keep hot. Repeat procedure with remaining egg mixture, making 8 patties in all.

To Prepare Sauce: Mix soy sauce, cornflour, vinegar and ginger, stirring to blend cornflour. Gradually stir in water. Stirring constantly, bring mixture to the boil and cook until sauce thickens. To serve, divide patties between 2 warmed plates and top each portion with half the sauce.

Each serving provides: 3 Protein Exchanges, 1 Vegetable Exchange, 1 Fat Exchange, 5 Calories Optional Exchange

— Eggs with — Olive-Anchovy Topping

SERVES 4

110 CALORIES PER SERVING

8 large black olives, stoned and chopped

1 tablespoon capers, drained and mashed

1 teaspoon each lemon juice and olive oil

1 drained canned anchovy fillet, mashed

pinch garlic powder

4 eggs, hard-boiled

8 large lettuce leaves

4 teaspoons chopped onion

parsley sprigs for garnish

Mix olives, capers, lemon juice, oil, anchovies and garlic powder. Cover and let stand for 1 hour to blend flavours. To serve, cut eggs lengthwise into halves. Arrange lettuce leaves on serving dish and top with egg halves. Spoon ⅛ of olive and anchovy mixture onto each half, mounding mixture. Sprinkle each egg half with ½ teaspoon chopped onion and garnish dish with parsley.

Each serving provides: 1 Protein Exchange, ½ Vegetable Exchange, 25 Calories Optional Exchange

— Egg and Chicory — Salad with Lemon-Mustard Vinaigrette

SERVES 4

170 CALORIES PER SERVING

2 heads chicory, each about 4oz (120g) and each cut lengthwise into eighths

12 small tomatoes, cut into halves

4 eggs, hard-boiled and cut into quarters

Lemon-Mustard Vinaigrette (see page 79)

On each of 4 salad plates arrange 4 sections of chicory. Top each portion with 6 small tomato halves, cut-side down, and 4 egg quarters. Cover and chill lightly in refrigerator before serving. To serve, pour ¼ of vinaigrette over each portion of salad.

Each serving provides (includes Lemon-Mustard Vinaigrette): 1 Protein Exchange, 1½ Vegetable Exchanges, 1 Fat Exchange

— Pepper Omelette —

SERVES 4

265 CALORIES PER SERVING

4 teaspoons olive oil

4oz (120g) onions, thinly sliced

3oz (90g) each red and green peppers, seeded and thinly sliced

½ garlic clove, crushed with ¼ teaspoon salt

8oz (240g) canned tomatoes, crushed

½ teaspoon salt

pinch pepper

8 large eggs, lightly beaten

4 teaspoons grated Parmesan cheese

Heat oil in large non-stick frying pan, add onions and saute until transparent, about 2 minutes. Add red and green peppers and crushed garlic and cook, stirring occasionally, until peppers are tender, 2 to 3 minutes longer. Reduce heat, stir in tomatoes and seasonings, and let simmer until liquid has evaporated. Beat eggs lightly with the Parmesan cheese and pour into the pan. Stir mixture gently with wooden spoon and remove from heat as soon as eggs are lightly set.

Each serving provides: 2 Protein Exchanges, 1½ Vegetable Exchanges, 1 Fat Exchange, 10 Calories Optional Exchange

— Tangy Egg Salad —

SERVES 2

240 CALORIES PER SERVING

2oz (60g) celery, chopped

2 tablespoons chopped spring onions

2 tablespoons low-fat natural yogurt

2 tablespoons low-calorie mayonnaise

1 tablespoon chilli sauce

2 teaspoons each pickle and chopped drained capers

¼ teaspoon pepper

pinch salt

4 eggs, hard-boiled and coarsely chopped

8 lettuce leaves

Combine chopped vegetables, dressings and seasonings. Add eggs and mix well. Cover and chill lightly in refrigerator. To serve, line serving plate with lettuce leaves and top with egg salad.

Each serving provides: 2 Protein Exchanges, 1 Vegetable Exchange, 1½ Fat Exchanges, 20 Calories Optional Exchange

•

— Egg, Cheese and — Asparagus Bake

SERVES 2

305 CALORIES PER SERVING

2 teaspoons margarine

2 tablespoons chopped spring onions

6oz (180g) cooked chopped asparagus

1oz (30g) low-fat dry milk, mixed with ¼ pint (150ml) water

2 eggs, beaten

2oz (60g) Cheddar cheese, grated

¼ teaspoon pepper

pinch each salt and cayenne pepper

Preheat oven to 375°F, 190°C, Gas Mark 5. Heat 1 teaspoon margarine in small frying pan, add spring onion and saute until softened. Mix with the asparagus, milk, eggs, 1oz (30g) cheese and the seasonings. Grease 7-inch (18-cm) pie plate with remaining teaspoon margarine and pour in egg mixture. Sprinkle with remaining cheese and bake for 35 minutes or until a knife inserted in centre comes out clean.

Each serving provides: 2 Protein Exchanges, 1½ Vegetable Exchanges, 1 Fat Exchange, ½ Milk Exchange

•

— Savoury — Baked Custard

SERVES 1

335 CALORIES PER SERVING

1oz (30g) low-fat dry milk, mixed with ¼ pint (150ml) water

1 large egg, beaten

1oz (30g) Cheddar cheese, grated

1 teaspoon imitation bacon bits

pinch pepper

1 teaspoon grated Parmesan cheese

Preheat oven to 350°F, 180°C, Gas Mark 4. Beat milk and egg together and stir in Cheddar cheese, bacon bits and pepper. Pour into individual non-stick baking tin and sprinkle with Parmesan cheese. Stand the tin in a larger baking tin or ovenproof dish and pour boiling water into dish to a depth of 1 inch (2.5 cm). Bake for 25 to 30 minutes or until a knife inserted in centre comes out clean. Remove from water and, keeping warm, let stand for about 5 minutes before serving.

Each serving provides: 2 Protein Exchanges, 1 Milk Exchange, 20 Calories Optional Exchange

•

— Broccoli-Cheese — Souffle

SERVES 4

335 CALORIES PER SERVING

4 large eggs, separated

4 teaspoons each margarine and finely chopped onion

2 tablespoons flour

8fl oz (240ml) skimmed milk, hot

¼ teaspoon salt

pinch each white pepper, cayenne pepper and nutmeg

4oz (120g) extra strong Cheddar cheese, grated

4oz (120g) cooked long grain rice

4oz (120g) cooked broccoli florets

pinch cream of tartar

½ teaspoon vegetable oil

Beat egg yolks in small bowl and set aside. Heat margarine in small saucepan, add onion and saute until softened. Reduce heat to low, add flour and cook, stirring constantly, for 3 minutes. Remove from heat and gradually stir in hot milk, stirring until mixture is smooth. Add salt, white and cayenne pepper and nutmeg. Return saucepan to moderate heat and cook, stirring constantly, until mixture is thickened. Reduce heat to low and cook, stirring frequently, for 10 minutes longer. Add cheese and cook, stirring constantly, until cheese is melted. Gradually stir beaten egg yolks into cheese sauce, stirring until well blended. Remove sauce from heat. Preheat oven to 350°F, 180°C, Gas Mark 4. Gently stir rice into cheese sauce, transfer mixture to a large mixing bowl and gently fold in broccoli. Beat egg whites with cream of tartar until stiff but not dry. Lightly stir ¼ of the whites into broccoli mixture, then fold in remaining whites. Grease a souffle dish or deep ovenproof dish with the vegetable oil. Turn broccoli mixture into dish. Using the back of a spoon, form a crown by making a shallow indentation about 1 inch (2.5 cm) from edge of dish all the way round souffle. Bake for 40 minutes and serve immediately.

Each serving provides: 2 Protein Exchanges, ½ Bread Exchange, ½ Vegetable Exchange, 1 Fat Exchange, 40 Calories Optional Exchange

•

— Baked Eggs in — Spinach Cups

SERVES 2

350 CALORIES PER SERVING

3 teaspoons margarine

1 garlic clove, chopped

6oz (180g) cooked chopped spinach

2 teaspoons flour

8fl oz (240ml) skimmed milk

¼ teaspoon salt

pinch each nutmeg and pepper

2oz (60g) Emmenthal cheese, grated

2 eggs

Preheat oven to 350°F, 180°C, Gas Mark 4. Heat 2 teaspoons margarine in frying pan, add garlic and saute for 1 minute. Add spinach and cook over moderate heat, stirring constantly, for 3 minutes. Sprinkle flour over spinach and stir quickly to combine. Gradually stir in milk and cook, stirring constantly, until slightly thickened. Remove from heat, stir in salt, nutmeg and pepper, add cheese and stir to combine. Grease 2 small individual ovenproof casseroles with remaining teaspoon margarine and divide spinach mixture between them. Using the back of a spoon, make a hollow in the centre of each portion of spinach. Break the eggs, one at a time, into a cup and slide them carefully into the hollows in the spinach mixture. Bake until eggs are firm, 12 to 15 minutes.

Each serving provides: 2 Protein Exchanges, 1 Vegetable Exchange, 1½ Fat Exchanges, 50 Calories Optional Exchange

— Apple Custard —

SERVES 2

245 CALORIES PER SERVING

2 teaspoons margarine

2 medium eating apples, cored, peeled and sliced

2 whole cloves

pinch cinnamon

8fl oz (240ml) skimmed milk

2 large eggs

1 tablespoon sugar

½ teaspoon vanilla flavouring

Preheat oven to 350°F, 180°C, Gas Mark 4. Heat margarine in small saucepan, add apples, cloves and cinnamon. Cover and cook, stirring occasionally, until apples begin to soften, about 2 minutes. Remove and discard cloves. Divide mixture into two small individual ovenproof dishes. Combine remaining ingredients and beat until well mixed. Pour half the mixture into each dish and bake until custard is set, 35 to 40 minutes. Serve warm or chilled.

Each serving provides: 1 Protein Exchange, 1 Fat Exchange, 1 Fruit Exchange, 70 Calories Optional Exchange

•

— Creamy — 'Eggnog' Dessert

SERVES 2

145 CALORIES PER SERVING

1 teaspoon unflavoured gelatine

1oz (30g) low-fat dry milk, mixed with 4fl oz (120ml) water

1 egg, separated

2 teaspoons sugar

1 teaspoon vanilla flavouring

¼ teaspoon rum flavouring

2 tablespoons thawed frozen whipped topping

nutmeg

Chill 2 dessert dishes. Sprinkle gelatine over 4 tablespoons milk in a small saucepan and let stand to soften. Mix remaining milk with egg yolk, sugar and flavourings and beat until combined. Pour into gelatine mixture and cook over low heat, stirring constantly, until gelatine is completely dissolved and mixture coats the back of a metal spoon. Remove from heat and let cool slightly. Cover and refrigerate until mixture begins to thicken, about 20 minutes. Using an electric mixer on high speed, beat egg white until stiff peaks form. Fold into chilled milk mixture and spoon into chilled dessert dishes. Cover with cling film and refrigerate until firm. Serve each portion topped with 1 tablespoon whipped topping and pinch of nutmeg.

Each serving provides: ½ Protein Exchange, ½ Milk Exchange, 40 Calories Optional Exchange

•

— Pimento-Egg Salad —

SERVES 4

260 CALORIES PER SERVING

2oz (60g) celery, finely chopped

2oz (60g) pickled cucumber, chopped

2oz (60g) drained canned pimentos, chopped

8 teaspoons mayonnaise

1 tablespoon chopped onion

2 teaspoons French mustard

8 eggs, hard-boiled and chopped

¼ teaspoon each salt and pepper

8 lettuce leaves

Mix celery, pickled cucumber, pimentos, mayonnaise, onion and mustard, mixing well. Add eggs, salt and pepper and combine. Cover and chill lightly in refrigerator. To serve, line serving dish with lettuce leaves and top with egg salad.

Each serving provides: 2 Protein Exchanges, 1 Vegetable Exchange, 2 Fat Exchanges

— Caramel Custard —

SERVES 2

160 CALORIES PER SERVING

Caramel

½ teaspoon margarine

2 tablespoons sugar

4 teaspoons water

Custard

4fl oz (120ml) skimmed milk

2 eggs, beaten

½ teaspoon vanilla flavouring

1 teaspoon sugar

Grease 2 individual ovenproof ramekins or dariole moulds with margarine. Stand dishes in a baking tin and pour boiling water into tin to a depth of about 1 inch (2.5 cm). Mix sugar and water in a small, heavy pan and cook over moderate heat, stirring constantly, until sugar dissolves and browns. Be very careful not to burn. Pour half of the caramel immediately into greased moulds, tilting moulds to coat sides.

To Prepare Custard: Preheat oven to 325°F, 160°C, Gas Mark 3. Mix all ingredients for custard and pour half of the mixture into each caramel-coated mould. Replace in tin of boiling water and bake 15 to 20 minutes or until knife inserted in centre of custard comes out clean. Remove dishes from water bath and let stand for 10 to 15 minutes. Loosen edges of custard with point of a knife and invert onto serving plate. Serve warm or chilled.

Each serving provides: 1 Protein Exchange, 100 Calories Optional Exchange

— Matzo 'Cheese Flan'—

SERVES 4

365 CALORIES PER SERVING

2 tablespoons margarine

6oz (180g) onion, chopped

1 garlic clove, crushed

4 eggs

¼ teaspoon each paprika and salt

pinch pepper

4oz (120g) strong Cheddar cheese, grated

3oz (90g) matzo boards, broken into halves

2 medium tomatoes, sliced

Preheat oven to 375°F, 190°C, Gas Mark 5. Heat margarine in small frying pan, add onions and garlic and saute until onions are softened. Beat eggs, add sauteed onions, paprika, salt and pepper and cheese and stir until well combined. Place half the matzo boards in 8-inch (20-cm) square baking tin and top with half the tomato slices, then half the egg mixture. Repeat layers with remaining matzo halves, tomato slices and egg mixture. Bake flan for 30 minutes or until a knife inserted in centre comes out clean. Remove from oven and, keeping the flan warm, let stand for 5 minutes before cutting.

Each serving provides: 2 Protein Exchanges, 1 Bread Exchange, 1 Vegetable Exchange, 1½ Fat Exchanges

— Chicken Egg-Drop — Soup

SERVES 1

95 CALORIES PER SERVING

½ chicken stock cube, crumbled

6fl oz (180ml) water

2 teaspoons thinly sliced spring onion

1 large egg, beaten

¼ teaspoon soy sauce (optional)

Mix crumbled stock cube and water in saucepan, stirring until cube is dissolved. Add spring onion and bring to the boil. Remove from heat and gradually stir in egg and, if desired, soy sauce. Serve immediately.

Each serving provides: 1 Protein Exchange, ½ Vegetable Exchange

— Devilled Eggs —

SERVES 4

135 CALORIES PER SERVING

4 eggs, hard-boiled and cut lengthwise into halves

4 teaspoons each mayonnaise and pickle or chutney

½ teaspoon spicy brown mustard

pinch each onion salt and garlic powder

¼ teaspoon paprika and 8 pimento strips, each 1 inch (2.5 cm) long, for garnish

parsley sprigs for garnish

Carefully remove yolks from egg halves to a small bowl and set whites aside. Mash yolks, add all remaining ingredients except egg whites and garnish and mix well. Fill each egg white half with ⅛ of the yolk mixture. Sprinkle each with an equal amount of paprika and top with a pimento strip and parsley sprig. Arrange eggs on serving dish, cover loosely and chill lightly in refrigerator before serving.

Each serving provides: 1 Protein Exchange, 1 Fat Exchange, 10 Calories Optional Exchange

PEANUT BUTTER

Peanut butter is not just for children's sandwiches – it's a high-protein food in its own right. Make the most of its distinctive flavour by trying some of our wide range of dishes. There's an oriental touch in Gingered Peanut Dressing, for instance, and an unusual vegetable treatment in Nutty Green Beans. Mouthwatering sweet treats, too, which the whole family will enjoy, such as Crunchy Peanut Butter Fudge and Nutty Chocolate Ice Cream.

— Nutty Chocolate — Ice Cream

SERVES 2

270 CALORIES PER SERVING

4oz (120g) chocolate ice cream, softened

2 tablespoons crunchy peanut butter

2 teaspoons chocolate sauce

1 digestive biscuit, made into crumbs

2 teaspoons desiccated coconut, toasted

Beat ice cream, peanut butter and chocolate sauce together with electric mixer, transfer to freezer container, cover and freeze until firm. Mix crumbs and coconut. Divide chocolate/peanut mixture into 2 dessert dishes and sprinkle each portion with half the crumb mixture.

Each serving provides: 1 Protein Exchange, ½ Bread Exchange, 1 Fat Exchange, 135 Calories Optional Exchange

— Gingered Peanut — Dressing

SERVES 4

95 CALORIES PER SERVING

4 tablespoons each wine vinegar and water

4 tablespoons crunchy peanut butter

2 teaspoons soy sauce

1 garlic clove, crushed

pinch ginger

Gradually stir vinegar and water into peanut butter, add remaining ingredients and stir to combine. Use as a dressing for raw or cooked vegetables.

Each serving provides: 1 Protein Exchange, 1 Fat Exchange

— Chicken and — Vegetable Saute with Peanut Sauce

SERVES 2

290 CALORIES PER SERVING

Chicken and Vegetables

8oz (240g) skinned and boned chicken breast, cut into thin strips

1 teaspoon each cornflour and peanut or vegetable oil

1 garlic clove, crushed

1 medium red pepper, seeded and cut into thin strips

4fl oz (120ml) water

1 teaspoon soy sauce

8oz (240g) broccoli florets, blanched

pinch each salt and pepper

Sauce

1oz (30g) onion, thinly sliced

8fl oz (240ml) water

½ chicken stock cube, crumbled

2 tablespoons peanut butter

1 teaspoon soy sauce

To Prepare Chicken and Vegetables: Sprinkle chicken with cornflour. Heat oil in large non-stick frying pan, add garlic and chicken and saute for 2 minutes. Add pepper strips, water and soy sauce and cook until pepper is tender-crisp, 2 to 3 minutes. Add broccoli, salt and pepper and cook until broccoli is heated through.
To Prepare Sauce: Cook onion in non-stick frying pan over moderate heat, stirring frequently, until transparent; stir in water and stock cube and bring to the boil. Reduce heat, stir in peanut butter and soy sauce and simmer until mixture is well blended. Serve over chicken and vegetables.

Each serving provides: 4 Protein Exchanges, 2 Vegetable Exchanges, 1½ Fat Exchanges, 5 Calories Optional Exchange

— Apple-Nut Squares —

SERVES 8

180 CALORIES PER SERVING

3oz (90g) flour

1 teaspoon baking powder

1 egg

8 teaspoons dark brown sugar

8 tablespoons crunchy peanut butter

1 teaspoon vanilla flavouring

½ teaspoon cinnamon

2fl oz (60ml) skimmed milk

2 medium eating apples, cored, peeled and chopped

1 teaspoon vegetable oil

Preheat oven to 350°F, 180°C, Gas Mark 4. Sift together flour and baking powder and set aside. Combine egg and sugar and, using an electric mixer, beat until thick. Add peanut butter, vanilla and cinnamon and beat until combined. Add sifted flour alternately with milk, about ⅓ at a time, beating after each addition. Stir in apple. Grease an 8 x 8 x 2-inch (20 x 20 x 5-cm) baking tin with the vegetable oil. Spread batter evenly in tin and bake until top is lightly browned, 30 to 35 minutes. Remove tin to wire rack and let cool for 5 minutes, then remove cake from tin and return to rack to cool completely. Cut into sixteen 2-inch (5-cm) squares.

Each serving provides: 1 Protein Exchange, ½ Bread Exchange, 1 Fat Exchange, 50 Calories Optional Exchange

— Peanut Butter — Fudge

SERVES 4

240 CALORIES PER SERVING

2oz (60g) low-fat dry milk

4 tablespoons peanut butter

2oz (60g) raisins, chopped

8 teaspoons thawed frozen concentrated apple juice

2 tablespoons ice water

¾oz (20g) cornflakes, crushed

4 teaspoons desiccated coconut

Mix milk powder with peanut butter, blending well, and stir in raisins, apple juice, water and cornflakes. Roll into 12 balls and roll each ball in the coconut. Refrigerate until firm, about 2 hours.

Each serving provides: 1 Protein Exchange, 1 Fat Exchange, 1 Fruit Exchange, ½ Milk Exchange, 25 Calories Optional Exchange

•

— Nut Squares —

SERVES 16

125 CALORIES PER SERVING

8 tablespoons caster sugar

1 egg

16 tablespoons crunchy peanut butter

1 teaspoon vanilla flavouring

½ teaspoon vegetable oil

Preheat oven to 350°F, 180°C, Gas Mark 4. Beat sugar and egg together with electric mixer until light and fluffy. Add peanut butter and vanilla, beating until combined. Grease a shallow baking tin approximately 8 x 8 inches (20 x 20 cm) with vegetable oil. Spread mixture evenly in the tin and bake until top is lightly browned, about 20 minutes. Remove tin to wire rack, cool for 5 minutes, then turn mixture out on to the rack and leave until completely cold. Cut into sixteen 2-inch (5-cm) squares. Wrap squares individually in cling film and store in refrigerator.

Each serving provides: 1 Protein Exchange, 1 Fat Exchange, 35 Calories Optional Exchange

•

— Creamy Peanut Dip —

SERVES 4

125 CALORIES PER SERVING

4 tablespoons smooth peanut butter

3 tablespoons water

2 tablespoons thawed frozen concentrated orange juice

1 tablespoon lemon juice

5fl oz (150ml) low-fat natural yogurt

dash vanilla flavouring

Combine peanut butter, water and juices, mixing until smooth. Stir in yogurt and vanilla. Cover and refrigerate until required. Serve with fresh fruits such as apples, bananas, pears etc, or with raw carrot and celery sticks.

Each serving provides: 1 Protein Exchange, 1 Fat Exchange, ¼ Milk Exchange, 15 Calories Optional Exchange

•

— Stuffed Dates —

SERVES 4

125 CALORIES PER SERVING

4 tablespoons smooth peanut butter

2 teaspoons grated fresh orange peel

8 stoned fresh dates, split open lengthwise

½ teaspoon icing sugar

Mix peanut butter and 1 teaspoon orange peel and spoon ⅛ of mixture into each date. Sift an equal amount of sugar over each filled date, then sprinkle each with ⅛ of the remaining orange peel.

Each serving provides: 1 Protein Exchange, 1 Fat Exchange, 1 Fruit Exchange, 5 Calories Optional Exchange

•

— Nutty Green Beans —

SERVES 2

125 CALORIES PER SERVING

2 tablespoons each crunchy peanut butter and sherry

2 teaspoons soy sauce

1 garlic clove, crushed

½ teaspoon chopped peeled ginger root

9oz (270g) cooked French beans, fresh or frozen, hot

Mix peanut butter, sherry, soy sauce, garlic and ginger in a small saucepan and bring to the boil. Reduce heat and simmer, stirring constantly, until mixture is creamy, about 1 minute. Pour over hot green beans and serve immediately.

Each serving provides: 1 Protein Exchange, 1½ Vegetable Exchanges, 1 Fat Exchange, 15 Calories Optional Exchange

•

Left: Peanut Butter Fudge
Right: Stuffed Dates
Bottom: Nut Squares

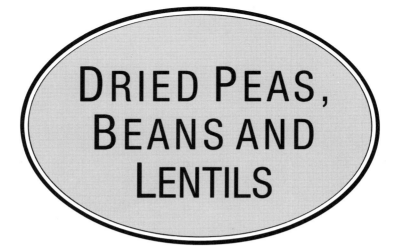

DRIED PEAS, BEANS AND LENTILS

Neglected for a long time, pulses are coming into their own again. They're economical, easy to store, good to eat and the variety's endless: little orange and brown lentils, dried peas and beans in all colours from yellow and white to green, pink and red. Use them in hearty one-dish soups such as Pasta and Bean Soup, classic Minestrone, and Split Pea and Ham Soup. Combine them with cheese and vegetables in Vegetarian Casserole, use them in dips and delicious salads from our recipes.

— Tofu-Peach — Shortcake

SERVES 2

205 CALORIES PER SERVING

4oz (120g) canned sliced peaches, no sugar added

3oz (90g) tofu (soybean curd)

1 tablespoon thawed frozen concentrated orange juice

1 teaspoon each demerara sugar and lemon juice

¼ teaspoon vanilla flavouring

4 digestive biscuits

Reserve 4 peach slices for garnish. Dice remaining peaches and set aside. Combine tofu, orange juice, sugar, lemon juice and vanilla in blender or food processor and puree until smooth, scraping down sides of container as necessary. Place 2 digestive biscuits on a serving plate, spread with half the tofu mixture and top with diced peaches. Top peaches with remaining 2 digestive biscuits and spread remaining tofu mixture over top and sides of shortcake. Garnish with reserved peach slices. Cover and refrigerate for at least 10 minutes before serving.

Each serving provides: ½ Protein Exchange, 2 Bread Exchanges, ½ Fruit Exchange, 25 Calories Optional Exchange

— Broccoli-Bean — Casserole

SERVES 4

245 CALORIES PER SERVING

4 teaspoons margarine

1½oz (45g) onion, chopped

1 medium garlic clove, crushed

1lb (480g) broccoli florets, blanched

6oz (180g) drained canned small haricot beans

4oz (120g) drained canned pimentos, chopped

¼ teaspoon salt

pinch each oregano and pepper

4oz (120g) strong Cheddar cheese, coarsely grated

3 tablespoons dried breadcrumbs

Preheat oven to 350°F, 180°C, Gas Mark 4. Heat 1 teaspoon margarine in small frying pan, add onion and garlic and saute until onion is softened. Spread onion mixture in 10 x 6 x 2-inch (25 x 15 x 5-cm) baking tin. Arrange broccoli florets over onions and top with beans, then pimentos. Sprinkle with salt, oregano and pepper and top with cheese, then breadcrumbs. Dot with remaining tablespoon margarine and bake until cheese is melted and crumbs are browned, about 30 minutes.

Each serving provides: 1½ Protein Exchanges, 2 Vegetable Exchanges, 1 Fat Exchange, 25 Calories Optional Exchange

— Vegetarian — Casserole

SERVES 2

285 CALORIES PER SERVING

2 teaspoons olive or vegetable oil

1½oz (45g) onion, chopped

1 medium garlic clove, crushed

9oz (270g) courgettes, thinly sliced

8oz (240g) canned tomatoes, crushed

6oz (180g) drained canned red kidney beans

¼ teaspoon oregano

pinch each salt and pepper

2oz (60g) Cheddar cheese, grated

Preheat oven to 350°F, 180°C, Gas Mark 4. Heat oil in frying pan, add onion and garlic and saute until onion is softened. Add courgettes and cook, stirring constantly, until tender-crisp, about 3 minutes. Stir in tomatoes, beans and seasonings and bring to the boil. Transfer bean mixture to shallow flameproof casserole, sprinkle with cheese and bake for 20 to 25 minutes, or until hot. Place under grill until cheese is lightly browned.

Each serving provides: 2 Protein Exchanges, 3 Vegetable Exchanges, 1 Fat Exchange

— Minestrone —

SERVES 2

275 CALORIES PER SERVING

2 teaspoons olive oil

6oz (180g) cabbage, shredded

4oz (120g) onion, sliced

4 garlic cloves, crushed

12fl oz (360ml) beef stock, prepared according to package directions

8oz (240g) canned tomatoes, chopped

8fl oz (240ml) water

2oz (60g) carrot, sliced

2oz (60g) celery, sliced

6oz (180g) drained canned haricot beans

3oz (90g) courgettes, diced

1 tablespoon chopped fresh basil or 2 teaspoons dried

½ teaspoon salt

pinch pepper

4oz (120g) cooked elbow macaroni

1 tablespoon chopped parsley

2 teaspoons grated Parmesan cheese

Heat oil in large saucepan, add cabbage, onion and garlic and saute, stirring occasionally, for about 10 minutes. Add stock, tomatoes, water, carrot and celery and cook for 15 to 20 minutes longer. Add beans, courgettes, basil, salt and pepper and simmer until vegetables are tender, about 15 minutes. Add macaroni and cook until heated through. Serve sprinkled with parsley and cheese.

Each serving provides: 1 Protein Exchange, 1 Bread Exchange, 4 Vegetable Exchanges, 1 Fat Exchange, 10 Calories Optional Exchange

•

— Sesame-Chick — Pea Dip

SERVES 4

75 CALORIES PER SERVING

6oz (180g) drained canned chick peas

4 tablespoons lemon juice

4 teaspoons sesame seeds, toasted

2 teaspoons vegetable oil

1 garlic clove, crushed

½ teaspoon salt

Puree all ingredients in blender or food processor. Cover and chill lightly in refrigerator. Serve with raw vegetables.

Each serving provides: ½ Protein Exchange, ½ Fat Exchange, 20 Calories Optional Exchange

•

— Marinated — Chick Pea Salad

SERVES 2

95 CALORIES PER SERVING

6oz (180g) drained canned chick peas

1 tablespoon each chopped onion, green pepper and red wine vinegar

1½ teaspoons lemon juice

1 teaspoon olive or vegetable oil

½ teaspoon chopped fresh basil or ¼ teaspoon dried

½ garlic clove, crushed

pinch each salt, pepper and oregano

Mix chick peas, onion and green pepper in a salad bowl. Mix remaining ingredients, pour dressing over chick pea mixture and toss gently to coat. Cover and refrigerate for at least 4 hours or overnight.

Each serving provides: 1 Protein Exchange, ¼ Vegetable Exchange, ½ Fat Exchange

•

— Black Bean Soup —

SERVES 2

200 CALORIES PER SERVING

2 teaspoons margarine

2 tablespoons chopped onion

1 garlic clove, chopped

12fl oz (360ml) water

6oz (180g) drained canned black beans

1oz (30g) carrot, chopped

1oz (30g) celery, chopped

1 chicken stock cube, crumbled

½ small bay leaf

1 tablespoon dry sherry

pinch each salt and pepper

1 egg, hard–boiled and chopped

Heat margarine in a saucepan, add onion and garlic and saute until onion is softened. Add water, beans, carrot, celery, stock cube and bay leaf to saucepan and bring mixture to the boil. Reduce heat, cover and cook until vegetables are very soft, about 45 minutes. Remove from heat and let cool slightly. Remove and discard bay leaf. Pour mixture into blender and puree at low speed until smooth. Return soup to saucepan and stir in sherry, salt and pepper. Simmer gently for about 5 minutes or until heated through. Pour into 2 bowls and sprinkle each portion with half the chopped egg.

Each serving provides: 1½ Protein Exchanges, ½ Vegetable Exchange, 1 Fat Exchange, 10 Calories Optional Exchange

•

— Split Pea and — Ham Soup

SERVES 2

240 CALORIES PER SERVING

3oz (90g) uncooked yellow split peas

1 teaspoon margarine

3oz (90g) carrot, chopped

1½oz (45g) onion, chopped

1oz (30g) celery, chopped

3oz (90g) ham, chopped

¾ pint (450ml) water

1 chicken stock cube, crumbled

1 small bay leaf, studded with 1 clove

pinch each cinnamon and white pepper

Pick over and rinse peas and set aside. Heat margarine in a saucepan, add carrot, onion, celery and ham and cook, stirring constantly, until onion is transparent. Stir in split peas and remaining ingredients and bring to the boil. Reduce heat, cover and simmer until peas and vegetables are soft, about 45 minutes. Let soup cool slightly and remove and discard bay leaf and clove. Transfer soup to blender and puree. Return to saucepan and heat through.

Each serving provides: 3 Protein Exchanges, 1 Vegetable Exchange, ½ Fat Exchange

— Vegetarian — Aubergine Rolls

SERVES 4

325 CALORIES PER SERVING

1 large aubergine, about 1lb 8oz (720g)

2 tablespoons olive or vegetable oil

3oz (90g) onion, chopped

2oz (60g) green pepper, seeded and chopped

1 tablespoon chopped parsley

¼ teaspoon each salt and oregano

9oz (270g) drained canned chick peas, mashed

5oz (150g) low-fat soft cheese

6oz (180g) cooked chopped spinach, well drained

1 egg, beaten

8oz (240g) canned tomatoes, pureed

4oz (120g) mozzarella cheese, grated

chopped parsley for garnish

Cut stem and very thin slice from top of aubergine, then cut aubergine in half lengthwise. Starting from cut sides and slicing lengthwise, cut four ¼-inch (5-mm) slices from each half. Reserve remaining aubergine for another use. Heat 1¼ teaspoons oil in large non-stick frying pan, add 2 aubergine slices and cook, turning once, until soft and lightly browned on both sides. Remove from pan and set aside. Repeat procedure with remaining aubergine, using 1¼ teaspoons oil for each 2 slices. Heat remaining teaspoon oil in saucepan, add onion and green pepper and saute until onion is transparent. Stir in 1 tablespoon parsley and the salt and oregano and remove from heat. Preheat oven to 350°F, 180°C, Gas Mark 4. Mix half the sauteed vegetables with chick peas, soft cheese, spinach and egg, mixing well. Spoon ⅛ of mixture on to each aubergine slice and, starting from narrow end, roll aubergine to enclose

filling. Arrange rolls seam-side down in a shallow casserole just large enough to hold them in one layer. Combine remaining onion mixture with pureed tomatoes and pour evenly over aubergine rolls. Sprinkle with mozzarella cheese and bake until cheese is melted and lightly browned, about 30 minutes. Serve garnished with chopped parsley.

Each serving provides: 2½ Protein Exchanges, 3½ Vegetable Exchanges, 1½ Fat Exchanges

— Bean Dip — Mexicali

SERVES 4

280 CALORIES PER SERVING

12oz (360g) drained canned haricot beans (reserve 3 tablespoons liquid)

1 tablespoon chopped onion

1 medium garlic clove, crushed

½ teaspoon each chilli powder and cumin

4oz (120g) strong Cheddar cheese, grated

2 teaspoons vegetable oil

4oz (120g) pitta bread, cut into 16 equal pieces

Place beans, reserved liquid, onion, garlic, chilli powder and cumin in blender and puree until smooth. Transfer bean mixture to a saucepan, add cheese and cook over low heat, stirring constantly, until cheese is melted. Stir in oil and serve with bread, dividing evenly.

Each serving provides: 2 Protein Exchanges, 1 Bread Exchange, ½ Fat Exchange

— Chick Pea Salad — with Mustard Vinaigrette

SERVES 2

130 CALORIES PER SERVING

6oz (180g) drained canned chick peas

2oz (60g) celery, chopped

4oz (120g) tomatoes, chopped

3oz (90g) cucumber, peeled and chopped

2 tablespoons wine vinegar

1 tablespoon each chopped parsley and lemon juice

2 teaspoons olive or vegetable oil

1 garlic clove, crushed, or pinch garlic powder

¼ teaspoon spicy brown mustard

pinch each salt, pepper and oregano

Combine all ingredients in salad bowl, cover and chill lightly in refrigerator, tossing occasionally.

Each serving provides: 1 Protein Exchange, 1½ Vegetable Exchanges, 1 Fat Exchange

•

— Hearty Lentil Soup —

SERVES 2

225 CALORIES PER SERVING

3oz (90g) uncooked lentils, rinsed

16fl oz (480ml) water

6oz (180g) peeled potatoes, diced

3oz (90g) onion, chopped

2oz (60g) celery, chopped

3oz (90g) carrot, chopped

1 beef stock cube, crumbled

2 tablespoons chopped parsley

1 garlic clove, crushed

1 bay leaf

pinch cumin

Place lentils and water in large saucepan and bring to the boil. Reduce heat, cover pan, and simmer until lentils are tender, about 20 minutes. Add remaining ingredients, stir to combine, cover and cook over low heat until potatoes are tender, 20 to 30 minutes. Remove bay leaf before serving. Serve with mixed green salad.

Each serving provides: 1½ Protein Exchanges, 1 Bread Exchange, 1½ Vegetable Exchanges

•

— Baked Beans — and Rice

SERVES 2

165 CALORIES PER SERVING

6oz (180g) drained canned haricot beans

2oz (60g) canned tomatoes, pureed

2 teaspoons ketchup

1 teaspoon molasses

½ teaspoon dry mustard

4oz (120g) cooked long grain rice

Preheat oven to 350°F, 180°C, Gas Mark 4. Combine beans, pureed tomatoes, ketchup, molasses and mustard in small shallow casserole and mix well. Stir in rice and bake until heated through, about 15 minutes.

Each serving provides: 1 Protein Exchange, 1 Bread Exchange, ½ Vegetable Exchange, 15 Calories Optional Exchange

•

— White Bean Soup —

SERVES 2

150 CALORIES PER SERVING

2 teaspoons olive or vegetable oil

3oz (90g) carrot, diced

2oz (60g) celery, chopped

1½oz (45g) onion, chopped

1 garlic clove, crushed

12fl oz (360ml) water

4oz (120g) canned tomatoes, pureed

¼ teaspoon each basil and salt

pinch each thyme and pepper

6oz (180g) drained canned small white beans

2 teaspoons chopped parsley

Heat oil in a saucepan, add carrots, celery, onion and garlic and saute until vegetables are tender. Stir in water, pureed tomatoes and seasonings and bring mixture to the boil. Reduce heat and simmer for 15 minutes. Stir in beans and cook until heated through, about 5 minutes longer. Serve each portion sprinkled with 1 teaspoon parsley.

Each serving provides: 1 Protein Exchange, 2 Vegetable Exchanges, 1 Fat Exchange

•

— Chick Peas —
Au Gratin

SERVES 2

360 CALORIES PER SERVING

2 teaspoons olive or vegetable oil

1 garlic clove, sliced

3oz (90g) onion, chopped

2oz (60g) green pepper, seeded and chopped

6oz (180g) cabbage, shredded

8oz (240g) canned tomatoes, chopped

1 teaspoon tomato puree

¼ teaspoon each salt and oregano

pinch each ginger and white pepper

9oz (270g) drained canned chick peas

2oz (60g) Cheddar cheese, grated

3 tablespoons dried breadcrumbs

parsley sprigs for garnish

Preheat oven to 450°F, 230°C, Gas Mark 8. Heat oil in frying pan, add garlic and saute until golden. Using a slotted spoon, remove and discard garlic. Add onion and green pepper to pan and saute until onion is transparent. Stir in cabbage and cook until cabbage is wilted, about 5 minutes. Stir in tomatoes and bring mixture to the boil. Stir in tomato puree and seasonings, reduce heat and simmer for 5 minutes. Stir in chick peas and remove from heat. Transfer mixture to shallow casserole. Combine cheese and breadcrumbs, sprinkle over chick pea mixture and bake for about 5 minutes or until mixture is heated through and cheese topping is browned. Serve garnished with parsley.

Each serving provides: 2½ Protein Exchanges, ½ Bread Exchange, 3 Vegetable Exchanges, 1 Fat Exchange, 5 Calories Optional Exchange

— Pasta and Bean —
Soup

SERVES 6

215 CALORIES PER SERVING

4 teaspoons olive oil

6oz (180g) onions, chopped

2oz (60g) celery, chopped

1 garlic clove, crushed

4 large tomatoes, blanched and chopped

2 pints (1 litre 200ml) water

6oz (180g) uncooked haricot beans, rinsed, soaked overnight and drained

5oz (150g) courgettes, sliced

5oz (150g) carrots, chopped

4oz (120g) green beans, sliced

2oz (60g) each green and red pepper, seeded and chopped

1½oz (45g) uncooked small macaroni

1 tablespoon each chopped fresh basil and parsley

1 teaspoon salt

2oz (60g) Parmesan cheese, grated

Heat oil in large saucepan, add onions, celery and garlic and saute until onions are transparent. Add tomatoes and cook, stirring constantly, for 1 to 2 minutes. Add water and haricot beans and bring to the boil. Reduce heat to moderate, cover and cook until beans are tender, 50 minutes to 1 hour. Add courgettes, carrots, green beans and peppers to soup, cover and cook until vegetables are tender, about 15 minutes. Stir in macaroni, basil, parsley and salt, cover and cook until macaroni is just soft, about 8 minutes. Sprinkle each portion with ½oz (15g) cheese. Serve with a mixed green salad.

Each serving provides: 1½ Protein Exchanges, ¼ Bread Exchange, 3 Vegetable Exchanges, ½ Fat Exchange, 25 Calories Optional Exchange

— Split Pea Fritters —

SERVES 4

195 CALORIES PER SERVING

3oz (90g) uncooked yellow split peas, rinsed and picked over

¾ pint (450ml) water

2oz (60g) onion, chopped

3oz (90g) carrot, grated

1 chicken stock cube, crumbled

2oz (60g) flour

1 teaspoon baking powder

pinch each salt and white pepper

1 egg, beaten

4 teaspoons vegetable oil

Place peas, water, onion, carrot and stock cube in a saucepan and bring to the boil. Reduce heat and simmer, uncovered, stirring occasionally, until peas are soft, about 30 minutes. Drain and mash. Cool. Mix flour, baking powder, salt and pepper. Add egg to cooled split pea mixture, stirring to combine, and stir into dry ingredients. Heat 1 teaspoon oil in a non-stick frying pan. Spoon 4 heaped tablespoons mixture into pan, forming 4 small fritters. Cook until edges bubble and fritters are browned on bottom. Turn fritters over and cook until browned on other side. Remove to warmed serving plate. Set aside and keep hot. Repeat procedure with remaining oil and batter, making a total of 16 fritters and using 1 teaspoon oil for each 4 fritters.

Each serving provides: 1 Protein Exchange, ½ Bread Exchange, ½ Vegetable Exchange, 1 Fat Exchange, 10 Calories Optional Exchange

Top: Pasta and Bean Soup
Bottom: Split Pea Fritters

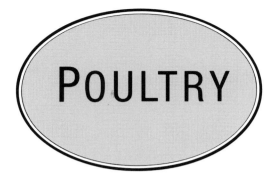

POULTRY

*L*ots of recipes in this section, for poultry is probably the most adaptable of all the protein foods. To prove it, we've collected recipes from as far afield as China, Spain and Italy, as well as favourites from closer to home, such as Sauteed Chicken in Mushroom-Tarragon Sauce and Creamed Parsley Chicken. It is good to know, too, that these days chicken and turkey won't break the budget – just add clever touches with vegetables, herbs and spices and you can have a lot of flavour for comparatively little money.

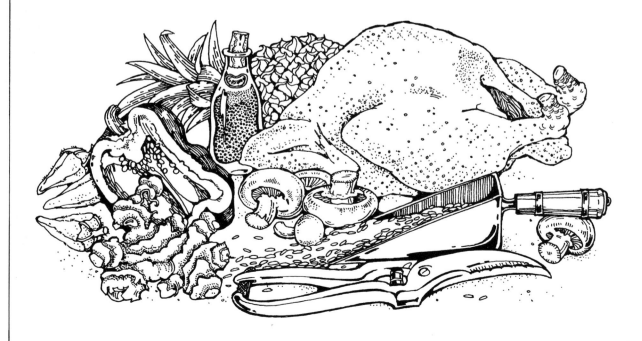

— Chicken Oriental — Soup

SERVES 2

60 CALORIES PER SERVING

1 chicken stock cube, crumbled

12fl oz (360ml) boiling water

2oz (60g) spinach leaves, well washed and chopped

2 tablespoons sliced spring onions

1 egg white

2oz (60g) skinned and boned cooked chicken, cut into thin strips

pinch each ginger and pepper

Mix stock cube and water in small saucepan, add spinach and spring onion and return to the boil. Reduce heat and slowly add egg white, stirring constantly, until egg white has set. Add chicken and seasonings and cook for 10 minutes.

Each serving provides: 1 Protein Exchange, ½ Vegetable Exchange, 10 Calories Optional Exchange

— 'Fried' Chinese — Chicken

SERVES 2

275 CALORIES PER SERVING

1 tablespoon each cornflour and wine vinegar

2½ teaspoons soy sauce

1½ teaspoons chopped peeled ginger root

1 teaspoon dry sherry

½ teaspoon brown sugar

10oz (300g) chicken breasts, skinned

1 tablespoon vegetable oil

3oz (90g) mange-tout peas, stem ends and strings removed

2oz (60g) red pepper, seeded and cut into strips

2oz (60g) spring onions, sliced into 2-inch (2.5-cm) pieces

coriander sprig for garnish

Mix cornflour with the vinegar, 1½ teaspoons soy sauce, the ginger, sherry and brown sugar. Rinse chicken pieces and pat dry on paper towels. Cut into cubes. Dip chicken in soy sauce mixture, turning to coat. Place on sheet of greaseproof paper and let stand for about 1 hour to dry. Brush any liquid that has exuded over chicken and let dry. Heat oil in large non-stick frying pan, add chicken and saute, turning frequently, until chicken is browned on all sides and juices run clear when chicken is pierced with a fork. Remove to serving plate and keep hot. Stir-fry all vegetables together in same pan until tender-crisp, add the chicken, sprinkle with remaining teaspoon soy sauce and stir to combine. Garnish with coriander sprig.

Each serving provides: 4 Protein Exchanges, 1½ Vegetable Exchanges, 1½ Fat Exchanges, 25 Calories Optional Exchange

— Tropical Chicken — Saute

SERVES 2

425 CALORIES PER SERVING

1½oz (45g) flour

¼ teaspoon each salt and pepper

9oz (270g) skinned and boned chicken breasts, cut into 4 pieces

1 egg, beaten

1 tablespoon vegetable oil

1 teaspoon fresh tarragon or ½ teaspoon dried

2fl oz (60ml) dry white wine

1 tablespoon lemon juice

1 teaspoon margarine

1 small mango, peeled, stoned and diced

parsley sprigs for garnish

Mix flour, salt and pepper. Dip chicken pieces into beaten egg, then dredge in seasoned flour, being sure to use all the egg and flour. Heat oil in large non-stick frying pan, add chicken and cook over high heat until bottom is golden brown. Turn chicken pieces over, sprinkle with tarragon and brown other side, reducing heat if necessary. Add wine, lemon juice and margarine, bring to the boil and cook until liquid is slightly reduced and thickened. Add mango, cover and cook until fruit is hot, 1 to 2 minutes. Serve garnished with parsley sprigs.

Each serving provides: 4 Protein Exchanges, 1 Bread Exchange, 2 Fat Exchanges, 1 Fruit Exchange, 25 Calories Optional Exchange

— Turkey Breasts — in Mushroom Sauce

SERVES 2

255 CALORIES PER SERVING

2 teaspoons margarine

10oz (300g) turkey breasts

4oz (120g) mushrooms, thinly sliced

3oz (90g) onion, chopped

2 teaspoons flour

5fl oz (150ml) low-fat natural yogurt

1 tablespoon chopped parsley

1 teaspoon paprika

½ teaspoon salt

pinch pepper

Heat margarine in non-stick frying pan, add turkey and cook gently until browned on both sides. Remove from pan and keep hot. Cook mushrooms and onion in same pan, stirring occasionally, until liquid has evaporated. Sprinkle with 1 teaspoon flour and cook, stirring constantly, for 1 minute. Remove from heat. Combine yogurt with remaining teaspoon flour and stir in 2 tablespoons vegetable mixture. Add all yogurt mixture to pan and stir to combine. Place pan over low heat and stir in parsley and seasonings. Add turkey and cook just until heated through. Do not boil.

Each serving provides: 4 Protein Exchanges, 1 Vegetable Exchange, 1 Fat Exchange, ½ Milk Exchange, 10 Calories Optional Exchange

●

— Chicken a la King —

SERVES 2

225 CALORIES PER SERVING

2 teaspoons margarine

3oz (90g) onion, chopped

1½oz (45g) mushrooms, chopped

1 teaspoon flour

4fl oz (120ml) skimmed milk

6oz (180g) skinned and boned cooked chicken, diced

3oz (90g) peas

2 tablespoons chopped drained canned pimentos

¼ teaspoon each salt, white pepper and paprika

Heat margarine in frying pan, add onion and mushrooms and saute, stirring occasionally, until mushrooms are lightly browned. Sprinkle flour over vegetables and stir quickly to combine. Gradually stir in milk and, stirring constantly, bring to the boil. Reduce heat and simmer until mixture thickens. Stir in remaining ingredients and cook 10 to 15 minutes.

Each serving provides: 3 Protein Exchanges, 1½ Vegetable Exchanges, 1 Fat Exchange, 5 Calories Optional Exchange

●

— Oriental Stir-Fry —

SERVES 2

345 CALORIES PER SERVING

1 tablespoon vegetable oil

10oz (300g) skinned and boned chicken breasts, cut into thin strips

1 garlic clove, thinly sliced

¼ teaspoon each grated peeled ginger root and salt

pinch each pepper and paprika

4oz (120g) onions, thinly sliced

2oz (60g) each red and green peppers, seeded and cut into thin strips

2oz (60g) celery, cut in thin diagonal slices

6fl oz (180ml) chicken stock, prepared according to package directions

1 tablespoon soy sauce

2 teaspoons cornflour

4oz (120g) cooked long grain rice, hot

Heat oil in a non-stick wok or large frying pan. Add chicken, garlic and ginger, sprinkle with salt, pepper and paprika and cook, stirring quickly and frequently, until chicken loses its pink colour, 1 to 2 minutes. Add vegetables and half the stock and stir to combine. Cover and cook until vegetables are tender-crisp, 1 to 2 minutes. Mix remaining stock with the soy sauce and cornflour, stirring well. Add to chicken mixture and cook, stirring constantly, until mixture is thickened. Arrange rice on serving dish and serve with chicken mixture.

Each serving provides: 4 Protein Exchanges, 1 Bread Exchange, 2 Vegetable Exchanges, 1½ Fat Exchanges, 10 Calories Optional Exchange

●

— Turkey-Rice Salad —

SERVES 2

260 CALORIES PER SERVING

6oz (180g) skinned and boned cooked turkey, diced

4oz (120g) cooked long-grain rice

1oz (30g) celery, chopped

2 tablespoons each chopped onion and red pepper

1 tablespoon mayonnaise

1½ teaspoons each chopped parsley, low-fat natural yogurt and lemon juice

¼ teaspoon French mustard

pinch each salt, pepper and garlic powder

2 lettuce leaves

radish rose for garnish

Mix turkey, rice, celery, onion and red pepper. Mix mayonnaise, parsley, yogurt, lemon juice, mustard and seasonings, pour over salad and toss well to coat. Cover and chill lightly in refrigerator. Toss again just before serving. Serve on lettuce leaves, garnished with radish rose.

Each serving provides: 3 Protein Exchanges, 1 Bread Exchange, ½ Vegetable Exchange, 1½ Fat Exchanges, 5 Calories Optional Exchange

— Orange Chicken —

SERVES 4

260 CALORIES PER SERVING

8 teaspoons low-fat spread

1lb 4oz (600g) skinned and boned chicken breasts

6oz (180g) mushrooms, sliced

2 teaspoons flour

¼ pint (150ml) water

2fl oz (60ml) thawed frozen concentrated orange juice

½ chicken stock cube, crumbled

2oz (60g) spring onions, thinly sliced

8oz (240g) canned mandarin orange sections, no sugar added, heated gently

Heat margarine in frying pan, add chicken and cook until browned on both sides. Remove from pan and set aside. Cook mushrooms in same pan over high heat, stirring occasionally, until all liquid has evaporated. Sprinkle in flour and stir quickly to combine. Gradually stir in water, add orange juice and stock cube and, stirring constantly, bring to the boil. Reduce heat, add chicken and simmer for about 3 minutes to allow flavours to blend. Serve sprinkled with spring onions and topped with orange sections.

Each serving provides: 4 Protein Exchanges, 1 Vegetable Exchange, 1 Fat Exchange, 1 Fruit Exchange, 5 Calories Optional Exchange

— Sauteed Chicken —

SERVES 2

270 CALORIES PER SERVING

2 chicken joints, each 6oz (180g), skinned, boned and cut into pieces

½ teaspoon salt

4 teaspoons flour

1 tablespoon margarine

1 garlic clove, crushed

4oz (120g) mushrooms, sliced

4fl oz (120ml) chicken stock, prepared according to package directions

2fl oz (60ml) dry sherry

pinch pepper

1 tablespoon chopped parsley for garnish

Sprinkle chicken with salt and dredge in flour to coat. Set aside. Heat margarine in large non-stick frying pan, add garlic and saute briefly, being careful not to burn. Add chicken pieces and brown well on all sides. Reduce heat to low, cover and cook until chicken is tender, 10 to 15 minutes. Add mushrooms to pan and cook uncovered, stirring occasionally, for about 3 minutes. Add stock, wine and pepper, cover and simmer for about 10 minutes. Serve sprinkled with parsley.

Each serving provides: 4 Protein Exchanges, 1½ Vegetable Exchanges, 1½ Fat Exchanges, 40 Calories Optional Exchange

— Curried Chicken — Open Sandwich

SERVES 1

460 CALORIES PER SERVING

2½fl oz (75ml) low-fat natural yogurt

1 tablespoon lemon juice

1½ teaspoons mayonnaise

¼ teaspoon curry powder

pinch each white pepper and salt

4oz (120g) skinned and boned cooked chicken, diced

2 tablespoons chopped celery

1oz (30g) sultanas

½ teaspoon sunflower seeds

2 slices wholemeal bread, toasted

Combine yogurt, lemon juice, mayonnaise, curry powder, pepper and salt. Add chicken, celery, raisins and sunflower seeds and mix to coat with dressing. Spread half the chicken salad on each slice of toast.

Each serving provides: 4 Protein Exchanges, 2 Bread Exchanges, ½ Vegetable Exchange, 1½ Fat Exchanges, 1 Fruit Exchange, ½ Milk Exchange, 10 Calories Optional Exchange

•

— Spanish Chicken — and Rice

SERVES 2

315 CALORIES PER SERVING

2 teaspoons olive oil

3oz (90g) onion, chopped

2oz (60g) green pepper, seeded and chopped

2 garlic cloves, crushed

4oz (120g) canned tomatoes, pureed

3fl oz (90ml) water

1 packet low-calorie chicken soup powder

¼ teaspoon cumin

pinch pepper

6oz (180g) skinned and boned cooked chicken, diced

4oz (120g) cooked long grain rice

3oz (90g) drained canned haricot beans

2 tablespoons chopped parsley

Heat oil in frying pan, add onion, green pepper and garlic and saute over low heat until vegetables are tender, about 5 minutes. Add pureed tomatoes, water, low-calorie soup powder and seasonings and bring to the boil. Reduce heat and simmer for 5 minutes. Stir in remaining ingredients and cook for 10 minutes longer.

Each serving provides: 3½ Protein Exchanges, 1 Bread Exchange, 1½ Vegetable Exchanges, 1 Fat Exchange, 20 Calories Optional Exchange

•

— Turkey Loaf —

SERVES 4

350 CALORIES PER SERVING

4 teaspoons margarine

2 medium apples, cored, peeled and diced

2oz (60g) carrot, grated

3oz (90g) onion, chopped

2oz (60g) celery, chopped

2oz (60g) green pepper, seeded and chopped

1lb 2oz (540g) minced turkey

4 slices white bread, cut into cubes

5fl oz (150ml) low-fat natural yogurt

2 eggs, beaten

¼ teaspoon each poultry seasoning and salt

Preheat oven to 375°F, 190°C, Gas Mark 5. Heat 3 teaspoons margarine in frying pan, add apples and vegetables and saute, stirring constantly, until apples are soft. Remove from heat and stir in remaining ingredients. Grease a 2lb (960g) loaf tin with remaining teaspoon margarine and transfer turkey mixture to tin. Smooth top and bake until set, 35 to 40 minutes (centre should be firm). Remove from oven, let stand for 5 minutes and invert onto serving plate.

Each serving provides: 4 Protein Exchanges, 1 Bread Exchange, 1 Vegetable Exchange, 1 Fat Exchange, ½ Fruit Exchange, ¼ Milk Exchange

•

— Chicken Schnitzel —

SERVES 2

475 CALORIES PER SERVING

3 tablespoons flour

pinch each salt and pepper

3 tablespoons dried breadcrumbs

pinch each paprika and garlic powder

2 chicken breasts (4oz/120g each), skinned and boned, cut into halves and pounded to ⅛ inch (3 mm) thick

1 egg, lightly beaten

4 teaspoons vegetable oil

3oz (90g) onion, chopped

1 medium apple, cored, peeled and thinly sliced

½ chicken stock cube, dissolved in 6fl oz (180ml) hot water

1lb (480g) sauerkraut, drained and rinsed

1oz (30g) raisins

1 lemon, thinly sliced, and parsley sprigs for garnish

Mix 2 tablespoons flour with the salt and pepper on a sheet of greaseproof paper. Mix breadcrumbs, paprika and garlic powder on another sheet of paper. Dredge each piece of chicken in seasoned flour, dip in beaten egg and coat with breadcrumbs. Heat oil in a large non-stick frying pan, add chicken pieces and quickly brown on both sides. Remove chicken to a plate and keep hot. Saute onion and apple together in same pan over moderate heat until softened. Sprinkle remaining tablespoon flour over mixture, stir quickly to combine and cook for 1 minute. Gradually stir in dissolved stock cube and, stirring constantly, bring to the boil. Reduce heat and simmer until mixture thickens. Stir in sauerkraut and raisins and cook, stirring, until mixture is well heated. Spoon sauerkraut mixture onto centre of serving plate and surround with chicken pieces. Garnish chicken with lemon slices and parsley sprigs.

Each serving provides: 3½ Protein Exchanges, ½ Bread Exchange, 2½ Vegetable Exchanges, 2 Fat Exchanges, 1 Fruit Exchange, 45 Calories Optional Exchange

•

— Herbed — Oven-Baked Chicken

SERVES 4

275 CALORIES PER SERVING

9 tablespoons dried breadcrumbs

1 teaspoon oregano

pinch each salt, pepper and garlic powder

1lb 4oz (600g) skinned and boned chicken breasts, cut into 1-inch (2.5-cm) strips

1 teaspoon vegetable oil

Mix crumbs and seasonings. Dip chicken strips in water, then into crumb mixture, pressing crumbs to make sure they adhere and chicken is thoroughly coated. Grease a non-stick baking sheet with the vegetable oil. Arrange chicken on baking sheet and sprinkle evenly with any remaining crumb mixture. Bake at 350°F, 180°C, Gas Mark 4, until tender, about 20 minutes.

Each serving provides: 4 Protein Exchanges, ¾ Bread Exchange, 15 Calories Optional Exchange

•

— Hot and Sour Soup —

SERVES 4

80 CALORIES PER SERVING

4 large dried black Chinese mushrooms

1 teaspoon vegetable oil

4oz (120g) skinned and boned chicken breast, cut into thin strips

1¼ pints (750ml) water

3oz (90g) each Chinese leaves, finely shredded, and drained canned bamboo shoots, sliced

2 chicken stock cubes

1 tablespoon cornflour, mixed with 2 tablespoons water

2 tablespoons wine vinegar

2 teaspoons soy sauce

3oz (90g) tofu (soybean curd) cut into 1 x ½-inch (2.5 x 1-cm) pieces

½ teaspoon white pepper

1 teaspoon chopped chives to garnish

Soak mushrooms for 30 minutes in water to cover. Drain mushrooms, cut off and discard stems. Slice caps thinly, squeeze to remove all moisture and set aside. Heat oil in saucepan, add chicken and saute just until meat is no longer pink, about 2 minutes. Add water, mushrooms, Chinese leaves, bamboo shoots and stock cubes and bring to the boil. Reduce heat and simmer for 5 minutes. Add cornflour mixed with water and stir into chicken mixture. Add vinegar and soy sauce and simmer, stirring constantly, until slightly thickened. Add tofu and pepper and stir to blend. Garnish with chopped chives and serve.

Each serving provides: 1 Protein Exchange, 1 Vegetable Exchange, 20 Calories Optional Exchange

•

Hot and Sour Soup

— Cheesy Chicken — with Sauteed Mushrooms

SERVES 1

340 CALORIES PER SERVING

2 teaspoons flour

pinch each salt and pepper

3oz (90g) skinned and boned chicken breast, pounded to ¼ inch (5 mm) thick

1½ teaspoons margarine

2oz (60g) mushrooms, sliced

1oz (30g) Emmenthal cheese, grated

parsley sprigs and 3 small tomatoes for garnish

Mix flour, salt and pepper and dredge chicken in seasoned flour, coating all sides. Heat 1 teaspoon margarine in small non-stick pan over moderate heat, add chicken, sprinkle evenly with any remaining seasoned flour and cook, turning once, until golden brown on both sides. Remove pan from heat and transfer chicken to an individual shallow flameproof baking dish. Set aside and keep hot. Saute mushrooms in the same pan with remaining ½ teaspoon margarine until lightly browned. Top chicken with mushrooms, then cheese. Grill 6 inches (15 cm) from heat source until cheese is melted, 3 to 5 minutes. Serve garnished with parsley sprigs and tomatoes.

Each serving provides: 3 Protein Exchanges, 2 Vegetable Exchanges, 1½ Fat Exchanges, 20 Calories Optional Exchange

— Caper Chicken — Saute

SERVES 2

265 CALORIES PER SERVING

2 teaspoons margarine

1oz (30g) each celery and onion, sliced

2 small garlic cloves, crushed

4oz (120g) tomatoes, seeded and chopped

1 tablespoon drained capers, rinsed

10oz (300g) skinned and boned chicken breasts, cut into cubes

pinch pepper

3fl oz (90ml) dry sherry

1 tablespoon chopped parsley, optional

Heat 1 teaspoon margarine in frying pan, add celery, onion and garlic and saute, stirring occasionally, until vegetables are tender. Add tomatoes and capers and continue sauteing until tomatoes begin to soften, about 3 minutes longer. Push vegetables to side of pan and add remaining teaspoon margarine and the chicken and pepper. Brown chicken lightly on all sides. Combine vegetables with chicken, stir in sherry and cook until some of the liquid has evaporated, about 1 minute. If desired, sprinkle with parsley just before serving.

Each serving provides: 4 Protein Exchanges, 1 Vegetable Exchange, 1 Fat Exchange, 50 Calories Optional Exchange

— Hearty Chicken — Stew

SERVES 2

325 CALORIES PER SERVING

1 tablespoon flour

½ teaspoon salt

¼ teaspoon pepper

8oz (240g) skinned and boned chicken breasts, cubed

2 teaspoons margarine

6oz (180g) onions, chopped

2oz (60g) ham, chopped

2oz (60g) okra, sliced

2oz (60g) celery, chopped

8oz (240g) canned tomatoes, crushed

8fl oz (240ml) water

3oz (90g) drained canned sweetcorn

Mix flour, ¼ teaspoon salt and the pepper. Sprinkle seasoned flour over chicken cubes and set aside. Heat margarine in a large saucepan, add onions and ham and saute until onions are softened. Add chicken cubes and cook until lightly browned on all sides. Add okra and celery and stir to combine. Add tomatoes, water and remaining ¼ teaspoon salt and bring to the boil. Reduce heat, cover and simmer until chicken is almost tender, about 20 minutes. Add sweetcorn and cook for a further 2 to 3 minutes.

Each serving provides: 4 Protein Exchanges, ½ Bread Exchange, 3 Vegetable Exchanges, 1 Fat Exchange, 15 Calories Optional Exchange

— Chicken and — Cheese Soup

SERVES 2

390 CALORIES PER SERVING

2 teaspoons margarine

2oz (60g) celery, finely chopped

3oz (90g) onion, finely chopped

3oz (90g) carrot, finely chopped

2 teaspoons flour

8fl oz (240ml) water

1 chicken stock cube, crumbled

3oz (90g) frozen peas

4fl oz (120ml) skimmed milk

2oz (60g) Cheddar cheese, grated

4oz (120g) skinned and boned cooked chicken or turkey, diced

4oz (120g) cooked long grain rice

1 teaspoon Worcestershire sauce

pinch each salt and cayenne pepper

Heat margarine in saucepan, add celery, onion and carrot and cook over moderate heat, stirring occasionally, until vegetables are tender. Add flour, stir quickly to combine, and gradually stir in water. Add stock cube and, stirring constantly, bring to the boil. Add peas and cook for 3 minutes. Reduce heat and add milk and cheese. Cook, stirring constantly, until cheese is melted. Add remaining ingredients and cook, stirring occasionally, for 10 minutes or until completely heated through.

Each serving provides: 3 Protein Exchanges, 1 Bread Exchange, 2 Vegetable Exchanges, 1 Fat Exchange, 30 Calories Optional Exchange

•

— Okra Soup Supper —

SERVES 4

195 CALORIES PER SERVING

1 medium green pepper, seeded and chopped

4oz (120g) onion, chopped

2oz (60g) celery, chopped

1 chicken stock cube, crumbled

1 garlic clove, crushed

10oz (300g) skinned and boned chicken breasts, diced

1lb 4oz (600g) canned whole tomatoes, chopped

¾ pint (450ml) water

12oz (360g) drained canned sweetcorn

6oz (180g) okra, sliced

1½ teaspoons salt

½ teaspoon hot pepper sauce

Combine green pepper, onion, celery, stock cube and garlic in a large saucepan and cook, stirring frequently, until all vegetables are tender. Add chicken, tomatoes and water to vegetables and bring to the boil. Reduce heat, cover and simmer for 30 minutes. Add sweetcorn, okra, salt and hot sauce to chicken mixture. Cook uncovered, stirring frequently, for 45 minutes.

Each serving provides: 2 Protein Exchanges, 1 Bread Exchange, 3 Vegetable Exchanges

•

— Chicken with — Vermicelli

SERVES 2

265 CALORIES PER SERVING

2 teaspoons vegetable oil

3oz (90g) spring onions, thinly sliced

½ teaspoon chopped peeled ginger root

8oz (240g) skinned and boned chicken breasts, cut into thin strips

4oz (120g) mushrooms, thinly sliced

2oz (60g) beansprouts

2 teaspoons soy sauce

4oz (120g) cooked vermicelli

Heat oil in frying pan, add spring onions and ginger root and saute for 1 minute. Add chicken and saute for 2 minutes. Add mushrooms and beansprouts and cook until vegetables are tender, 3 to 5 minutes. Stir in soy sauce. Add vermicelli and stir to combine. Cook until heated through, about 1 minute.

Each serving provides: 3 Protein Exchanges, 1 Bread Exchange, 1½ Vegetable Exchanges, 1 Fat Exchange

•

— Chicken Fontina —

SERVES 4

275 CALORIES PER SERVING

4 chicken breasts, each 3oz (90g), skinned and boned, pounded to ¼ inch (5 mm) thick

4 slices Fontina cheese (1oz/30g each)

4 teaspoons each flour and margarine

4oz (120g) mushrooms, thinly sliced

1 garlic clove, crushed

6fl oz (180ml) water

1 chicken stock cube, crumbled

1 teaspoon each tomato puree and salt

¼ teaspoon rosemary leaves, crushed

pinch pepper

4 teaspoons white wine

chopped parsley for garnish

Top each breast with 1 slice cheese and fold chicken to enclose. Pound open edges together with meat mallet or end of rolling pin to seal. Dust each breast with 1 teaspoon flour and set aside. Heat margarine in non-stick frying pan, add chicken and brown quickly on both sides. Remove chicken from pan and set aside. Saute mushrooms and garlic together in same pan until mushrooms are tender. Add water, stock cube, tomato puree and seasonings and simmer for 5 minutes. Return chicken to pan and simmer for about 5 minutes, basting frequently with sauce. Stir in wine and serve sprinkled with parsley.

Each serving provides: 3 Protein Exchanges, ½ Vegetable Exchange, 1 Fat Exchange, 15 Calories Optional Exchange

— Turkey Kebabs — with Soya-Pineapple Sauce

SERVES 2

330 CALORIES PER SERVING

3oz (90g) onions, chopped

2½fl oz (75ml) pineapple juice

2 tablespoons each soy sauce and lemon juice

2 teaspoons each spicy brown mustard and dry sherry

1 garlic clove, cut in quarters

1-inch (2.5-cm) piece peeled ginger root, cut in quarters

10oz (300g) skinned and boned turkey, cut into 1-inch (2.5-cm) cubes

½ each medium red and green peppers, seeded and cut into 1-inch (2.5-cm) squares

8 medium mushroom caps (about 1½-inch/4-cm diameter each)

8 spring onions, bulbs only

1 tablespoon vegetable oil

4oz (120g) canned crushed pineapple, no sugar added

1 teaspoon cornflour

Mix onion, pineapple juice, soy sauce, lemon juice, mustard, sherry, garlic and ginger in a bowl, add turkey and remaining vegetables and toss to coat. Cover and refrigerate for 1 hour. Using slotted spoon, remove turkey, pepper squares, mushrooms and spring onions from marinade. Divide turkey cubes, pepper squares, mushroom caps and spring onions between four 8-inch (20-cm) kebab skewers. Thread carefully onto skewers, alternating ingredients. Arrange kebabs in a shallow flameproof casserole large enough to hold them in one layer and set aside. Strain marinade; reserving liquid, pick out garlic and ginger pieces, leaving onion. Heat oil in small frying pan, add reserved onion and saute until softened. Stir in crushed pineapple. Add cornflour to reserved marinade liquid and mix well. Add to

the pan and, stirring constantly, bring mixture to the boil. Reduce heat and simmer until mixture thickens. Pour pineapple sauce into blender and puree at low speed until smooth. Preheat grill. Lightly brush kebabs with some of the pineapple sauce and grill, turning once and brushing again with some of the sauce, until turkey is browned, about 5 minutes on each side. Reheat remaining sauce and serve with kebabs.

Each serving provides: 4 Protein Exchanges, 2 Vegetable Exchanges, 1½ Fat Exchanges, 1 Fruit Exchange, 10 Calories Optional Exchange

— Honey-Glazed — Chicken Joints

SERVES 2

210 CALORIES PER SERVING

2 tablespoons finely chopped mint

2 teaspoons each honey, warmed, and olive oil

1 garlic clove, crushed

2 chicken joints, each 6oz (180g), skinned

½ teaspoon salt

2 tablespoons lemon juice

mint sprigs for garnish

Mix chopped mint, honey, oil and garlic. Place chicken joints in a non-stick baking tin and sprinkle with salt on all sides. Brush with mint-honey mixture and sprinkle with lemon juice. Bake at 400°F, 200°C, Gas Mark 6 until tender, 25 to 30 minutes. Remove baking tin from oven and baste chicken with pan juices. Place under hot grill for about 1 minute or until browned and crisp. Garnish with mint sprigs before serving.

Each serving provides: 4 Protein Exchanges, 1 Fat Exchange, 20 Calories Optional Exchange

Turkey Kebabs with Soya-Pineapple Sauce

— Turkey-Vegetable — Saute

SERVES 2

265 CALORIES PER SERVING

2 teaspoons peanut or vegetable oil

4oz (120g) onions, thinly sliced

1 garlic clove, crushed

10oz (300g) skinned and boned turkey breast, cut into 2 x 1-inch (5 x 2.5-cm) strips

8oz (240g) broccoli florets, blanched

3oz (90g) red pepper, seeded and thinly sliced

6fl oz (180ml) water

4 teaspoons dry sherry

1 tablespoon soy sauce

½ chicken stock cube, crumbled

2 teaspoons cornflour, mixed with 1½ teaspoons water

Heat oil in a frying pan, add onions and garlic and saute until onions are transparent. Add turkey and continue sauteing until turkey is browned. Add broccoli and red pepper and saute until vegetables are tender-crisp, about 5 minutes. Add water, sherry, soy sauce and stock cube and bring to the boil. Stir in cornflour mixed with water and cook, stirring constantly, until mixture thickens.

Each serving provides: 4 Protein Exchanges, 3 Vegetable Exchanges, 1 Fat Exchange, 20 Calories Optional Exchange

•

— Potted Turkey — Patties

SERVES 2

280 CALORIES PER SERVING

2 teaspoons margarine

2 tablespoons chopped onion

1 garlic clove, crushed

1½oz (45g) mushrooms, chopped

8oz (240g) minced turkey

1 egg

1 slice white bread, made into crumbs

2 teaspoons chopped parsley

¼ teaspoon thyme

pinch each salt and pepper

2 teaspoons flour

½ chicken stock cube, dissolved in 8fl oz (240ml) hot water

2fl oz (60ml) skimmed milk

Heat 1 teaspoon margarine in small non-stick frying pan, add onion and garlic and saute until onion is transparent, about 2 minutes. Add mushrooms and saute until softened, about 5 minutes. Transfer mushroom mixture to a bowl and add turkey, egg, breadcrumbs, 1 teaspoon parsley and the thyme, salt and pepper. Stir to combine. Form turkey mixture into 4 equal patties and sprinkle each with ¼ teaspoon flour. Heat remaining teaspoon margarine in a frying pan, add turkey patties and cook until browned on both sides. Add dissolved stock cube and bring to the boil. Reduce heat, cover and simmer for about 10 minutes. Mix milk with remaining teaspoon flour. Gradually stir into pan juices and cook over moderate heat, stirring constantly, until mixture becomes slightly thickened. Serve sprinkled with remaining teaspoon parsley.

Each serving provides: 3½ Protein Exchanges, ½ Bread Exchange, ½ Vegetable Exchange, 1 Fat Exchange, 20 Calories Optional Exchange

•

— Turkey Burgers —

SERVES 2

370 CALORIES PER SERVING

8oz (240g) minced turkey

4 teaspoons margarine, softened

1½ teaspoons water

1 packet low-calorie chicken soup powder

½ teaspoon vegetable oil

2oz (60g) onion, thinly sliced

4 teaspoons tomato ketchup

2 baps, each 2oz (60g), cut into halves and toasted

Mix turkey, margarine, water and low-calorie soup powder and form into 2 equal patties. Grease a non-stick frying pan with the vegetable oil. Heat pan over moderate heat, add patties and brown on both sides. Reduce heat to low and add onions. Cover pan and cook until patties are no longer pink inside, 5 to 8 minutes. Serve each burger, topped with 2 teaspoons ketchup and half the cooked onion slices, on a toasted bap.

Each serving provides: 3 Protein Exchanges, 2 Bread Exchanges, ½ Vegetable Exchange, 2 Fat Exchanges, 15 Calories Optional Exchange

•

— Turkey Balls in — Tomato Sauce

SERVES 2

265 CALORIES PER SERVING

Turkey Balls

10oz (300g) minced turkey

4oz (120g) cooked long grain rice

1½oz (45g) onion, chopped

2 tablespoons chopped parsley

1 teaspoon salt

pinch each marjoram, thyme and pepper

½ teaspoon vegetable oil

Sauce

8oz (240g) canned tomatoes, pureed

4fl oz (120ml) chicken stock, prepared according to package directions

½ small garlic clove, crushed

To Prepare Turkey Balls: Preheat oven to 350°F, 180°C, Gas Mark 4. Place all ingredients for turkey balls in a bowl and mix well. Shape into 8 equal balls. Grease a casserole with vegetable oil and arrange turkey balls in casserole. *To Prepare Sauce:* Mix together all ingredients for sauce and pour over turkey balls. Cover casserole and bake for 1 hour, turning turkey balls once during baking.

Each serving provides: 4 Protein Exchanges, 1 Bread Exchange, 1½ Vegetable Exchanges, 15 Calories Optional Exchange

— Vegetable-Turkey — Stir-Fry

SERVES 2

275 CALORIES PER SERVING

1 tablespoon peanut or vegetable oil

6oz (180g) onion, chopped

2oz (60g) celery, thinly sliced

2oz (60g) red pepper, seeded and cut into thin strips

2oz (60g) cauliflower florets, blanched

8oz (240g) skinned and boned cooked turkey, cut into thin strips

6fl oz (180ml) water

1 teaspoon cornflour

½ chicken stock cube, crumbled

1 teaspoon soy sauce

few drops hot pepper sauce

pinch garlic powder

Heat oil in wok or large frying pan over high heat, add vegetables and cook, stirring quickly and frequently, until celery and pepper are tender-crisp, 1 to 2 minutes. Stir in turkey. Mix water and cornflour, stirring well, and stir in crumbled stock cube. Pour into the pan and bring to the boil, stirring constantly. Reduce heat and cook, stirring until mixture thickens. Stir in soy sauce, hot sauce and garlic powder and cook for 1 minute longer.

Each serving provides: 4 Protein Exchanges, 2 Vegetable Exchanges, 1½ Fat Exchanges, 5 Calories Optional Exchange

— Curried Chicken — and Vegetable Saute

SERVES 2

215 CALORIES PER SERVING

2 teaspoons flour

¼ teaspoon salt

pinch pepper

12oz (360g) chicken pieces, skinned

2 teaspoons vegetable oil

2oz (60g) onion, chopped

1 garlic clove, crushed

2oz (60g) celery, chopped

2oz (60g) green pepper, seeded and chopped

1½ teaspoons curry powder

8oz (240g) canned tomatoes, crushed

Mix flour, salt and pepper, sprinkle flour mixture over chicken pieces. Heat oil in large frying pan, add chicken and cook until browned on all sides. Remove chicken from pan and set aside. Saute onion and garlic in same pan until onion is softened. Add celery, green pepper and curry powder and saute until vegetables are softened. Return chicken to pan, stir in tomatoes and bring mixture to the boil. Reduce heat, cover and simmer for 20 minutes. Remove lid and simmer until chicken is tender, about 5 to 10 minutes.

Each serving provides: 4 Protein Exchanges, 2½ Vegetable Exchanges, 1 Fat Exchange, 10 Calories Optional Exchange

— Mixed Fruit and — Chicken Saute

SERVES 4

270 CALORIES PER SERVING

3 tablespoons flour

½ teaspoon salt

pinch pepper

1lb 8oz (720g) chicken pieces, skinned

4 teaspoons vegetable oil

4oz (120g) onions, sliced

1 tablespoon chopped garlic

1 teaspoon chopped peeled ginger root

4oz (120g) spinach, well washed

2 each medium peaches and apricots, blanched, peeled, stoned and sliced

¼ small pineapple, peeled and cut into 1-inch (2.5-cm) pieces

1 teaspoon wine vinegar

Mix flour, salt and pepper. Rinse chicken, dry on paper towels and dredge in seasoned flour to coat. Heat oil in large non-stick frying pan. Add chicken, one piece at a time, and cook, turning frequently, until browned on all sides. Juices should run clear when chicken is pierced with a fork. Remove chicken to serving plate and keep hot. Saute onion, garlic and ginger together in same pan until onion is browned, 2 to 3 minutes. Add spinach, fruit and vinegar and cook, stirring occasionally, until spinach is wilted. Return chicken to pan and stir to combine.

Each serving provides: 4 Protein Exchanges, 1 Vegetable Exchange, 1 Fat Exchange, 1 Fruit Exchange, 25 Calories Optional Exchange

•

— Creamed Parsley — Chicken

SERVES 2

195 CALORIES PER SERVING

2 tablespoons each chopped carrot and celery

½ chicken stock cube, crumbled

6fl oz (180ml) water

2 teaspoons each margarine and flour

6oz (180g) skinned and boned cooked chicken, cut into 1-inch (2.5-cm) cubes

2fl oz (60ml) skimmed milk

2 tablespoons chopped parsley

pinch pepper

Place carrot, celery and stock cube in a small saucepan with the water. Bring to the boil and simmer for 5 minutes. Heat margarine in a saucepan, add flour and cook, stirring constantly, for 2 minutes. Remove from heat and gradually stir in vegetable mixture. Return to heat and simmer, stirring constantly, for 5 minutes. Add chicken, milk and parsley and stir to combine. Simmer for 10 minutes and season with pepper.

Each serving provides: 3 Protein Exchanges, ½ Vegetable Exchange, 1 Fat Exchange, 20 Calories Optional Exchange

•

— Fruited Ginger — Chicken

SERVES 2

330 CALORIES PER SERVING

1 tablespoon soy sauce

1 tablespoon thawed frozen concentrated orange juice

1 garlic clove, chopped

2 teaspoons grated peeled ginger root

2 teaspoons dry white wine

2 teaspoons chilli sauce

10oz (300g) skinned and boned chicken breasts, cut into thin strips

2 teaspoons peanut or vegetable oil

4oz (120g) onions, sliced

1 teaspoon cornflour

12oz (360g) canned sliced peaches, no sugar added

4oz (120g) thawed frozen mange-tout peas, blanched

Mix soy sauce, orange juice, half the garlic, ginger, wine and chilli sauce in a bowl, add chicken and toss to coat thoroughly. Cover and refrigerate for at least 1 hour (may be marinated overnight). Remove chicken from marinade and strain marinade, reserving liquid and discarding garlic and ginger. Heat oil in a frying pan, add onions and remaining garlic and saute until onions are transparent. Add chicken and cook until lightly browned on all sides. Mix cornflour with the reserved marinade, add to the pan and bring to the boil, stirring constantly. Reduce heat and simmer until liquid thickens. Add peaches and mange-tout peas and stir to combine. Cook until well heated through.

Each serving provides: 4 Protein Exchanges, 1½ Vegetable Exchanges, 1 Fat Exchange, ½ Fruit Exchange, 30 Calories Optional Exchange

•

Fruited Ginger Chicken

— Chicken Curry —

SERVES 4

220 CALORIES PER SERVING

5fl oz (150ml) low-fat natural yogurt

2 garlic cloves, crushed

1 teaspoon curry powder

¼ teaspoon each ground coriander, ginger and salt

pinch cayenne pepper

1lb 4oz (600g) chicken pieces, skinned

2 teaspoons vegetable oil

3oz (90g) onion, chopped

8oz (240g) tomatoes, chopped

1 bay leaf

Mix yogurt and seasonings in a bowl, add chicken pieces, turning to coat, and let stand at room temperature for 30 minutes. Heat oil in large frying pan, add onion and saute until lightly browned. Add tomatoes and bay leaf and simmer for 5 minutes. Add chicken and marinade mixture and stir to combine. Bring mixture to the boil. Reduce heat, cover and simmer, turning once or twice, until chicken is tender, about 30 minutes. Remove bay leaf before serving.

Each serving provides: 3 Protein Exchanges, 1 Vegetable Exchange, ½ Fat Exchange, ¼ Milk Exchange

— Creamy Broccoli- Chicken Casserole

SERVES 2

440 CALORIES PER SERVING

2 teaspoons margarine

1½oz (45g) onion, chopped

4 teaspoons flour

10fl oz (300ml) skimmed milk

2oz (60g) Cheddar cheese, grated

pinch each salt and pepper

6oz (180g) skinned and boned cooked chicken, diced

4oz (120g) cooked chopped broccoli

4oz (120g) cooked macaroni

2oz (60g) chopped drained canned pimentos

Preheat oven to 375°F, 190°C, Gas Mark 5. Heat margarine in small saucepan, add onion and saute briefly. Do not brown. Add flour and stir quickly to mix. Remove from heat and gradually stir in milk, stirring until well blended. Return to heat and cook, stirring constantly, until slightly thickened. Add cheese and cook over low heat, stirring occasionally, until sauce is thick and creamy, about 2 minutes. Remove from heat and stir in salt and pepper. Combine remaining ingredients in a casserole. Stir cheese sauce into chicken mixture and bake for 30 minutes.

Each serving provides: 4 Protein Exchanges, 1 Bread Exchange, 1½ Vegetable Exchanges, 1 Fat Exchange, ½ Milk Exchange, 20 Calories Optional Exchange

— Sesame Chicken — Saute

SERVES 4

320 CALORIES PER SERVING

1½oz (45g) cornflakes, crushed

6 tablespoons dried breadcrumbs

2 teaspoons sesame seeds

pinch each salt, onion powder and garlic powder

1lb 4oz (600g) skinned and boned chicken breasts, pounded to ¼ inch (5 mm) thick

5fl oz (150ml) buttermilk

2 tablespoons peanut or vegetable oil

Mix cornflakes, breadcrumbs, sesame seeds and seasonings. Dip chicken into buttermilk and then into crumb mixture. Heat oil in a large frying pan, add chicken and cook, turning once, until browned on both sides, 3 to 4 minutes on each side.

Each serving provides: 4 Protein Exchanges, 1 Bread Exchange, 1½ Fat Exchanges, 25 Calories Optional Exchange

— Baked Stuffed — Chicken Breasts

SERVES 2

350 CALORIES PER SERVING

2 teaspoons margarine

1½oz (45g) mushrooms, finely chopped

2oz (60g) onion, chopped

2 teaspoons dry sherry

1 small garlic clove, crushed

½ teaspoon salt

pinch pepper

4oz (120g) cooked long grain rice

2 skinned and boned chicken breasts (5oz/150g each), pounded to ⅛ inch (3 mm) thick

3 tablespoons dried breadcrumbs

½ teaspoon vegetable oil

pinch paprika

parsley sprigs for garnish

Heat 1 teaspoon margarine in small non-stick pan, add mushrooms, onion, sherry, garlic, salt and pepper and saute, stirring occasionally, until onion is tender. Remove from heat and stir in rice. Place chicken breasts hollow side up and spread half the rice mixture on each, leaving a border of about ½ inch (1 cm). Fold long sides over, then roll breast from short end to enclose filling. Secure each roll with wooden cocktail sticks. Preheat oven to 350°F, 180°C, Gas Mark 4. Melt remaining teaspoon margarine in small non-stick frying pan and remove from heat. Roll each stuffed breast in margarine, then in breadcrumbs, coating all sides. Grease a small shallow baking tin with the vegetable oil. Transfer chicken rolls to the tin and sprinkle with any remaining breadcrumbs. Sprinkle with paprika and bake until chicken is tender, 20 to 25 minutes. Remove cocktail sticks before serving. Garnish with parsley sprigs.

Each serving provides: 4 Protein Exchanges, 1 Bread Exchange, ½ Vegetable Exchange, 1 Fat Exchange, 20 Calories Optional Exchange

— Velvet Chicken — and Vegetables

SERVES 4

325 CALORIES PER SERVING

2 tablespoons cornflour

1 tablespoon soy sauce

1 egg white

1lb 4oz (600g) skinned and boned chicken breasts, cut into 2-inch (5-cm) strips

¾ pint (450ml) water

1 chicken stock cube, crumbled

4 teaspoons vegetable oil

2oz (60g) each red and green pepper, seeded and cut into thin strips

2 garlic cloves, crushed

1 teaspoon chopped peeled ginger root

4oz (120g) broccoli florets, blanched

8oz (240g) drained canned button mushrooms

8oz (240g) cooked long grain rice, hot

Mix cornflour, soy sauce and egg white well together, add chicken and toss to coat evenly. Refrigerate, uncovered, for 30 minutes so that coating will adhere to chicken. Mix water and stock cube in a frying pan and bring to the boil. Gradually add chicken, stirring gently to separate chicken pieces. Return mixture to the boil. Remove from heat and drain chicken, reserving 1 teacupful of liquid from the pan. Set aside chicken and pan liquid. Heat oil in same pan, add peppers, garlic and ginger and saute over gentle heat until peppers are tender, about 5 minutes. Add broccoli, mushrooms, chicken and reserved pan liquid to pan and cook, stirring occasionally, until ingredients are thoroughly hot and mixture is slightly thickened. Serve over rice.

Each serving provides: 4 Protein Exchanges, 1 Bread Exchange, 1½ Vegetable Exchanges, 1 Fat Exchange, 20 Calories Optional Exchange

— Chicken Fricassee —

SERVES 2

220 CALORIES PER SERVING

4 teaspoons flour

¼ teaspoon salt

pinch each pepper and thyme

12oz (360g) chicken pieces, skinned

1 teaspoon margarine

3oz (90g) onion, chopped

3oz (90g) mushrooms, sliced

1oz (30g) celery, chopped

6fl oz (180ml) water

½ small bay leaf

2fl oz (60ml) skimmed milk

2 teaspoons chopped parsley for garnish

Mix 2 teaspoons flour with the salt, pepper and thyme. Dredge chicken pieces in seasoned flour to coat. Heat margarine in saucepan, add chicken and cook, turning frequently, until browned on all sides. Remove chicken to plate and set aside, reserving pan drippings. Saute onion in the pan drippings until softened, add mushrooms and celery and saute until tender, about 3 minutes. Return chicken to pan, add water and bay leaf and bring to the boil. Reduce heat, cover and simmer until chicken is tender, 30 to 35 minutes. Mix remaining 2 teaspoons flour with the milk, stirring well. Stir into chicken mixture and cook, stirring constantly, until sauce is thickened, 3 to 5 minutes. Remove and discard bay leaf. Serve sprinkled with parsley.

Each serving provides: 4 Protein Exchanges, 1½ Vegetable Exchanges, ½ Fat Exchange, 30 Calories Optional Exchange

— Stuffed Turkey — Roll

SERVES 4
230 CALORIES PER SERVING

1 tablespoon margarine

3oz (90g) onion, chopped

1 garlic clove, crushed

3oz (90g) mushrooms, chopped

6oz (180g) cooked chopped spinach, well drained

2½oz (75g) low-fat soft cheese

3 tablespoons dried breadcrumbs

½ teaspoon salt

¼ teaspoon pepper

1 large skinned and boned turkey breast, 14oz (420g)

2fl oz (60ml) dry white wine

½ chicken stock cube, dissolved in 8fl oz (240ml) hot water

1 tablespoon water

1 teaspoon cornflour

Heat margarine in frying pan, add onion and garlic and saute until softened. Add mushrooms and saute until browned, about 5 minutes. Stir in spinach, cheese, breadcrumbs, ¼ teaspoon salt and pinch of pepper. Remove from heat, set aside and let cool. Pound turkey breast to ¼ inch (5 mm) thick between 2 sheets of cling film. Remove top sheet and sprinkle chicken with remaining ¼ teaspoon salt and pinch of pepper. Spread with cooled spinach mixture, leaving a 1-inch (2.5-cm) border all round. Preheat oven to 350°F, 180°C, Gas Mark 4. Carefully roll turkey breast lengthwise to enclose filling and tie with butcher's twine or secure with small skewers. Transfer to a baking tin. Add wine and dissolved stock cube, cover with foil and bake for 40 minutes. Remove foil and continue baking, basting with pan juices, until turkey is tender, 10 to 15 minutes longer. Remove turkey roll to a dish and keep hot. Bring pan juices to the boil in a small saucepan. Mix water and cornflour, stir into pan juices and cook, stirring constantly, until mixture is slightly thickened. Pour over turkey roll.

Each serving provides: 3 Protein Exchanges, 1 Vegetable Exchange, ½ Fat Exchange, 50 Calories Optional Exchange

— Sauteed Chicken — in Mushroom-Tarragon Sauce

SERVES 2
250 CALORIES PER SERVING

2 teaspoons flour

¼ teaspoon salt

pinch pepper

10oz (300g) skinned and boned chicken breasts

2 teaspoons margarine

4oz (120g) mushrooms, sliced

2oz (60g) spring onions, chopped

½ teaspoon tarragon

2fl oz (60ml) each dry white wine and water

Mix flour, salt and pepper and sprinkle chicken breasts with the mixture. Heat margarine in a frying pan, add chicken and cook, turning once, until lightly browned on both sides. Add mushrooms, spring onions and tarragon and cook until vegetables are softened. Stir in wine and bring to the boil. Add water, reduce heat, cover and simmer, turning chicken once, until chicken is tender, about 15 minutes.

Each serving provides: 4 Protein Exchanges, 1 Vegetable Exchange, 1 Fat Exchange, 40 Calories Optional Exchange

— Chicken Oriental —

SERVES 2
280 CALORIES PER SERVING

10oz (300g) skinned and boned chicken breasts, thinly sliced

4 teaspoons soy sauce

½ teaspoon grated peeled ginger root

2 teaspoons peanut or vegetable oil

3oz (90g) spring onions, chopped

1 garlic clove, crushed

4oz (120g) mushrooms, sliced

5oz (150g) courgettes, cut into thin strips

3fl oz (90ml) water

2 teaspoons cornflour

½ packet low-calorie chicken soup powder

4oz (120g) cauliflower florets, blanched

Mix chicken with the soy sauce and ginger and set aside. Heat oil in a large frying pan, add spring onions and garlic and saute until spring onions are soft. Add mushrooms and courgettes and saute, stirring constantly, until vegetables are just tender. Add chicken mixture and cook, stirring and turning, until chicken loses its pink colour. Mix together the water, cornflour and low-calorie soup powder, stirring well. Add to chicken mixture and stir to combine. Add cauliflower and cook over moderate heat, stirring constantly, until thickened.

Each serving provides: 4 Protein Exchanges, 3 Vegetable Exchanges, 1 Fat Exchange, 20 Calories Optional Exchange

— Turkey in Lemon — and Mushroom Sauce

SERVES 2

280 CALORIES PER SERVING

1 medium onion, chopped

6oz (180g) mushrooms, chopped

1 tablespoon chopped parsley

juice and thinly peeled rind of ½ lemon

½ pint (300ml) chicken stock, made with 1 cube

3oz (90g) pickled cucumber, chopped

8oz (240g) cooked turkey, chopped

1 tablespoon cornflour

1oz (30g) low-fat dry milk

6oz (180g) cooked green beans, hot

Combine onion, mushrooms, parsley, lemon rind and juice, chicken stock and pickled cucumber in a saucepan. Bring to the boil and simmer until vegetables are tender. Remove lemon rind, add turkey, bring back to the boil and simmer for a further 10 minutes. Mix cornflour with a little water, add to turkey mixture and cook until thickened. Remove from heat, add milk powder and stir until powder is completely dissolved. Serve at once with green beans.

Each serving provides: 4 Protein Exchanges, 3 Vegetable Exchanges, ½ Milk Exchange, 15 Calories Optional Exchange

— Chicken — Tandoori

SERVES 4

220 CALORIES PER SERVING

4 x 6oz (180g) skinned chicken portions

grated rind of 1 lemon

6 tablespoons lemon juice

2 teaspoons salt

1 teaspoon ground coriander

½ teaspoon cumin

1 teaspoon ground ginger

½ teaspoon garlic powder

2 tablespoons paprika

¼ teaspoon cayenne

10fl oz (300ml) low-fat natural yogurt

1 tablespoon wine vinegar

lemon wedges for garnish

Skin chicken portions, make cuts at 1-inch (2.5-cm) intervals about ½-inch (1.25-cm) deep. Mix together lemon rind, 2 tablespoons lemon juice and salt. Rub into chicken flesh. Combine coriander, cumin, ginger, garlic, paprika and cayenne in a bowl and blend to a smooth paste with the remaining lemon juice. Stir in yogurt and vinegar. Spread over chicken portions. Cover with cling film and allow to stand for 2 hours. Preheat oven to 400°F, 200°C, Gas Mark 6. Place portions on rack in roasting tin and cook in oven for 15 minutes. Spoon over the remaining marinade and return to oven. Reduce heat to 350°F, 180°C, Gas Mark 4. Bake for 1 hour or until chicken is cooked through. Increase temperature to 400°F, 200°C, Gas Mark 6 for 15 minutes to brown. Garnish with lemon wedges. The flavour of this dish may be strengthened by marinating the raw chicken overnight.

Each serving provides: 4 Protein Exchanges, ½ Milk Exchange

— Turkey and — Asparagus Mould

SERVES 2

170 CALORIES PER SERVING

6oz (180g) drained canned asparagus (reserve liquid)

1 chicken stock cube

1 tablespoon unflavoured gelatine

6oz (180g) cooked turkey

1 small lettuce

½ bunch watercress

Make reserved liquid up to ½ pint (300ml) with water. Add stock cube and sprinkle in the gelatine. Heat gently in a small pan, stirring well. Do not allow mixture to boil. Cut turkey meat into small pieces. Arrange asparagus in a 1 pint (600ml) mould, add chopped turkey and pour in the gelatine mixture. Leave in a cool place to set. Turn out and serve on a bed of lettuce and watercress.

Each serving provides: 3 Protein Exchanges, 2 Vegetable Exchanges

135

VEAL

Veal is delicious and our recipes show how to enjoy it to the full. Use it with onion and peppers in Veal and Pepper Saute, make Baked Veal Stuffed Aubergine or team it with pasta for Veal and Spinach Pancakes. For a special dinner party dish, add wine and herbs for Veal Steaks Piccata or Sauteed Veal with Sherry Sauce.

— Minced Veal Rolls —

SERVES 2

330 CALORIES PER SERVING

1 tablespoon margarine

1½oz (45g) onion, chopped

10oz (300g) minced veal

1½oz (45g) cornflakes, crushed

2 teaspoons each imitation bacon bits, crushed, and spicy brown mustard

1 tablespoon low-fat natural yogurt

4 thin spring onions, white portion only (each about 3 inches/ 8 cm long), blanched

1 teaspoon flour

6fl oz (180ml) water

½ chicken stock cube, crumbled

Heat 1 teaspoon margarine in a frying pan, add onion and saute until transparent. Transfer to a bowl and add veal, ¾oz (20g) crushed cornflakes and the bacon bits, mustard and yogurt. Mix well. Divide veal mixture into 4 equal portions. Place 1 portion of veal mixture on a sheet of cling film and flatten into a circle. Top with a spring onion, and roll up to enclose onion. Repeat with remaining 3 portions of veal and spring onions. Coat veal rolls evenly in remaining crushed cornflakes, arrange on a plate, cover and refrigerate for 30 minutes. Heat remaining 2 teaspoons margarine in the same pan, add chilled veal rolls and cook over medium heat until rolls are browned on all sides. Remove to warmed serving dish and keep hot. Sprinkle flour into pan drippings and stir quickly to combine. Gradually stir in water. Add stock cube and, stirring constantly, bring to the boil. Reduce heat and simmer until mixture thickens slightly. Pour gravy over veal rolls and serve immediately.

Each serving provides: 4 Protein Exchanges, 1 Bread Exchange, ½ Vegetable Exchange, 1½ Fat Exchanges, 20 Calories Optional Exchange

— Veal Stuffed — Cutlets

SERVES 4

550 CALORIES PER SERVING

8 teaspoons margarine

8oz (240g) onions, thinly sliced

1oz (30g) celery, chopped

4 garlic cloves, crushed, or 1 teaspoon garlic powder

6oz (180g) mushrooms, thinly sliced

pinch each salt and pepper

8oz (240g) cooked long grain rice

4 tablespoons chopped parsley

4 teaspoons grated Parmesan cheese

8 veal cutlets, each 3oz (90g), pounded to ¼ inch (5 mm) thick

8fl oz (240ml) dry sherry

4fl oz (120ml) chicken stock, prepared according to package directions

Heat 4 teaspoons margarine in large frying pan, add onions, celery and garlic and saute for 2 minutes. Do not brown. Add mushrooms, salt and pepper and continue cooking until most of liquid has evaporated, about 5 minutes. Transfer mixture to bowl, add rice, 2 tablespoons parsley and the cheese and stir to combine. Mound an equal amount of rice mixture on to each cutlet (about 3 heaped tablespoons) and roll veal to enclose filling, folding in edges. Secure each with a wooden cocktail stick. Heat remaining 4 teaspoons margarine in same pan, add veal cutlets and cook, turning occasionally, until browned on all sides. Remove cocktail sticks and transfer veal cutlets to a warmed serving dish. Keep hot. Cook wine and stock together in same pan over high heat, stirring occasionally and scraping particles from sides and bottom of pan, until sauce is slightly thickened. Pour over veal cutlets, garnish with remaining 2 tablespoons parsley and serve immediately.

Each serving provides: 4 Protein Exchanges, 1 Bread Exchange, 1½ Vegetable Exchanges, 2 Fat Exchanges, 75 Calories Optional Exchange

— Minced Veal — with Cabbage

SERVES 4

300 CALORIES PER SERVING

4 teaspoons margarine

6oz (180g) onions, chopped

2 garlic cloves, crushed

1lb 4oz (600g) minced veal

1 teaspoon paprika

½ teaspoon salt

¼ teaspoon pepper

6oz (180g) cabbage, shredded

12fl oz (360ml) water

8oz (240g) canned tomatoes, chopped

1 chicken stock cube, crumbled

2 teaspoons flour

2 tablespoons water

8oz (240g) cooked elbow macaroni

Heat margarine in large frying pan, add onions and garlic and saute until softened. Add veal, paprika, salt and pepper and saute until veal is lightly browned. Add cabbage, water and the tomatoes and stock cube and stir to combine. Cover and cook over moderate heat, stirring occasionally, for 30 minutes. Mix flour with the 2 tablespoons water and stir into veal mixture. Bring to the boil, stirring constantly and cook until thickened. Stir in macaroni and cook until hot.

Each serving provides: 4 Protein Exchanges, 1 Bread Exchange, 2 Vegetable Exchanges, 1 Fat Exchange, 10 Calories Optional Exchange

— Baked Veal-Stuffed — Aubergine

SERVES 4

315 CALORIES PER SERVING

2 medium aubergines, each about 1lb 4oz (600g)

4 teaspoons olive or vegetable oil

6oz (180g) onions, chopped

1 garlic clove, crushed

6oz (180g) mushrooms, sliced

10oz (300g) minced veal

8oz (240g) canned tomatoes, crushed

1 teaspoon basil leaves

½ teaspoon salt

pinch freshly ground pepper

4oz (120g) cooked elbow macaroni

4oz (120g) mozzarella cheese, grated

4 teaspoons grated Parmesan cheese

Cut each aubergine in half lengthwise. Blanch halves in boiling water for 1 to 2 minutes, then drain. Cool slightly. Scoop pulp from each half with a spoon, leaving shells about ¼ inch (5 mm) thick. Place shells cut-side down on paper towels and set aside. Chop pulp and reserve. Heat oil in large saucepan, add onion and garlic and saute over moderate heat just until onions soften, about 1 minute. Increase heat to high, add mushrooms and saute, stirring constantly, until all liquid evaporates, about 3 minutes. Add veal and stir quickly to break up large pieces. Cook, stirring constantly, until veal loses pink colour and begins to brown. Stir in tomatoes, seasonings and reserved aubergine pulp. Reduce heat to low and cook until mixture is slightly thickened, 5 to 8 minutes. Preheat oven to 375°F, 190°C, Gas Mark 5. Remove pan from heat and stir in macaroni. Fill each reserved aubergine shell with ¼ of the veal mixture, top each with 1oz (30g) mozzarella cheese, then sprinkle with

1 teaspoon Parmesan cheese. Bake until cheese is bubbly, 20 to 25 minutes.

Each serving provides: 3 Protein Exchanges, ½ Bread Exchange, 3½ Vegetable Exchanges, 1 Fat Exchange, 10 Calories Optional Exchange

•

— Sauteed Veal with — Sherry Sauce

SERVES 2

295 CALORIES PER SERVING

4 teaspoons margarine

10oz (300g) veal, thinly sliced

3oz (90g) mushrooms, sliced

1 garlic clove, crushed

3fl oz (90ml) dry sherry

4 tablespoons chicken stock, prepared according to package directions

1 teaspoon flour

¼ teaspoon salt

pinch freshly ground pepper

Heat margarine in non-stick frying pan, add veal and quickly saute on both sides. Remove veal from pan and set aside. Cook mushrooms and garlic quickly in same pan, stirring constantly, until liquid evaporates. Add wine and cook, stirring occasionally, for 3 to 4 minutes. Mix stock and flour, stirring well, add to pan and cook, stirring constantly, until sauce thickens. Add veal, any juices remaining from veal and salt and pepper and cook until hot. Serve immediately.

Each serving provides: 4 Protein Exchanges, ½ Vegetable Exchange, 2 Fat Exchanges, 55 Calories Optional Exchange

•

— Veal and Spinach — Pancakes

SERVES 4

410 CALORIES PER SERVING

4 teaspoons margarine

2 tablespoons chopped shallots or onions

4 garlic cloves, crushed

1lb 2oz (540g) minced veal

12oz (360g) cooked chopped spinach, well drained

3oz (90g) mushrooms, chopped

8oz (240g) canned tomatoes, pureed

½ teaspoon salt

¼ teaspoon each nutmeg and pepper

8 pancakes (½ Crepes Suzette recipe, page 37)

White Sauce (see page 82)

4 teaspoons grated Parmesan cheese

Heat margarine in large frying pan, add shallots or onion and garlic and saute until transparent, about 3 minutes. Add veal and cook, stirring constantly, until veal loses its pink colour, about 5 minutes. Stir in spinach and mushrooms and cook for 5 minutes longer. Add half the pureed tomatoes and the salt, nutmeg and pepper. Stir to combine and remove from heat. Preheat oven to 400°F, 200°C, Gas Mark 6. Spoon ⅛ of veal mixture onto centre of each pancake and fold sides to enclose. Place pancakes seam-side down in shallow casserole. Combine White Sauce with remaining pureed tomatoes and spoon over pancakes. Sprinkle with Parmesan cheese and bake until hot and bubbly, 20 to 25 minutes.

Each serving, including White Sauces and Crepes Suzettes, provides: 4 Protein Exchanges, 1 Bread Exchange, 2 Vegetable Exchanges, 3 Fat Exchanges, ¾ Milk Exchange, 35 Calories Optional Exchange

•

Top: Veal and Spinach Pancakes
Bottom: Baked Veal-Stuffed Aubergine

— Veal Balls in — Beer Sauce

SERVES 4

335 CALORIES PER SERVING

4 slices white bread, torn into small pieces

8fl oz (240ml) beer

4fl oz (120ml) water

2 teaspoons honey

2 tablespoons margarine

6oz (180g) onions, chopped

1 garlic clove, crushed

1lb 3oz (570g) minced veal

1 egg

1 tablespoon chopped parsley

½ teaspoon salt

pinch pepper

Mix bread pieces with 4 tablespoons beer, set aside and let soak. Mix remaining beer with the water and honey in another bowl and set aside. Heat 1 teaspoon margarine in a large non-stick frying pan, add onions and garlic and saute until onions are transparent. Add sauteed onions to soaked bread, add veal, egg, parsley, salt and pepper and mix until thoroughly combined. Shape into 16 balls, each about 2 inches (5 cm) in diameter. Heat remaining 5 teaspoons margarine in same pan, add meatballs, one at a time, and brown quickly on all sides. Be careful not to burn. Reduce heat if necessary. Add reserved honey mixture to pan and bring to the boil. Reduce heat to low and simmer 1 minute.

Each serving provides: 4 Protein Exchanges, 1 Bread Exchange, ½ Vegetable Exchange, 1½ Fat Exchanges, 30 Calories Optional Exchange

•

— Duchess Veal — Loaf

SERVES 2

445 CALORIES PER SERVING

Veal Mixture

2 teaspoons margarine

2 tablespoons each chopped celery, onion and green pepper

5oz (150g) minced veal

2½oz (75g) low-fat soft cheese

1 egg, beaten

3 tablespoons dried breadcrumbs

2 tablespoons chopped parsley

1 tablespoon water

1 teaspoon Worcestershire sauce

¼ teaspoon pepper

Topping

6oz (180g) peeled cooked potatoes, hot

2 tablespoons each grated Parmesan cheese and skimmed milk

1 tablespoon chopped chives

2 teaspoons margarine

pinch each salt and pepper

pimento strips (about 2 tablespoons) for garnish

To Prepare Veal Mixture: Heat margarine in small frying pan, add celery, onion and green pepper and saute until vegetables are tender, about 3 minutes. Mix sauteed vegetables with remaining ingredients for veal mixture and shape into a loaf. Transfer to roasting tin and bake at 375°F, 190°C, Gas Mark 5 until browned, 30 to 35 minutes.

To Prepare Topping: Combine all ingredients for topping and beat until smooth with electric mixer. Place baked loaf in an 8 x 8 x 2-inch (20 x 20 x 5-cm) baking tin and top with potato mixture, covering entire loaf. Bake at 425°F, 220°C, Gas Mark 7,

until topping is browned, about 15 minutes. Garnish with pimento strips.

Each serving provides: 3 Protein Exchanges, 1½ Bread Exchanges, ½ Vegetable Exchange, 2 Fat Exchanges, 35 Calories Optional Exchange

•

— Veal Steaks — Piccata

SERVES 2

275 CALORIES PER SERVING

¾oz (20g) flour

½ teaspoon salt

pinch pepper

2 boneless veal shoulder steaks, each 5oz (150g)

1 tablespoon margarine

3oz (90g) mushrooms, thinly sliced

1 garlic clove, crushed

4 tablespoons dry white wine

2 tablespoons each chopped parsley and lemon juice

1 small lemon, thinly sliced

Mix flour, salt and pepper and dredge steaks in seasoned flour, turning to coat all sides. Set aside remaining flour mixture. Heat margarine in large non-stick frying pan, add veal steaks and brown gently on both sides. Remove to warmed serving plate, set aside and keep hot. Saute mushrooms and garlic together in same pan, stirring constantly, until mushrooms are browned, about 1 minute. Sprinkle with remaining flour mixture and stir quickly to combine. Gradually stir in wine, add parsley and lemon juice and, stirring constantly, bring to the boil. Reduce heat and simmer until slightly thickened. Add lemon slices and stir to combine. To serve, pour sauce over veal steaks.

Each serving provides: 4 Protein Exchanges, ½ Bread Exchange, ½ Vegetable Exchange, 1½ Fat Exchanges, 30 Calories Optional Exchange

— Veal Stew —

SERVES 4

235 CALORIES PER SERVING

2 tablespoons flour

¼ teaspoon each salt and pepper

1lb 4oz (600g) boneless veal shoulder, cut into 1-inch (2.5-cm) cubes

4 teaspoons margarine

1½oz (45g) shallots or onions, chopped

8 teaspoons dry white wine

4oz (120g) mushrooms, cut in quarters

2oz (60g) celery, sliced

2oz (60g) carrot, sliced

1½ teaspoons chopped parsley

8fl oz (240ml) water

½ chicken stock cube, crumbled

1 bay leaf

Mix flour, salt and pepper. Dredge veal cubes in seasoned flour, coating all sides. Heat margarine in a saucepan, add veal cubes and saute until lightly browned on all sides. Add shallots or onion and any remaining flour mixture. Saute until transparent. Gradually stir in wine and bring to the boil, stirring constantly. Add mushrooms, celery, carrot and parsley and cook for 3 minutes. Stir in water, stock cube and bay leaf and bring mixture back to the boil. Reduce heat, cover and cook until veal is tender, 45 to 50 minutes. Remove bay leaf before serving.

Each serving provides: 4 Protein Exchanges, 1 Vegetable Exchange, 1 Fat Exchange, 25 Calories Optional Exchange

— Veal Stew with — Sherry

SERVES 6

255 CALORIES PER SERVING

1 tablespoon vegetable oil

1lb 14oz (900g) lean veal, cut into cubes

6oz (180g) onions, chopped

1 tablespoon chopped fresh garlic

2 tablespoons flour

6oz (180g) mushrooms, sliced

6oz (180g) carrots, thinly sliced

12fl oz (360ml) water

6fl oz (180ml) dry sherry

4oz (120g) fresh tomatoes, chopped, or canned tomatoes, crushed

1 chicken stock cube, crumbled

1 teaspoon salt

pinch pepper

3oz (90g) frozen peas

Heat oil in a large saucepan, add veal and brown on all sides. Add onions and garlic and saute briefly, about 3 minutes. Do not brown. Add flour and stir until well mixed, add all remaining ingredients except peas and bring to the boil, stirring occasionally. Reduce heat, cover and simmer until meat is tender, about 40 minutes. Add peas, cover and cook for 10 minutes longer. Serve immediately or cool and freeze for future use.

Each serving provides: 4 Protein Exchanges, 1½ Vegetable Exchanges, ½ Fat Exchange, 45 Calories Optional Exchange

— Sauteed Veal — Patties

SERVES 2

365 CALORIES PER SERVING

1 tablespoon margarine

3oz (90g) onion, chopped

1 garlic clove, crushed

9oz (270g) minced veal

6 tablespoons dried breadcrumbs

1 egg

1 tablespoon each chopped parsley and lemon juice

½ teaspoon salt

pinch each nutmeg and pepper

1 teaspoon flour

½ chicken stock cube, dissolved in 6fl oz (180ml) hot water

Heat 1 teaspoon margarine in small non-stick frying pan, add onion and garlic and saute until onion is transparent. Transfer to a bowl, add veal, 3 tablespoons breadcrumbs and the egg, parsley, lemon juice and seasonings. Mix well, shape into 2 patties and dredge in remaining 3 tablespoons breadcrumbs to coat. Heat remaining 2 teaspoons margarine in same pan, add patties and cook over moderate heat, turning once, until browned on both sides and done to taste. Do not overcook. Remove to serving dish, set aside and keep hot. Stir flour into remaining pan juices. Gradually stir in dissolved stock cube and cook, stirring constantly, until mixture comes to the boil. Reduce heat and simmer until thickened. Pour over patties and serve immediately.

Each serving provides: 4 Protein Exchanges, 1 Bread Exchange, ½ Vegetable Exchange, 1½ Fat Exchanges, 5 Calories Optional Exchange

— Veal Chilli —

SERVES 4

440 CALORIES PER SERVING

1lb 6oz (660g) canned tomatoes

4 teaspoons olive or vegetable oil

6oz (180g) onion, chopped

4oz (120g) green pepper, seeded and chopped

4 garlic cloves, crushed

12oz (360g) minced veal

1 teaspoon each chilli powder and crushed chillies, or to taste

½ teaspoon salt

¼ teaspoon pepper

1½oz (45g) uncooked cornmeal

6oz (180g) drained canned red kidney beans

3oz (90g) extra strong Cheddar cheese, grated

8oz (240g) cooked long grain rice, hot

Puree 2oz (60g) of the canned tomatoes and chop the remainder, reserving the liquid. Heat oil in large saucepan, add onions, green pepper and garlic and saute until onions are transparent. Add veal and cook, stirring constantly, until meat loses its pink colour, 3 to 5 minutes. Stir in tomatoes, reserved liquid, pureed tomatoes and seasonings and bring to the boil. Reduce heat, cover and simmer, stirring occasionally, for 20 minutes. Stir cornmeal into veal mixture, cover pan and simmer for 5 minutes longer. Add beans and cook until hot. To serve, transfer mixture to a shallow serving dish, sprinkle with cheese and arrange cooked rice round edge of veal mixture.

Each serving provides: 4 Protein Exchanges, 1 Bread Exchange, 2½ Vegetable Exchanges, 1 Fat Exchange

— Veal and Pepper— Saute

SERVES 4

305 CALORIES PER SERVING

2 teaspoons olive or vegetable oil

2 garlic cloves, sliced

8oz (240g) onions, thinly sliced

6oz (180g) each red and green peppers, seeded and cut into thin strips

3 tablespoons flour

½ teaspoon salt

pinch pepper

1lb 4oz (600g) veal cutlets, cut into 6 x 1-inch (15 x 2.5-cm) strips

4 teaspoons margarine

4fl oz (120ml) dry white wine

2 tablespoons chopped fresh basil or 1 tablespoon dried basil

¼ teaspoon oregano

Heat 1 teaspoon oil in a large non-stick frying pan, add garlic and saute until browned. Be careful not to burn. Using a slotted spoon, remove and discard garlic. Saute onions in the same pan, stirring occasionally until brown. Remove to bowl and set aside. Add peppers and saute until tender-crisp. Set aside with the onions. Mix flour, salt and pepper in large plastic bag, add veal and shake until pieces are lightly coated. Heat the margarine and remaining teaspoon oil in the pan, add veal, a few pieces at a time, and saute until browned on both sides. Return onions and peppers to pan, stirring to combine. Add wine and seasonings and bring to the boil. Reduce heat and simmer for 2 to 3 minutes to blend flavours. Serve immediately.

Each serving provides: 4 Protein Exchanges, 2 Vegetable Exchanges, 1½ Fat Exchange, 50 Calories Optional Exchange

— Veal-Stuffed — Cabbage in Wine Sauce

SERVES 2

260 CALORIES PER SERVING

1½oz (45g) shallots or onions, chopped

9oz (270g) minced veal

1 egg, lightly beaten with 1 tablespoon water

3 tablespoons dried breadcrumbs

¼ teaspoon salt

pinch each white pepper and nutmeg

4 medium cabbage leaves, blanched

4oz (120g) canned tomatoes, pureed

4 tablespoons chicken stock, prepared according to package directions

2 tablespoons dry red wine

pinch each garlic powder and onion powder

Cook shallots or onions in a small non-stick frying pan until softened. Transfer to a bowl and mix well with the veal, egg, breadcrumbs, salt, pepper and nutmeg. Remove about 1 inch (2.5 cm) from core end of each blanched cabbage leaf. Place ¼ of meat mixture in centre of each leaf and roll tightly, tucking in sides to enclose filling. Arrange filled leaves in the frying pan, seam-side down. Mix remaining ingredients, pour over cabbage rolls, bring to the boil and cook for 10 minutes. Reduce heat to low, cover and simmer until cabbage is tender, about 25 minutes.

Each serving provides: 4 Protein Exchanges, ½ Bread Exchange, 2 Vegetable Exchanges, 15 Calories Optional Exchange

—Hungarian—
Veal

SERVES 4

270 CALORIES PER SERVING

1lb (480g) lean veal, cut in cubes

1 tablespoon paprika

4 teaspoons oil

6oz (180g) onion, chopped

6oz (180g) tomatoes, peeled and cut into wedges

5 tablespoons tomato puree

4fl oz (120ml) water

12oz (360g) green pepper, seeded and chopped

1½ teaspoons salt

8oz (240g) hot cooked noodles

Coat veal with paprika. Heat oil in frying pan and brown veal on all sides. Add onion and brown lightly. Add tomatoes, tomato puree, water, green pepper and salt. Cover pan and simmer gently about 1 hour or until veal is tender. Serve with noodles.

Each serving provides: 3 Protein Exchanges, 2 Vegetable Exchanges, 1 Bread Exchange, 15 Calories Optional Exchange

— Veal in Aspic —

SERVES 2

280 CALORIES PER SERVING

1 tablespoon unflavoured gelatine

6fl oz (180ml) cold chicken stock, made with ½ stock cube

2oz (60g) onion, grated

2 tablespoons low-calorie mayonnaise

2 tablespoons lemon juice

1 teaspoon Worcestershire sauce

½ teaspoon dry mustard

¼ teaspoon salt or to taste

dash hot pepper sauce

6oz (180g) cooked veal, chopped

2 sticks celery, chopped

2 tablespoons chopped red pepper

lettuce leaves and strips red pepper for garnish

Sprinkle gelatine over cold stock in small saucepan. Place over low heat; stir constantly until gelatine dissolves, about 3 minutes. Remove from heat. Combine onion, mayonnaise, lemon juice, Worcestershire sauce, dry mustard, salt and hot pepper sauce; mix thoroughly with gelatine mixture. Chill, stirring occasionally until mixture thickens to the consistency of unbeaten egg whites. Mix cooked veal, celery and red pepper. Stir into thickened gelatine mixture. Pour into 1 pint (600ml) mould. Chill until set. Turn out on a bed of lettuce leaves. Crisscross red pepper strips across the top before serving.

Each serving provides: 3 Protein Exchanges, 1 Vegetable Exchange, 1½ Fat Exchanges

— Grilled Veal —
Chops

SERVES 2

200 CALORIES PER SERVING

2 veal loin chops, each 6oz (180g)

¼ teaspoon rosemary

pinch pepper

2 teaspoons margarine

1 teaspoon lemon juice

¼ teaspoon salt (optional)

Sprinkle one side of each veal chop with ¼ each of the rosemary and pepper and place in a shallow baking tin. Dot each chop with ½ teaspoon margarine and sprinkle each with ¼ teaspoon lemon juice. Grill 6 inches (15 cm) from heat for 5 minutes. Turn chops over and sprinkle with remaining rosemary, pepper and lemon juice. Dot each with ½ teaspoon margarine and grill until lightly browned, 4 to 5 minutes. If desired, sprinkle with salt. Serve topped with any accumulated pan juices.

Each serving provides: 4 Protein Exchanges, 1 Fat Exchange

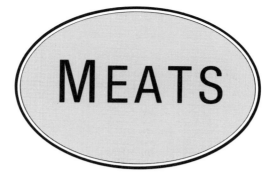

MEATS

*F*rom a succulent roast to cheap and cheerful mince, meat is still the top family favourite. You can whip up 'short order' grills and sauteed meals in a trice, and you can make economical dishes such as Beef Curry. Make a friend of your butcher and ask his advice about cuts which have the least waste and give best value for money. Look for good freezer buys, too, and try to keep a stock of cooked dishes in your freezer, ready prepared to thaw and heat.

— Pork Chow Mein —

SERVES 4

305 CALORIES PER SERVING

4 teaspoons peanut or vegetable oil

8oz (240g) onions, sliced

2 garlic cloves, crushed

4oz (120g) celery, sliced

3oz (90g) red or green pepper, seeded and sliced

3oz (90g) mushrooms, sliced

4oz (120g) bean sprouts

12oz (360g) cooked pork, cut into thin strips

2 teaspoons soy sauce

½ chicken stock cube, crumbled

6fl oz (180ml) water

1 teaspoon cornflour

2 tablespoons chopped spring onion

8oz (240g) cooked long grain rice, hot

Heat oil in a frying pan, add onions and garlic and saute briefly. Do not brown. Add celery and pepper strips and saute until tender-crisp, about 3 minutes. Add mushrooms and bean sprouts and saute, stirring occasionally, for 3 minutes. Add pork, soy sauce and stock cube and stir to combine. Mix water and cornflour, stirring well. Add to pan and cook, stirring constantly, until mixture is thickened. Sprinkle with spring onion and serve over rice.

Each serving provides: 3 Protein Exchanges, 1 Bread Exchange, 2 Vegetable Exchanges, 1 Fat Exchange, 5 Calories Optional Exchange

•

— Lamb Chops with — Wine and Vegetable Sauce

SERVES 2

340 CALORIES PER SERVING

1 tablespoon olive or vegetable oil

2oz (60g) onion, sliced

2 garlic cloves, crushed

4oz (120g) drained canned artichoke hearts

2 medium tomatoes, blanched, peeled, seeded and chopped

6fl oz (180ml) chicken stock, prepared according to package directions

2 teaspoons tomato puree

½ teaspoon rosemary

4 tablespoons dry sherry

½ teaspoon salt

pinch freshly ground pepper

12oz (360g) lamb loin chops

1 tablespoon chopped parsley for garnish

Heat oil in a frying pan, add onion and garlic and saute until onion slices are transparent. Add artichoke hearts, cover and cook over moderate heat for 5 minutes. Stir in tomatoes, stock, tomato puree and rosemary. Cover and simmer, stirring occasionally, for about 10 minutes. Add sherry, salt and pepper and cook uncovered, over moderate heat, until mixture thickens slightly. While vegetable sauce is cooking, grill chops on rack for 6 to 9 minutes on each side or until done to taste. Transfer to warmed serving dish, top with vegetable sauce and sprinkle with parsley.

Each serving provides: 4 Protein Exchanges, 2 Vegetable Exchanges, 1½ Fat Exchanges, 35 Calories Optional Exchange

•

— Pork Salad —

SERVES 1

215 CALORIES PER SERVING

4oz (120g) boned cooked pork, cut into 1-inch (2.5-cm) strips

2oz (60g) celery, chopped

2oz (60g) red pepper, seeded and chopped

1 tablespoon chopped spring onion

2 tablespoons wine vinegar

1 teaspoon mayonnaise

½ teaspoon French mustard

1 small garlic clove, crushed

¼ teaspoon salt

pinch pepper

2 lettuce leaves

Mix pork, celery, red pepper and spring onion. Combine vinegar, mayonnaise, mustard, garlic, salt and pepper, mixing well. Pour over salad and toss to coat. Serve on lettuce leaves.

Each serving provides: 4 Protein Exchanges, 1½ Vegetable Exchanges, 1 Fat Exchange

•

— Oriental Beef —
with Vegetables

SERVES 2

325 CALORIES PER SERVING

1 slice (10oz/300g) beef top rump

2 tablespoons each soy sauce and dry sherry

¼ teaspoon hot pepper sauce

1 teaspoon chopped peeled ginger root

1 garlic clove, crushed

2 teaspoons peanut or vegetable oil

4oz (120g) carrots, shredded or coarsely grated

3oz (90g) cabbage, shredded

4oz (120g) onions, thinly sliced

To make slicing easier, chill steak in freezer until slightly firm for 10 to 15 minutes. Remove to cutting board and slice diagonally across the grain into ¼-inch (5-mm) thick strips. Mix soy sauce, sherry, hot pepper sauce, ginger and garlic in a bowl, add beef and toss to coat. Let stand at room temperature for 1 hour. Heat oil in a non-stick frying pan, add vegetables and saute, stirring until carrots are soft. Remove from heat. Preheat grill. Remove meat from marinade, reserving marinade. Thread ⅛ of the steak strips on to each of eight 8-inch (20-cm) kebab skewers, set on rack in grill pan and grill until done to taste. While steak is grilling, add reserved marinade to sauteed vegetables and cook until mixture is hot. Transfer vegetables to serving dish and top with skewers of steak.

Each serving provides: 4 Protein Exchanges, 2 Vegetable Exchanges, 1 Fat Exchange, 15 Calories Optional Exchange

— Marinated —
Sweet and Sour Lamb

SERVES 2

245 CALORIES PER SERVING

4fl oz (120ml) lemon juice

2 teaspoons chilli sauce

1 teaspoon grated orange peel

1 teaspoon Worcestershire sauce

1 teaspoon grated lemon peel

½ teaspoon each sugar and honey

1 garlic clove, crushed

10oz (300g) fillet of lamb, cut in 1-inch (2.5-cm) cubes

Mix all ingredients except lamb in a bowl. Add lamb and toss to coat well. Cover and refrigerate for at least 1 hour, turning lamb occasionally. Transfer meat to rack in grill pan, reserving marinade. Grill for 6 minutes. Turn cubes over, brush with marinade and grill 6 minutes longer or until done to taste.

Each serving provides: 4 Protein Exchanges, 15 Calories Optional Exchange

— Apricot-Glazed —
Lamb Steaks

SERVES 2

350 CALORIES PER SERVING

4 teaspoons apricot jam

1 teaspoon each French mustard, honey and soy sauce

½ garlic clove, mashed to a paste

12oz (360g) lamb leg steaks

Mix all ingredients except lamb leg steaks. Place steaks on rack 2 to 5 inches (5 to 13 cm) from heat, depending on thickness of steaks. (Thinner steaks should be closer to heat). Grill 1 to 2 minutes, brush steaks with half the apricot mixture and grill for 5 to 7 minutes longer. Turn steaks over and grill for 1 to 2 minutes. Brush with remaining apricot mixture and grill for 5 to 7 minutes longer or until done to taste.

Each serving provides: 4 Protein Exchanges, 40 Calories Optional Exchange

— Roast Pork and —
Peaches with Peach Sauce

SERVES 6

350 CALORIES PER 4OZ (120G) SERVING
(LEAN MEAT WITHOUT CRACKLING)

2lb 4oz (1kg 80g) loin of pork

pinch salt

2 garlic cloves, crushed

3 medium peaches, blanched, peeled, halved and stoned

6fl oz (180ml) dry sherry

4 tablespoons peach jam

1 tablespoon soy sauce

sprigs of watercress to garnish

Put loin of pork on rack in roasting tin and sprinkle with salt. Insert meat thermometer into centre of roast, being careful thermometer does not touch bone. Roast at 325°F, 170°C, Gas Mark 3, until thermometer registers 170°F, 75°C, about 1½ hours. Remove tin from oven. Poach peaches in sherry for 2 to 3 minutes, lift out and keep warm. Add jam and soy sauce to sherry and bring to the boil. Reduce heat and simmer until sauce is thickened, about 3 minutes. Arrange peach halves round joint, fill hollow with watercress sprigs. Serve with peach sauce.

Each serving provides: 4 Protein Exchanges, ½ Fat Exchange, ½ Fruit Exchange, 55 Calories Optional Exchange

Roast Pork and Peaches with Peach Sauce

— Baked Pork Chops — with Stuffing

SERVES 2

290 CALORIES PER SERVING

2 pork loin chops, each 6oz (180g)

¼ teaspoon each salt, pepper and thyme

4fl oz (120ml) chicken stock, prepared according to package directions

1 teaspoon margarine

2 tablespoons chopped onion

1 garlic clove, crushed

3oz (90g) mushrooms, chopped

2 tablespoons chopped celery

1 slice bread, thinly toasted and cut into ¼-inch (5-mm) cubes

Grill pork chops on rack, turning once, until rare. Preheat oven to 325°F, 170°C, Gas Mark 3. Arrange chops in casserole large enough to hold them in one layer and sprinkle with pinch each salt, pepper and thyme. Add stock, cover casserole and bake for about 45 minutes. While pork chops are baking, heat margarine in small frying pan, add onion and garlic and saute until onion is transparent. Add mushrooms, celery and remaining pinch each salt, pepper and thyme. Saute for 5 minutes. Stir in bread cubes. Spoon an equal amount of stuffing mixture onto each baked pork chop and bake, uncovered, for 15 minutes longer.

Each serving provides: 4 Protein Exchanges, ½ Bread Exchange, 1 Vegetable Exchange, ½ Fat Exchange

•

— Bean and — Frankfurter Casserole

SERVES 2

450 CALORIES PER SERVING

2 teaspoons vegetable oil

3oz (90g) onion, chopped

2oz (60g) green pepper, seeded and chopped

1 garlic clove, crushed

4oz (120g) canned tomatoes, chopped

2 teaspoons each Worcestershire sauce and red wine vinegar

1 teaspoon brown sugar

½ teaspoon paprika

¼ teaspoon dry mustard

6oz (180g) frankfurters, cut diagonally into 1-inch (2.5-cm) pieces

6oz (180g) drained canned haricot beans

2 tablespoons grated Parmesan cheese

Heat oil in a saucepan, add onion, green pepper and garlic and saute until vegetables are lightly browned. Stir in tomatoes, Worcestershire sauce, vinegar, sugar, paprika and mustard and bring to the boil. Reduce heat, cover and simmer, stirring occasionally, for 15 minutes. Preheat oven to 450°F, 230°C, Gas Mark 8. Add frankfurters and beans to saucepan and stir to combine. Transfer to a casserole. Sprinkle with cheese and bake until cheese is melted, about 15 minutes.

Each serving provides: 4 Protein Exchanges, 1½ Vegetable Exchanges, 1 Fat Exchange, 40 Calories Optional Exchange

•

— Boiled Fresh — Tongue

66 CALORIES PER 1 OZ

1 fresh ox tongue, about 2lb 8oz (1 kilo 200g), washed and drained

4 pints (2 ltr 250ml) water

2 medium tomatoes, cut into quarters

2 large carrots, trimmed and scraped

1 large onion, cut into quarters

2 celery sticks

3 garlic cloves, crushed

2 parsley sprigs

1½ teaspoons salt

½ teaspoon thyme

6 peppercorns

3 cloves

2 bay leaves

Place tongue in large saucepan, add remaining ingredients and bring to the boil. Reduce heat, cover and simmer until tongue is fork-tender, 2½ to 3 hours. Allow meat to cool in the pot liquor. Remove tongue from pan and drain. On underside of tongue, slit skin lengthwise from root to tip and peel off skin. Cut off root end, any small bones and gristle. Starting at large end, cut thin slices diagonally across the grain. Serve hot or cold.

1oz (30g) cooked tongue provides: 1 Protein Exchange

•

— Fresh Tongue with — Horseradish Sauce

SERVES 2

390 CALORIES PER SERVING

5fl oz (150ml) low-fat natural yogurt

1 tablespoon each chopped parsley and horseradish sauce

2 teaspoons French mustard

1 teaspoon chopped shallots or onion

¼ teaspoon sugar

8oz (240g) sliced cooked fresh ox tongue, cold

Mix together all ingredients except the tongue. Arrange tongue on serving dish and serve with sauce.

Each serving provides: 4 Protein Exchanges, ½ Milk Exchange, 5 Calories Optional Exchange

•

— Tongue and — Aubergine Salad

SERVES 4

325 CALORIES PER SERVING

1 teaspoon margarine

1 medium aubergine, about 1lb (480g) sliced into ½-inch (1-cm) rounds

12oz (360g) cooked tongue, cut into thin strips

2 medium tomatoes, blanched, peeled, seeded and chopped

3oz (90g) red pepper, seeded and thinly sliced

1oz (30g) spring onion, chopped

2 tablespoons each red wine vinegar and lemon juice

4 teaspoons olive oil

1 garlic clove, crushed

¼ teaspoon pepper

pinch salt

1 tablespoon chopped parsley

Grease a baking sheet with the margarine. Arrange aubergine slices on sheet and bake at 350°F, 180°C, Gas Mark 4, turning once, until soft, about 30 minutes. Cut aubergine into ½-inch (1-cm) cubes. Mix aubergine with the tongue, tomatoes, red pepper and spring onion and arrange in a salad bowl. Mix all remaining ingredients except parsley. Pour dressing over salad and toss to combine. Cover and chill lightly in refrigerator. Just before serving, toss again and sprinkle with parsley.

Each serving provides: 3 Protein Exchanges, 2½ Vegetable Exchanges, 1 Fat Exchange, 15 Calories Optional Exchange

•

— Ham Salad — Open Sandwich

SERVES 2

285 CALORIES PER SERVING

5oz (150g) ham, minced

1 egg, hard-boiled and mashed

1 tablespoon each chopped celery, chopped onion and low-fat natural yogurt

2 teaspoons each pickle and mayonnaise

½ teaspoon French mustard

2 slices rye bread, toasted

2 lettuce leaves

1 medium tomato, sliced

Combine ham, egg, chopped vegetables, yogurt, pickle, mayonnaise and mustard, mixing well. Cover and chill lightly in refrigerator. Top each slice of toast with a lettuce leaf, stir salad again, then spoon half the salad on to each lettuce leaf. Serve with tomato slices.

Each serving provides: 3 Protein Exchanges, 1 Bread Exchange, 1 Vegetable Exchange, 1 Fat Exchange, 15 Calories Optional Exchange

•

— Beef Curry —

SERVES 2

310 CALORIES PER SERVING

10oz (300g) boneless chuck steak, cut into 1-inch (2.5-cm) cubes

2 teaspoons vegetable oil

6oz (180g) onions, chopped

1 garlic clove, crushed

1 to 1½ teaspoons curry powder

6fl oz (180ml) water

2oz (60g) canned tomatoes, pureed

½ beef stock cube, crumbled

3oz (90g) frozen peas

pinch salt

Grill beef cubes on rack, turning to brown all sides, until rare, about 6 minutes. Set aside. Heat oil in a saucepan, add onions and garlic and saute until onions are transparent. Stir in beef and curry powder, then water, pureed tomatoes and stock cube. Cover and simmer, stirring occasionally, for about 1 hour. Add peas and salt and cook for 5 minutes longer.

Each serving provides: 4 Protein Exchanges, 2 Vegetable Exchanges, 1 Fat Exchange

•

— Cheese-Topped — Burgers

SERVES 2

425 CALORIES PER SERVING

½ teaspoon vegetable oil

1½oz (45g) onion, chopped

10oz (300g) chuck steak, minced

1 tablespoon each chopped parsley and low-fat natural yogurt

¼ teaspoon Worcestershire sauce

pinch each salt, pepper and thyme

1oz (30g) Cheddar cheese, sliced

2 baps, each 2oz (60g)

2 lettuce leaves

½ medium tomato, sliced

1½oz (45g) pickled cucumber, sliced

Heat oil in small non-stick frying pan, add onion and saute until golden. Transfer to a bowl, add minced beef, parsley, yogurt, Worcestershire sauce and seasonings and mix well. Shape into 2 equal patties and place on rack in grill pan. Grill, turning once, for 7 to 10 minutes on each side or until done to taste. Top each patty with ½oz (15g) cheese and grill just until cheese is melted. To serve, line bottom half of each bap with a lettuce leaf, half the tomato and pickle slices, a cheese-topped patty and top half of bap.

Each serving provides: 4½ Protein Exchanges, 2 Bread Exchanges, 1 Vegetable Exchange, 15 Calories Optional Exchange

— Lamb Primavera —

SERVES 2

395 CALORIES PER SERVING

2 x 6oz (180g) lamb leg steaks

2 teaspoons olive or vegetable oil

2oz (60g) onion, sliced

2 garlic cloves, crushed

3oz (90g) mushrooms, quartered

2 medium tomatoes, blanched, peeled, seeded and chopped

6fl oz (180ml) water

2 teaspoons tomato puree

½ chicken stock cube, crumbled

½ teaspoon rosemary

3oz (90g) peas

3oz (90g) cooked asparagus, chopped

4 tablespoons rose wine

Grill lamb on rack, turning once, until done, 6 to 8 minutes on each side depending on thickness of steaks. While meat is grilling, heat oil in non-stick frying pan, add onion and garlic and saute until onion is transparent. Add mushrooms and cook, stirring occasionally, until mushrooms are just tender, about 3 minutes. Add tomatoes, water, tomato puree, stock cube and rosemary and cook over moderate heat, stirring occasionally, until mixture thickens, about 5 minutes. Stir in peas, asparagus and wine and continue cooking until hot, about 3 minutes. Transfer lamb steaks to serving dish and surround with vegetable mixture.

Each serving provides: 4 Protein Exchanges, 3 Vegetable Exchanges, 1 Fat Exchange, 35 Calories Optional Exchange

— Chilli Beef Salad —

SERVES 2

390 CALORIES PER SERVING

4oz (120g) cooked minced beef, crumbled and chilled

3oz (90g) drained canned red kidney beans

2 very ripe medium tomatoes, chopped

3 tablespoons lemon juice

2 tablespoons chopped onion

2 teaspoons olive oil

pinch each salt, chilli powder and ground cumin

1 to 2 drops hot sauce

4 lettuce leaves

1oz (30g) Cheddar cheese, grated

2 slices bread, toasted and cut into quarters

Mix all ingredients except lettuce, cheese and toast, cover and refrigerate lightly until ready to serve. Line each of 2 bowls with 2 lettuce leaves. Spoon an equal amount of beef mixture over each portion of lettuce, then sprinkle each with ½oz (15g) cheese. Surround each portion with half the toast quarters.

Each serving provides: 3 Protein Exchanges, 1 Vegetable Exchange, 1 Fat Exchange, 1 Bread Exchange

— Glazed Meat —
Loaf Ring

SERVES 4

335 CALORIES PER SERVING

5 fl oz (150ml) buttermilk

1 egg

4 slices wholemeal bread, cut into cubes

1 teaspoon vegetable oil

3oz (90g) onion, chopped

2oz (60g) celery, chopped

2oz (60g) red pepper, seeded and chopped

2oz (60g) carrot, shredded or coarsely grated

1 garlic clove, crushed

1lb 3oz (570g) chuck steak, minced

½ teaspoon salt

pinch each pepper, oregano, basil and thyme

3 tablespoons chilli sauce

2 teaspoons brown sugar

½ teaspoon dry mustard

1 teaspoon vegetable oil

Mix buttermilk and egg, add bread cubes and toss to coat. Set aside. Heat oil in non-stick frying pan, add vegetables and garlic and saute, stirring constantly, until vegetables are tender. Add sauteed vegetables to bread mixture, then add meat, salt, pepper and herbs and mix well. Mix chilli sauce, sugar and mustard and set aside. Preheat oven to 350°F, 180°C, Gas Mark 4. Cover roasting rack with foil and grease with vegetable oil, pierce foil at intervals to allow juices from loaf to drop through while cooking. Set meat mixture on rack and shape into ring. Place rack in roasting tin and bake until loaf is browned, 35 to 40 minutes. Brush chilli sauce mixture over meat and bake for 15 minutes longer.

Each serving provides: 4 Protein Exchanges, 1 Vegetable Exchange, ½ Fat Exchange, 1 Bread Exchange, 30 Calories Optional Exchange

— Baked Ham with —
Pineapple Rings

SERVES 8

200 CALORIES PER SERVING

2lb (960g) joint ham

20 whole cloves

4 canned pineapple slices, no sugar added

4 fl oz (120ml) low-calorie ginger ale

cinnamon

Preheat oven to 325°F, 170°C, Gas Mark 3. Using a sharp knife, score top of ham in a diamond pattern (cut long diagonal slashes, about 1½ inches (4 cm) apart, then cut across these slashes in the other direction). Stud the intersection of each 'diamond' with a clove. Transfer ham to a casserole and arrange pineapple slices on top of meat. Pour ginger ale over ham and sprinkle each pineapple slice with pinch cinnamon. Bake until hot, 20 to 30 minutes. Serve 4oz (120g) sliced ham and ½ pineapple slice per portion.

Each serving provides: 4 Protein Exchanges, 10 Calories Optional Exchange

— Sweet and Sour —
Pineapple Pork

SERVES 2

325 CALORIES PER SERVING

2 teaspoons peanut oil

2oz (60g) green pepper, seeded and cut into strips

1oz (30g) each carrot and spring onion, thinly sliced

2 garlic cloves, crushed

8oz (240g) boned, cooked pork, cut into 1-inch (2.5-cm) cubes

4 fl oz (120ml) chicken stock, prepared according to package directions

2 teaspoons each red wine vinegar and soy sauce

1 teaspoon brown sugar

1 tablespoon water

2 teaspoons cornflour

4oz (120g) canned pineapple chunks, no sugar added

Heat oil in frying pan, add pepper, carrot, spring onion and garlic and saute until vegetables are tender-crisp, about 5 minutes. Stir in pork cubes, chicken stock, vinegar, soy sauce and sugar and bring to the boil. Reduce heat and simmer for 5 minutes. Mix water and cornflour, stirring well, add to pan with the pineapple and cook, stirring constantly, until mixture is slightly thickened.

Each serving provides: 4 Protein Exchanges, 1 Vegetable Exchange, 1 Fat Exchange, ½ Fruit Exchange, 20 Calories Optional Exchange

— Braised Pork Chops —

SERVES 4

285 CALORIES PER SERVING

4 pork loin chops, each 6oz (180g)

4 teaspoons margarine

6oz (180g) each onions and mushrooms, chopped

½ teaspoon salt

¼ teaspoon pepper

12fl oz (360ml) water

4 teaspoons chopped parsley

Grill chops on rack, turning once, for about 3 minutes each side. Heat margarine in a large frying pan, add onions and saute until softened. Add pork chops, mushrooms, salt and pepper and cook for 5 minutes. Add water, cover and simmer until meat is tender, about 45 minutes. Serve sprinkled with parsley.

Each serving provides: 4 Protein Exchanges, 1 Vegetable Exchange, 1 Fat Exchange

— Spicy Pork and — Bean Casserole

SERVES 4

295 CALORIES PER SERVING

15oz (450g) fillet of pork, cut into 1–inch (2.5-cm) cubes

2 teaspoons vegetable oil

3oz (90g) onion, chopped

2 garlic cloves, crushed

1 medium green pepper, seeded and cut into 1-inch (2.5-cm) squares

4 teaspoons chilli powder

½ teaspoon ground cumin

8oz (240g) canned tomatoes, pureed

8fl oz (240ml) water

¼ teaspoon salt

pinch cayenne pepper

6oz (180g) drained canned white kidney beans

2oz (60g) strong Cheddar cheese, coarsely grated

Grill pork cubes on a rack until rare and set aside. Heat oil in saucepan, add onion and garlic and saute until onion is transparent. Stir in pork cubes, green pepper, chilli powder and cumin. Add pureed tomatoes, water, salt and cayenne pepper and stir to combine. Cover and simmer, stirring occasionally, until pork is fork-tender, about 45 minutes. Add beans and simmer, uncovered, for 10 minutes longer. Transfer pork mixture to flameproof casserole, sprinkle with cheese and grill until cheese is bubbly, about 3 minutes.

Each serving provides: 4 Protein Exchanges, 1½ Vegetable Exchanges, ½ Fat Exchange

— Oriental Steak — and Pepper

SERVES 2

335 CALORIES PER SERVING

10oz (300g) sirloin steak

2 teaspoons peanut or vegetable oil

1 medium green pepper, seeded and thinly sliced

3oz (90g) onion, sliced

1 garlic clove, crushed

6fl oz (180ml) water

½ beef stock cube, crumbled

1 tablespoon soy sauce

2 teaspoons cornflour

1 medium tomato, cut into eighths

pinch pepper

Place steak on a rack and grill 2 to 4 inches (5 to 10 cm) from heat until rare, about 3 minutes on each side. Grill thicker steak farther away from heat. Cut steak across the grain into thin slices and set aside. Heat oil in a frying pan, add green pepper, onion and garlic and saute until onion is transparent and pepper is tender-crisp. Add steak slices and saute for 1 minute. Add water and stock cube and bring liquid to the boil. Mix soy sauce and cornflour and stir into steak mixture. Add tomatoes and cook, stirring constantly, until tomatoes are just cooked and mixture is slightly thickened. Sprinkle with pepper and serve immediately.

Each serving provides: 4 Protein Exchanges, 2 Vegetable Exchanges, 1 Fat Exchange, 10 Calories Optional Exchange

— Oriental Pork — Saute

SERVES 2

290 CALORIES PER SERVING

2 teaspoons peanut or vegetable oil

1½oz (45g) onion, chopped

1 garlic clove, crushed

8oz (240g) boned cooked pork, cut into 2 x 1-inch (5 x 2.5-cm) strips

6oz (180g) Chinese leaves, shredded

2oz (60g) drained canned bamboo shoots, sliced

4fl oz (120ml) chicken stock, prepared according to package directions

2 teaspoons soy sauce

pinch each pepper and ginger

½ teaspoon cornflour, mixed with 1 tablespoon water

Heat oil in a large frying pan, add onion and garlic and saute until onion is transparent. Add pork strips, Chinese leaves and bamboo shoots and saute for 2 minutes. Stir in chicken stock, soy sauce, pepper and ginger and bring to the boil. Cook, stirring constantly, until mixture is slightly thickened.

Each serving provides: 4 Protein Exchanges, 1½ Vegetable Exchanges, 1 Fat Exchange, 5 Calories Optional Exchange

— Baked Pork Chops — in Wine Sauce

SERVES 2

290 CALORIES PER SERVING

1 teaspoon vegetable oil

1oz (30g) onion, sliced

1oz (30g) celery, chopped

1 garlic clove, crushed

2 pork loin chops, each 6oz (180g), grilled until rare

3oz (90g) mushrooms, sliced

4 tablespoons dry white wine

¼ teaspoon each basil and salt

pinch pepper

8fl oz (240ml) water

1 medium tomato, blanched, peeled, seeded and chopped

½ chicken stock cube, crumbled

1 teaspoon cornflour, mixed with 2 tablespoons water

2 teaspoons chopped parsley

Preheat oven to 325°F, 170°C, Gas Mark 3. Heat oil in a non-stick frying pan with ovenproof or removable handle. Add onion, celery and garlic and saute until transparent. Add pork chops, mushrooms, wine, basil, salt and pepper and bring the liquid to the boil. Cook for 2 minutes. Stir in water and the tomato and stock cube and bring back to the boil. Remove pan from heat, cover and transfer to oven. Bake for 45 to 50 minutes. Return pan to the cooker and stir in blended cornflour, bring to the boil, stirring constantly, and cook until mixture is thickened. Serve sprinkled with parsley.

Each serving provides: 4 Protein Exchanges, 1½ Vegetable Exchanges, ½ Fat Exchange, 35 Calories Optional Exchange

— Beef Stir-Fry —

SERVES 2

360 CALORIES PER SERVING

2 teaspoons peanut or vegetable oil

4oz (120g) onions, thinly sliced

3oz (90g) mushrooms, thinly sliced

2oz (60g) carrot, diagonally sliced

4fl oz (120ml) beef stock, prepared according to package directions

2 tablespoons dry sherry

2 tablespoons soy sauce

1 teaspoon cornflour

¼ teaspoon five spice powder

8oz (240g) grilled rump steak, thinly sliced diagonally across the grain

4oz (120g) torn well-washed spinach leaves

4oz (120g) long grain rice, hot

Heat oil in a wok or frying pan, add onions, mushrooms and carrot and cook, stirring quickly and frequently, until carrot is tender. Mix stock, sherry, soy sauce, cornflour and spice, stirring well, pour over vegetables and, stirring constantly, bring to the boil. Reduce heat and stir in beef and spinach. Simmer, stirring occasionally, for 10 minutes. Serve over hot rice.

Each serving provides: 4 Protein Exchanges, 1 Bread Exchange, 2 Vegetable Exchanges, 1 Fat Exchange, 20 Calories Optional Exchange

— Creamed Apple — and Pork Saute

SERVES 2

370 CALORIES PER SERVING

2 teaspoons margarine

1½oz (45g) onion, chopped

1 medium apple, cored, peeled and cut into ¼-inch (5-mm) thick slices

1 teaspoon brown sugar

2 teaspoons flour

2½fl oz (75ml) apple juice

4 tablespoons dry sherry

8oz (240g) boned cooked pork, cut into strips

¼ teaspoon salt

pinch white pepper

2½fl oz (75ml) low-fat natural yogurt

Heat margarine in frying pan, add onion and saute until transparent. Add apple slices and brown sugar and stir to combine. Stir in flour. Cook, stirring constantly, for 2 minutes. Gradually stir in apple juice. Add sherry and bring to the boil. Add pork, salt and pepper and cook over moderate heat, stirring constantly, for 10 minutes. Stir in yogurt and heat through. Do not boil.

Each serving provides: 4 Protein Exchanges, ¼ Vegetable Exchange, 1 Fat Exchange, 1 Fruit Exchange, ¼ Milk Exchange, 50 Calories Optional Exchange

— Savoury Pork — Balls

SERVES 2

345 CALORIES PER SERVING

3oz (90g) onion, chopped

2 small garlic cloves, crushed

10oz (300g) minced pork

1 slice white bread, cut into cubes

2 tablespoons low-fat natural yogurt

1 tablespoon chopped parsley

¼ teaspoon each salt and rosemary

pinch pepper

1 teaspoon vegetable oil

8oz (240g) canned tomatoes, crushed

1 teaspoon Worcestershire sauce

Mix half the onion and garlic in a small non-stick frying pan and cook, stirring constantly, until onion is soft but not brown. Transfer to a bowl and add pork, bread cubes, yogurt, parsley, salt, rosemary and pepper. Mix well together and form into 8 balls, each about 2½ inches (6 cm) in diameter. Arrange pork balls on a rack and grill, turning once, until browned. Heat oil in a frying pan, add remaining onion and garlic and saute until onion is soft. Add pork balls and toss with onion. Stir in crushed tomatoes and Worcestershire sauce. Cover and simmer for 30 minutes, turning pork balls once.

Each serving provides: 4 Protein Exchanges, ½ Bread Exchange, 2 Vegetable Exchanges, ½ Fat Exchange, 10 Calories Optional Exchange

— Chilli-Cheese Pie —

SERVES 4

345 CALORIES PER SERVING

4 teaspoons margarine

6oz (180g) onions, chopped

3oz (90g) red pepper, seeded and chopped

1 garlic clove, crushed

8oz (240g) cooked minced beef, crumbled

2 canned mild green chillies, chopped

4 teaspoons tomato puree

1 teaspoon chilli powder

salt

pinch freshly ground pepper

2oz (60g) Cheddar cheese, grated

3oz (90g) flour

5fl oz (150ml) buttermilk

2 large eggs

¼ teaspoon baking powder

Preheat oven to 425°F, 220°C, Gas Mark 7. Heat 1 teaspoon margarine in non-stick frying pan, add onions, red pepper and garlic and saute until pepper is tender, about 3 minutes. Add beef, chillies, tomato puree, chilli powder, ½ teaspoon salt and the ground pepper. Cook, stirring occasionally, for about 5 minutes to blend flavours. Transfer mixture to a 9-inch (23-cm) pie plate and sprinkle with cheese. Place remaining tablespoon margarine in blender container with the flour, milk, eggs, baking powder and pinch salt. Blend until smooth. Pour batter over beef mixture and bake until crust is golden brown, about 30 minutes.

Each serving provides: 3 Protein Exchanges, 1 Bread Exchange, 1 Vegetable Exchange, 1 Fat Exchange, 15 Calories Optional Exchange

— Spicy Pork — and Vegetables

SERVES 2

340 CALORIES PER SERVING

1 tablespoon peanut or vegetable oil

2 garlic cloves, sliced

4oz (120g) onion, sliced

3oz (90g) mushroom caps

8oz (240g) boned cooked pork, cut into 3 x 1-inch (7.5 x 2-cm) strips

2-3 drained canned mild green chillies, seeded and thinly sliced

2 tablespoons each lime juice and soy sauce

1 tablespoon dark brown sugar

Heat oil in large non-stick frying pan, add garlic and saute until browned. Be careful not to burn. Remove and discard garlic. Add onions and mushroom caps to pan and saute until lightly browned. Add pork and chillies and stir to combine. Cook for 10 minutes. Mix remaining ingredients, pour over pork mixture, stir to combine, and bring to the boil. Reduce heat and simmer until mixture is hot, about 3 minutes.

Each serving provides: 4 Protein Exchanges, 1½ Vegetable Exchanges, 1½ Fat Exchanges, 30 Calories Optional Exchange

— Creamy Pork and — Apple Stew

SERVES 2

415 CALORIES PER SERVING

2 teaspoons margarine

1oz (30g) onion, sliced

1 garlic clove, crushed

6fl oz (180ml) water

½ chicken stock cube, crumbled

8oz (240g) cooked pork, cubed

¼ teaspoon each salt and sage

1 medium apple, cored, peeled and cut into ½-inch (1-cm) thick slices

1oz (30g) sultanas

2 teaspoons cornflour

2½fl oz (75ml) low-fat natural yogurt

4oz (120g) cooked long grain rice, hot

Heat margarine in a saucepan, add onion and garlic and saute, stirring constantly, until onion is transparent, about 3 minutes. Stir in water and stock cube and bring to the boil. Add pork and seasonings. Cover and cook for about 10 minutes. Stir in apple slices and sultanas and cook until apple slices are tender, about 10 minutes. Add cornflour to yogurt and mix well. Stir into pork mixture and simmer gently for 2 to 3 minutes. Serve over cooked rice.

Each serving provides: 4 Protein Exchanges, 1 Bread Exchange, ¼ Vegetable Exchange, 1 Fat Exchange, 1 Fruit Exchange, ¼ Milk Exchange, 10 Calories Optional Exchange

— Spaghetti with — Italian Meat Sauce

SERVES 4

460 CALORIES PER SERVING

4 teaspoons olive or vegetable oil

6oz (180g) onions, chopped

4oz (120g) red or green pepper, seeded and chopped

2 garlic cloves, crushed

2lb (960g) canned tomatoes, pureed

1lb (480g) grilled minced beef, crumbled

4 tablespoons dry red wine

2 tablespoons each chopped parsley and tomato puree

1 bay leaf

¼ teaspoon each oregano, fennel seeds, salt and pepper

1lb (480g) cooked spaghetti, hot

8 teaspoons grated Parmesan cheese

Heat oil in large non-stick frying pan or saucepan, add onions, pepper and garlic and saute until onion is transparent. Add all remaining ingredients except spaghetti and cheese and stir to combine. Reduce heat and simmer, stirring occasionally, until sauce is thick, 1½ to 2 hours. Remove and discard bay leaf before serving. For each serving, top 4oz (120g) hot spaghetti with ¼ of the sauce and sprinkle with 2 teaspoons cheese.

Each serving provides: 4 Protein Exchanges, 2 Bread Exchanges, 3½ Vegetable Exchanges, 1 Fat Exchange, 40 Calories Optional Exchange

— Steak Provencale —

SERVES 4

275 CALORIES PER SERVING

4 rump steaks, each 5oz (150g)

4 teaspoons margarine

2oz (60g) spring onions, thinly sliced

1 garlic clove, crushed

2 tablespoons dry vermouth

2 medium tomatoes, cut into ¼-inch (5-mm) slices

1 tablespoon chopped fresh basil

Preheat grill. Grill steaks on rack until browned on both sides, about 5 minutes on each side, or until done to taste. While steaks are grilling, heat margarine in non-stick frying pan, add spring onions and garlic and saute until spring onions are softened, 1 to 2 minutes. Add vermouth and cook, stirring constantly, for 1 minute. Add tomato slices and basil and cook, stirring gently, until hot. To serve, spoon tomato mixture over grilled steaks.

Each serving provides: 4 Protein Exchanges, 1 Vegetable Exchange, 1 Fat Exchange, 15 Calories Optional Exchange

— Mexican Cornmeal — Casserole

SERVES 4

355 CALORIES PER SERVING

1 tablespoon vegetable oil

12oz (360g) freshly cooked cornmeal, hot (follow package directions)

6oz (180g) onions, chopped

3 garlic cloves, crushed

8oz (240g) cooked minced beef, crumbled

8oz (240g) canned tomatoes, pureed

2 tablespoons chopped drained canned mild green chillies

1 packet low-calorie chicken soup powder

1 teaspoon each chilli powder and oregano

4oz (120g) Cheddar cheese, grated

10fl oz (300ml) low-fat natural yogurt

Grease a baking sheet with 1 teaspoon vegetable oil, pour cornmeal onto sheet and spread in an even layer, about ½ inch (1 cm) thick. Allow to cool, cut into 2½-inch (6-cm) squares and set aside. Preheat oven to 400°F, 200°C, Gas Mark 6. Heat oil in non-stick frying pan, add onions and garlic and saute until onions are transparent, about 2 minutes. Add all remaining ingredients except cornmeal, cheese and yogurt and cook, stirring constantly, for about 5 minutes to blend flavours. Arrange a layer of half the cornmeal squares in a casserole, top with meat mixture, then 2oz (60g) cheese, then yogurt, then remaining cornmeal squares. Sprinkle remaining 2oz (60g) cheese over cornmeal and bake until cheese is completely melted, about 20 minutes. Remove from oven and let stand for 10 minutes before serving.

Each serving provides: 3 Protein Exchanges, 1½ Bread Exchanges, 1½ Vegetable Exchanges, ½ Fat Exchange, ½ Milk Exchange, 25 Calories Optional Exchange

— Beef-Barley Soup —

SERVES 4

240 CALORIES PER SERVING

2 beef stock cubes

1¼ pints (750ml) hot water

12oz (360g) cooked beef, cut into cubes

8oz (240g) cooked barley

3oz (90g) mushrooms, sliced

6oz (180g) onion, chopped

3oz (90g) cabbage, shredded

2oz (60g) celery, chopped

2½oz (75g) carrot, chopped

4oz (120g) canned tomatoes, pureed

1 bay leaf

1 teaspoon salt

½ teaspoon thyme

pinch pepper

chopped parsley for garnish

Mix stock cubes and hot water in a saucepan, add all remaining ingredients except parsley, partially cover pan and simmer until vegetables are tender, about 30 minutes. Remove and discard bay leaf. Serve soup sprinkled with parsley.

Each serving provides: 3 Protein Exchanges, 1 Bread Exchange, 2 Vegetable Exchanges

— Ginger Beef and — Vegetables

SERVES 2

330 CALORIES PER SERVING

2 teaspoons peanut or vegetable oil

4oz (120g) onions, thinly sliced

3oz (90g) red peppers, seeded and thinly sliced

2 garlic cloves, crushed

½ teaspoon chopped peeled ginger root

6fl oz (180ml) water

1 tablespoon soy sauce

1 teaspoon cornflour

2 beef stock cubes, crumbled

4oz (120g) broccoli florets, blanched

10oz (300g) sirloin steak

Heat oil in frying pan, add onions, red peppers, garlic and ginger and saute over moderate heat until vegetables are tender-crisp, about 4 minutes. Mix water, soy sauce and cornflour, stirring well. Add to vegetable mixture with the stock cubes and, stirring constantly, bring to the boil. Continue stirring and cook until thickened. Add broccoli and stir to combine. Reduce heat to lowest setting, just hot enough to keep mixture warm while beef is cooking. Grill steak on rack, allowing 4 to 5 minutes on each side, depending on thickness of meat. Remove from rack and slice across the grain into thin strips. Transfer vegetable mixture to serving dish and top with steak.

Each serving provides: 4 Protein Exchanges, 2 Vegetable Exchanges, 1 Fat Exchange, 5 Calories Optional Exchange

— Lamb Chops — Oriental

SERVES 2

325 CALORIES PER SERVING

4 lamb loin chops, each 3oz (90g)

1 tablespoon vegetable oil

2oz (60g) onion, thinly sliced

2oz (60g) celery, chopped

2oz (60g) green pepper, seeded and cut into thin strips

1 small garlic clove, crushed

pinch ginger

1 tablespoon soy sauce

2 teaspoons dry sherry

2 teaspoons cornflour mixed with 2 teaspoons water

1 medium tomato, blanched, peeled and cut into 8 wedges

2oz (60g) drained canned or fresh bean sprouts

pinch each salt and pepper

Grill chops on rack, turning once, until rare, at least 3 minutes on each side. Remove from grill and keep hot. Heat oil in non-stick frying pan, add onion, celery, green pepper, garlic and ginger and saute, stirring constantly, until onion is transparent and vegetables are tender-crisp. Reduce heat and add soy sauce and sherry. Stir in cornflour and cook, stirring constantly, until mixture thickens. Add lamb chops, tomato wedges and bean sprouts and cook, stirring occasionally, until thoroughly hot, about 3 minutes. Season with salt and pepper and serve immediately.

Each serving provides: 4 Protein Exchanges, 2 Vegetable Exchanges, 1½ Fat Exchanges, 15 Calories Optional Exchange

— Lamb Burgers — a la Grecque

SERVES 2

315 CALORIES PER SERVING

2 teaspoons olive oil

3oz (90g) onion, chopped

1 garlic clove, crushed

8oz (240g) canned tomatoes

8oz (240g) canned artichoke hearts

4 tablespoons water

½ teaspoon salt

¼ teaspoon each pepper and oregano

10oz (300g) minced lamb

4 black olives, stoned and cut into quarters

Heat oil in a frying pan, add onion and garlic and saute until onion is transparent. Add tomatoes, artichoke hearts, water, ¼ teaspoon salt, pinch pepper and the oregano. Cover and simmer, stirring occasionally, for about 15 minutes. While sauce is simmering, mix lamb with remaining ¼ teaspoon salt and pinch pepper. Shape into 4 equal patties. Grill on rack, turning once, for about 7 minutes. Add lamb burgers and olives to frying pan, cover and simmer for 5 minutes.

Each serving provides: 4 Protein Exchanges, 3 Vegetable Exchanges, 1 Fat Exchange, 10 Calories Optional Exchange

— Hearty Beef — Stew

SERVES 4

410 CALORIES PER SERVING

1lb 4oz (600g) stewing steak, cut into 1½-inch (4-cm) cubes

3 tablespoons flour

4 teaspoons vegetable oil

8oz (240g) celery, sliced

6oz (180g) onions, chopped

2 garlic cloves, crushed

1¼ pints (750ml) water

8fl oz (240ml) beef stock, prepared according to package directions

1 tablespoon each chopped parsley, Worcestershire sauce and French mustard

2 bay leaves, broken into halves

1 teaspoon salt

½ teaspoon pepper

8oz (240g) carrots, sliced or cut into thin strips

12oz (360g) peeled potatoes, cut into cubes

3oz (90g) frozen peas

Preheat grill and grill meat on rack, turning once, for about 6 minutes. Transfer meat to a bowl, add 2 tablespoons flour and toss to combine. Heat oil in a large saucepan or flameproof casserole. Add meat a few pieces at a time and cook, stirring constantly, until seared on all sides. Remove meat to a bowl and set aside. Cook celery, onions and garlic in same pan and stir constantly until onions are transparent. Return meat to pan and stir to combine. Sprinkle remaining tablespoon flour over mixture and stir quickly to combine. Gradually stir in water. Add beef stock, bay leaf and seasonings and, stirring constantly, bring to the boil. Reduce heat, cover and simmer until meat is tender, 45 to 60 minutes. Add carrots and potatoes to meat mixture, cover and simmer for 30 minutes. Stir in peas and cook until hot, about 5 minutes. Remove and discard bay leaves before serving.

Each serving provides: 4 Protein Exchanges, 1 Bread Exchange, 2 Vegetable Exchanges, 1 Fat Exchange, 25 Calories Optional Exchange

•

— Beef and — Vegetable Saute

SERVES 4

310 CALORIES PER SERVING

1lb 4oz (600g) chuck steak, minced

4 teaspoons vegetable oil

6oz (180g) onion, chopped

2 garlic cloves, crushed

6oz (180g) green pepper, seeded and thinly sliced

4oz (120g) carrots, thinly sliced

1 pint (600ml) water

6oz (180g) Chinese leaves, shredded

8 teaspoons soy sauce

4 teaspoons cornflour

Shape minced steak into 4 patties, place on rack in grill pan and grill, turning once, until browned on both sides, 4 to 5 minutes. Heat oil in large non-stick frying pan, add onions and garlic and saute until onions are transparent. Crumble patties into pan, add green pepper and carrot and saute for 5 minutes. Stir in ¾ pint (450ml) water, cover pan and simmer for 5 minutes. Add cabbage, cover and simmer for 10 minutes longer, stirring occasionally. Mix remaining ¼ pint (150ml) water with the soy sauce and cornflour, stirring well, add to minced steak mixture and cook, stirring constantly, until slightly thickened.

Each serving provides: 4 Protein Exchanges, 2 Vegetable Exchanges, 1 Fat Exchange, 10 Calories Optional Exchange

•

— Spicy Minced Beef — with Rice

SERVES 2

350 CALORIES PER SERVING

10oz (300g) minced beef

1 teaspoon margarine

3oz (90g) onion, chopped

1 garlic clove, crushed

1½oz (45g) mushrooms, sliced

8oz (240g) canned tomatoes, pureed

1 tablespoon chopped parsley

½ teaspoon French mustard

¼ teaspoon each oregano and Worcestershire sauce

pinch salt

dash hot pepper sauce

4oz (120g) cooked long grain rice, hot

Form beef into patties and place on rack in grill pan. Grill, turning once, for about 5 minutes. Cool slightly, then crumble. Heat margarine in a frying pan, add onion and garlic and saute until onion is softened. Stir in crumbled meat and mushrooms and saute for 5 minutes. Stir in pureed tomatoes, 1½ teaspoons parsley and the mustard, oregano, Worcestershire sauce, salt and hot sauce. Cover pan and simmer for 10 to 15 minutes. Serve over hot rice and sprinkle with remaining 1½ teaspoons parsley.

Each serving provides: 4 Protein Exchanges, 1 Bread Exchange, 2 Vegetable Exchanges, ½ Fat Exchange

•

— Marinated — Lamb Kebabs

SERVES 2

255 CALORIES PER SERVING

4fl oz (120ml) lemon juice

1 tablespoon water

2 teaspoons tomato ketchup

1 teaspoon honey

1 garlic clove, chopped

½ teaspoon each onion flakes, grated lemon peel and oregano

¼ teaspoon mint flakes

pinch salt

10oz (300g) fillet of lamb, cut into 1-inch (2.5-cm) cubes

6oz (180g) aubergine, cubed and blanched (1-inch/2.5-cm cubes)

1 medium green pepper, seeded and cut into 1-inch (2.5-cm) squares

Place lemon juice, water, ketchup, honey and seasonings in blender and puree until smooth. Transfer to shallow dish. Add lamb and aubergine and toss to coat. Cover dish and refrigerate for at least 1 hour, turning meat and aubergine occasionally. Preheat grill. Thread ¼ of the lamb, aubergine cubes and pepper squares on to each of 4 kebab skewers, alternating ingredients. Reserve marinade. Transfer skewers to rack in grill pan and grill, turning skewers often and basting with reserved marinade, until vegetables are tender and meat is done, about 8 minutes.

Each serving provides: 4 Protein Exchanges, 2 Vegetable Exchanges, 15 Calories Optional Exchange

— Beef in Creamy — Mushroom Sauce

SERVES 2

415 CALORIES PER SERVING

10oz (300g) rump steak, cut into 1-inch (2.5-cm) slices

1 tablespoon margarine

2 tablespoons chopped onion

½ garlic clove, crushed

3oz (90g) mushrooms, thinly sliced

1 tablespoon flour

6fl oz (180ml) beef stock, prepared according to package directions

2 teaspoons tomato puree

5fl oz (150ml) low-fat natural yogurt

pinch freshly ground pepper

1 tablespoon chopped parsley

4oz (120g) cooked noodles or long grain rice, hot

Grill rump steak on rack, turning once, until rare. While meat is grilling, heat margarine in a frying pan, add onion and garlic and saute until onion is transparent, about 2 minutes. Add mushrooms and cook, stirring occasionally, for 3 minutes. Sprinkle flour over vegetables, stir quickly to combine and gradually stir in stock. Add tomato puree and cook, stirring constantly, until mixture is slightly thickened. Remove pan from heat and stir in yogurt, pepper and parsley. Add meat and cook just until heated through. Do not boil. Serve over hot noodles or rice.

Each serving provides: 4 Protein Exchanges, 1 Bread Exchange, 1 Vegetable Exchange, 1½ Fat Exchanges, ½ Milk Exchange, 20 Calories Optional Exchange

— Courgette and — Ham Frittata (Italian Omelette)

SERVES 4

210 CALORIES PER SERVING

4 eggs

4 tablespoons water

pinch each pepper and garlic powder

4 teaspoons margarine

3oz (90g) onion, chopped

6oz (180g) courgettes, thinly sliced

2oz (60g) ham, chopped

2oz (60g) mozzarella cheese, grated

Mix eggs, water and seasoning and set aside. Heat margarine in a non-stick frying pan with metal or removable handle, add onion and saute until transparent. Add courgettes and saute until fork-tender, 5 to 7 minutes. Add meat and cook over moderate heat, stirring occasionally, for about 2 minutes. Pour egg mixture over courgettes, stirring quickly to combine before eggs begin to set. Sprinkle with cheese and cook until bottom of frittata begins to set. Transfer pan to grill and grill until frittata is puffed and lightly browned. Slide onto warm plate and serve immediately.

Each serving provides: 2 Protein Exchanges, 1 Vegetable Exchange, 1 Fat Exchange

Courgette and Ham Frittata (Italian Omelette)

— Beef with — Vegetable-Yogurt Sauce

SERVES 4

300 CALORIES PER SERVING

2 teaspoons olive or vegetable oil

6oz (180g) onions, chopped

3oz (90g) mushroom caps, sliced

2 teaspoons flour

12fl oz (360ml) water

1 beef stock cube, crumbled

1 tablespoon grated Parmesan cheese

1 teaspoon Worcestershire sauce

½ teaspoon paprika

pinch pepper

4 slices topside beef, each 5oz (150g), grilled for 3 minutes each side

5fl oz (150ml) low-fat natural yogurt

1 tablespoon chopped parsley

Preheat oven to 350°F, 180°C, Gas Mark 4. Heat oil in non-stick frying pan, add onions and mushrooms and saute, stirring, until onions are transparent. Sprinkle flour over vegetables and cook, stirring constantly, for 1 minute. Gradually stir in water. Add stock cube and, stirring constantly, bring to the boil. Reduce heat and simmer until mixture thickens. Stir in cheese, Worcestershire sauce, paprika and pepper and remove from heat. Transfer beef slices to a casserole and pour vegetable sauce over meat. Cover and bake until beef slices are tender, about 45 minutes. Remove beef slices from casserole and set aside. Spoon 2 tablespoons of vegetable sauce into yogurt and stir to combine. Pour yogurt mixture into casserole and stir until well blended. Return beef slices to casserole and serve sprinkled with parsley.

Each serving provides: 4 Protein Exchanges, 1 Vegetable Exchange, ½ Fat Exchange, ¼ Milk Exchange, 15 Calories Optional Exchange

— Grilled Steak with — Onion, Pepper and Mushroom Sauce

SERVES 4

295 CALORIES PER SERVING

1lb 4oz (600g) rump steak

4 teaspoons vegetable oil

2 garlic cloves, sliced

1-inch (2.5-cm) piece ginger root, peeled and sliced

8oz (240g) green pepper, seeded and cut into strips

4oz (120g) onions, sliced

3oz (90g) mushrooms, sliced

8fl oz (240ml) beef stock, prepared according to package directions

2 tablespoons dry sherry

1 tablespoon soy sauce

2 teaspoons cornflour

Preheat grill. Place steak on rack and grill, turning once, until rare, about 5 minutes on each side. Slice steak diagonally across the grain and cut each strip in half lengthwise. Keep warm. Heat oil in large non-stick frying pan, add garlic and ginger and saute until garlic is browned. Be careful not to burn. Remove and discard garlic and ginger. Add vegetables to pan and saute, stirring constantly, until tender-crisp. Mix stock, sherry, soy sauce and cornflour, stirring well. Add to vegetables and, stirring constantly, bring to the boil. Cook for 1 minute. Serve over steak slices.

Each serving provides: 4 Protein Exchanges, 1½ Vegetable Exchanges, 1 Fat Exchange, 15 Calories Optional Exchange

— Beef Steaks in — Tomato Sauce

SERVES 4

270 CALORIES PER SERVING

12oz (360g) canned tomatoes

2 teaspoons olive or vegetable oil

3oz (90g) onions, chopped

2oz (60g) celery, chopped

2 teaspoons flour

6fl oz (180ml) water

1 beef stock cube, crumbled

4oz (120g) green pepper, seeded and cut into strips

4 slices topside beef, each 5oz (150g), grilled for 3 minutes on each side

2 tablespoons chopped parsley

Preheat oven to 350°F, 180°C, Gas Mark 4. Puree 4oz (120g) of the canned tomatoes and chop the remainder. Heat oil in non-stick frying pan, add onion and celery and saute until onion is transparent. Sprinkle flour over vegetables and cook, stirring constantly, for 1 minute. Gradually stir in water. Stir in tomatoes, pureed tomatoes and stock cube and, stirring constantly, bring to the boil. Remove from heat and stir in pepper strips. Arrange steaks in a casserole and top with vegetable mixture. Cover and bake until steaks are tender, about 45 minutes. Serve sprinkled with parsley.

Each serving provides: 4 Protein Exchanges, 2 Vegetable Exchanges, ½ Fat Exchange, 5 Calories Optional Exchange

— Shepherd's Pie —

SERVES 4

430 CALORIES PER SERVING

1lb 4oz (600g) minced lamb

1 teaspoon vegetable oil

2 tablespoons margarine

8oz (240g) carrots, thinly sliced

6oz (180g) mushrooms, thinly sliced

6oz (180g) onions, chopped

1 packet low-calorie beef soup powder

2 teaspoons flour

12fl oz (360ml) skimmed milk

12oz (360g) potatoes, peeled, cooked and mashed, hot

½ teaspoon paprika

Preheat grill. Form lamb into 4 patties and place on rack in grill pan. Grill, turning once, until meat is rare, about 5 minutes. Remove and set aside. Grease a flameproof casserole with the vegetable oil. Heat margarine in a large non-stick frying pan, add carrots, mushrooms and onions and saute, stirring, until onion is transparent. Sprinkle low-calorie soup powder and flour over vegetables and stir quickly to combine. Cook, stirring constantly, for 1 minute. Gradually stir in 8fl oz (240ml) skimmed milk and, stirring constantly, bring to the boil. Reduce heat and simmer until mixture thickens. Crumble lamb into vegetable mixture and stir to combine. Transfer to casserole and set aside. Preheat oven to 375°F, 190°C, Gas Mark 5. Heat remaining 4fl oz (120ml) skimmed milk and beat into hot mashed potatoes. Spread over meat mixture, sprinkle with paprika and bake for 15 to 20 minutes or until completely heated through. Place under hot grill until potatoes are browned, 1 to 2 minutes.

Each serving provides: 4 Protein Exchanges, 1 Bread Exchange, 2 Vegetable Exchanges, 1½ Fat Exchanges, ¼ Milk Exchange, 35 Calories Optional Exchange

— Ham and Beans —

SERVES 2

225 CALORIES PER SERVING

2 teaspoons vegetable oil

1½oz (45g) onion, chopped

1 garlic clove, crushed

6oz (180g) ham, cut into thin strips

4oz (120g) canned tomatoes, pureed

4 tablespoons water

¼ teaspoon Worcestershire sauce

pinch each salt, pepper and thyme

4oz (120g) drained cooked broad beans

Heat oil in a frying pan, add onion and garlic and saute until onion is softened. Add ham and saute for about 3 minutes. Stir in pureed tomatoes, water and seasonings and simmer, stirring occasionally, for 15 minutes. Add beans and simmer until beans are hot, about 5 minutes.

Each serving provides: 3 Protein Exchanges, 1½ Vegetable Exchanges, 1 Fat Exchange

— Ham Sandwich — with Spicy Russian Dressing

SERVES 4

365 CALORIES PER SERVING

Dressing

8 teaspoons each mayonnaise and tomato ketchup

4 teaspoons spicy brown mustard

Sandwich

12oz (360g) ham, sliced

8 slices wholemeal bread, toasted

2 medium tomatoes, thinly sliced

8 lettuce leaves

To Prepare Dressing: Mix mayonnaise, ketchup and mustard.
To Prepare Sandwiches: Brown ham in large non-stick frying pan, 1 to 2 minutes. Divide onto 4 slices of toast. Top each portion with ¼ of the tomato slices, 2 lettuce leaves and 1 of the remaining toast slices. Cut each sandwich into quarters and serve each portion with ¼ of the dressing.

Each serving provides: 3 Protein Exchanges, 2 Bread Exchanges, 1 Vegetable Exchange, 2 Fat Exchanges, 10 Calories Optional Exchange

— Glazed Ham Steak —

SERVES 4

240 CALORIES PER SERVING

2 tablespoons each pineapple jam and dry sherry

1 teaspoon each dark brown sugar and French mustard

1lb (480g) cooked ham steak

12 whole cloves

Mix jam, sherry, sugar and mustard in a small saucepan and cook over low heat until sugar is melted and mixture is hot. Preheat grill. Score one side of ham steak in a crisscross pattern and stud with cloves. Transfer to a shallow flameproof casserole just large enough to hold ham flat. Pour glaze over surface and grill until glaze is bubbly and browned, about 3 minutes.

Each serving provides: 4 Protein Exchanges, 40 Calories Optional Exchange

— Ham and — Artichoke Bake

SERVES 2

485 CALORIES PER SERVING

½ pint (300ml) skimmed milk

3 eggs

3oz (90g) Emmenthal cheese, grated

1 tablespoon margarine

3oz (90g) onion, chopped

2oz (60g) ham, diced

8oz (240g) drained canned artichoke hearts, chopped

pinch pepper

Beat together milk and eggs, stir in cheese and set aside. Grease a casserole with 1 teaspoon margarine. Preheat oven to 375°F, 190°C, Gas Mark 5. Heat remaining 2 teaspoons margarine in a small frying pan, add onion and saute briefly. Do not brown. Add ham and continue sauteing until onion is soft. Add artichokes and cook until hot, stirring occasionally. Sprinkle with pepper and add to milk mixture, stirring to combine. Transfer to casserole and bake until eggs are set, 35 to 40 minutes.

Each serving provides: 4 Protein Exchanges, 2 Vegetable Exchanges, 1½ Fat Exchanges, ½ Milk Exchange

•

— Frankfurters — with Beans

SERVES 4

390 CALORIES PER SERVING

4 teaspoons margarine

12oz (360g) frankfurters, cut into 1-inch (2.5-cm) pieces

6oz (180g) onion, chopped

4oz (120g) green pepper, seeded and chopped

12oz (360g) drained canned red kidney beans

8 teaspoons tomato ketchup

2 teaspoons brown sugar

½ teaspoon garlic powder

Heat margarine in large frying pan, add frankfurters and chopped vegetables and saute until meat is browned. Reduce heat to low and add remaining ingredients. Cook, stirring occasionally, for 10 minutes.

Each serving provides: 4 Protein Exchanges, 1 Vegetable Exchange, 1 Fat Exchange, 20 Calories Optional Exchange

•

— Frankfurters — with Vegetables

SERVES 2

315 CALORIES PER SERVING

2 teaspoons vegetable oil

2oz (60g) each onion and carrot, sliced

2oz (60g) green pepper, seeded and thinly sliced

1 small garlic clove, crushed, or pinch garlic powder

3oz (90g) cabbage, shredded

6oz (180g) frankfurters, cut crosswise into thin slices

4 tablespoons chicken stock, prepared according to package directions

1 teaspoon each soy sauce and cornflour

Heat oil in frying pan, add onion, carrot, green pepper and garlic or garlic powder and saute until onion is transparent, about 5 minutes. Stir in cabbage. Reduce heat, cover and cook, stirring occasionally, until cabbage is soft, about 10 minutes. Add frankfurters and cook, uncovered, until hot . Mix stock, soy sauce and cornflour, stirring well. Pour over frankfurter mixture and cook, stirring constantly, until slightly thickened.

Each serving provides: 3 Protein Exchanges, 1½ Vegetable Exchanges, 1 Fat Exchange, 5 Calories Optional Exchange

•

— Kidney and Ham — Saute

SERVES 4

275 CALORIES PER SERVING

1lb 2oz (540g) trimmed kidneys (tubes and fat removed), cut into halves lengthwise, soaked in water for 1 hour and drained

2 teaspoons vegetable oil

6oz (180g) onions, chopped

1 garlic clove, crushed

2oz (60g) ham, diced

1 tablespoon flour

4fl oz (120ml) dry red wine

4fl oz (120ml) beef stock, prepared according to package directions

2 tablespoons chopped parsley

pinch each salt and pepper

8oz (240g) cooked long grain rice, hot

Chop drained kidneys and set aside. Heat oil in a non-stick frying pan, add onions and garlic and saute until onions are transparent. Stir in ham and saute until onions and ham are browned. Transfer mixture to a bowl and set aside. Saute kidneys in same pan until browned, return onion mixture to pan and stir to combine. Sprinkle mixture with flour and stir quickly to combine. Cook, stirring constantly, for 1 minute. Gradually stir in wine, add stock and, stirring constantly, bring to the boil. Reduce heat, cover pan and simmer until kidneys are tender, 30 to 35 minutes. Stir in parsley, salt and pepper and serve on hot rice.

Each serving provides: 4 Protein Exchanges, 1 Bread Exchange, ½ Vegetable Exchange, ½ Fat Exchange, 35 Calories Optional Exchange

and bake until kidneys are tender, about 45 minutes. To serve, place 2 toast triangles on each of 2 plates and spoon half the kidney mixture over each portion of toast. Sprinkle with parsley.

Each serving provides: 4 Protein Exchanges, 1 Bread Exchange, 1 Vegetable Exchange, 1 Fat Exchange, 40 Calories Optional Exchange

vegetables from pan. Puree in batches in blender, being careful not to overfill the container. Combine with mixture remaining in pan and, if necessary, reheat. Slice roast and pour sauce over meat. Serve each portion with 2oz (60g) cooked spaghetti.

Each serving provides: 4 Protein Exchanges, 1 Bread Exchange, 2½ Vegetable Exchanges, ½ Fat Exchange, 20 Calories Optional Exchange

---

— Sauteed Lamb — Kidneys in Sherry-Mushroom Sauce

SERVES 2

295 CALORIES PER SERVING

2 teaspoons margarine

3oz (90g) onion, finely chopped

2oz (60g) mushrooms, sliced

10oz (300g) trimmed lamb kidneys (tubes and fat removed), cut into quarters, soaked in water for 1 hour and drained

2 teaspoons flour

pinch pepper

1 packet low-calorie beef and vegetable soup powder, dissolved in 3fl oz (90ml) hot water

4 teaspoons dry sherry

2 slices white bread, toasted and cut diagonally into halves

2 teaspoons chopped parsley

Heat 1 teaspoon margarine in a frying pan, add onion and saute until transparent. Add mushrooms and saute until lightly browned. Transfer to a casserole. Preheat oven to 350°F, 180°C, Gas Mark 4. Sprinkle drained kidneys with flour and pepper and toss to coat. Heat remaining teaspoon margarine in same pan, add kidneys and saute until lightly browned. Arrange sauteed kidneys over mushroom mixture in casserole, add dissolved soup powder and sherry and stir to combine. Cover casserole

---

— Pot Roast — Italienne

SERVES 10

345 CALORIES PER SERVING

3lb 2oz (1kg 500g) top side beef

5 teaspoons vegetable oil

12oz (360g) onions, chopped

10oz (300g) red or green peppers, seeded and chopped

2 garlic cloves

8oz (240g) tomatoes, pureed

8fl oz (240ml) dry red wine

2 tablespoons each chopped basil and parsley

1 teaspoon salt

½ teaspoon each oregano and pepper

1lb 4oz (600g) carrots, chopped

1lb 4oz (600g) cooked spaghetti, hot

Preheat oven to 325°F, 160°C, Gas Mark 3. Place meat on rack in roasting tin and roast until rare, about 1 hour. Heat oil in large saucepan or flameproof casserole, add roast meat, onions, peppers and garlic and sear meat on all sides, stirring vegetables to prevent burning. Add all remaining ingredients except carrots and spaghetti and stir to combine. Reduce heat to low, cover pan and simmer for 1 hour, turning meat occasionally. Add carrots, cover and cook until tender, about 30 minutes. Remove meat from pan and keep hot. Remove half the liquid and half the

---

— Grilled — Marinated Chuck Steak

SERVES 4

220 CALORIES PER SERVING

8fl oz (240ml) beer

4oz (120g) onions, sliced

1 tablespoon grated lemon peel

1 garlic clove, sliced

½ teaspoon each salt and pepper

1lb 4oz (600g) chuck steak, cut about 2 inches (5 cm) thick

1 medium tomato, thinly sliced

1 tablespoon chopped parsley

Mix beer, onions, lemon peel and seasonings in a bowl and add steak, turning to coat with marinade. Cover bowl and refrigerate for at least 8 hours, turning meat several times in marinade. Preheat grill. Transfer steak to rack in grill pan, discarding marinade. Grill 3 inches (8 cm) from heat until steak is browned on both sides, 5 to 7 minutes on each side, or until done to taste. Arrange tomato slices over surface of steak and grill until tomatoes are lightly browned. Serve sprinkled with parsley.

Each serving provides: 4 Protein Exchanges, ½ Vegetable Exchange, 20 Calories Optional Exchange

LIVER

If you have only ever tried grilled liver or liver and onions, you'll find lots of new ideas in this section, from Chicken Liver Pate to Calf Liver with Vegetables Julienne. Try to buy liver the day you intend to use it, but if that's not possible, refrigerate it and use within forty-eight hours. As well as the time-honoured combination of liver with bacon and onions, it goes well with rice, mushrooms, celery and peppers, and you will even find recipes teaming liver with fruits such as pineapple and raisins.

— Grilled Oriental —
Liver Rolls

SERVES 4

125 CALORIES PER SERVING

4oz (120g) ham

5oz (150g) chicken livers, cut into chunks

1½oz (45g) drained canned water chestnuts

4 tablespoons soy sauce

2 teaspoons vegetable oil

½ teaspoon brown sugar

1-inch (2.5-cm) piece ginger root, peeled and sliced

Cut each ham slice into 3 strips. There should be the same number of ham strips as liver chunks and water chestnuts (if necessary, cut water chestnuts into halves). Place 1 liver chunk and 1 water chestnut on each strip of ham, roll up and secure each with a cocktail stick. Place in shallow bowl. Mix soy sauce, 1 teaspoon oil, sugar and ginger root, pour over rolls and toss gently to coat. Cover and refrigerate for about 1 hour, tossing occasionally. Preheat grill. Grease a non-stick baking sheet with remaining 1 teaspoon vegetable oil. Transfer rolls to the baking sheet, reserving marinade. Grill, turning frequently and brushing with reserved marinade, until livers are no longer pink. Transfer to serving dish and serve piping hot.

Each serving provides: 2 Protein Exchanges, ½ Fat Exchange, 15 Calories Optional Exchange

•

— Chopped Chicken —
Livers

SERVES 2

205 CALORIES PER SERVING

1 tablespoon margarine

1½oz (45g) onion, chopped

4oz (120g) chicken livers

1 egg, hard-boiled and chopped

pinch each salt and white pepper

4 lettuce leaves

1 medium tomato, cut into 8 wedges

1 medium carrot, cut into 6 sticks

1oz (30g) onion, sliced and separated into rings

Heat ½ teaspoon margarine in small non-stick frying pan, add chopped onion and saute until transparent. Add livers and cook, stirring frequently, until livers are browned on the outside but still pink on the inside, about 5 minutes. Transfer mixture to blender or food processor and puree until smooth. Transfer to a bowl, stir in remaining 2½ teaspoons margarine and the egg, salt and pepper. Cover and chill lightly in refrigerator. When ready to serve, line each plate with 2 lettuce leaves. Mound half the liver mixture on each portion of lettuce and garnish each with 4 tomato wedges, 3 carrot sticks and half the onion rings.

Each serving provides: 2 Protein Exchanges, 2 Vegetable Exchanges, 1½ Fat Exchanges

•

— Easy Ox Liver —
Saute

SERVES 2

300 CALORIES PER SERVING

2 teaspoons margarine

10oz (300g) ox liver, cut into 3 x 1-inch (8 x 2.5-cm) strips

4oz (120g) onion, thinly sliced

2 medium tomatoes, blanched, peeled and cut into wedges

1 teaspoon salt

¼ teaspoon pepper

chopped parsley for garnish

Heat margarine in large frying pan. Turn up heat, add liver and onions and saute, stirring occasionally, until liver is browned and onions are tender, about 5 minutes. Reduce heat and add tomatoes, salt and pepper. Cook, stirring occasionally, until tomatoes are hot. Serve garnished with parsley.

Each serving provides: 4 Protein Exchanges, 2 Vegetable Exchanges, 1 Fat Exchange

•

— Devilled —
Calf Liver

SERVES 2

325 CALORIES PER SERVING

5 fl oz (150ml) low-fat natural yogurt

½ teaspoon mustard

¼ teaspoon Worcestershire sauce

2 teaspoons margarine

3oz (90g) onion, chopped

10oz (300g) calf liver, cut into ½-inch (1-cm) wide strips

2 teaspoons flour

pinch each thyme, pepper and salt

Mix yogurt, mustard and Worcester-shire sauce and set aside. Heat margarine in frying pan, add onion and saute until softened. Add liver and sprinkle with flour. Add thyme and pepper and saute over fairly high heat until liver strips are browned on the outside but still pink on the inside, about 5 minutes. Reduce heat to low and stir in yogurt mixture. Heat through, but do not boil. Season with salt.

Each serving provides: 4 Protein Exchanges, ½ Vegetable Exchange, 1 Fat Exchange, ½ Milk Exchange, 10 Calories Optional Exchange

•

— Ox or Calf Liver —
in Wine

SERVES 2

350 CALORIES PER SERVING

2 teaspoons margarine

3oz (90g) onion, chopped

1 small garlic clove, crushed

10oz (300g) ox or calf liver, thinly sliced

8 teaspoons white wine

pinch thyme

2 slices white bread, toasted and cut diagonally into halves

2 teaspoons chopped parsley

Heat margarine in frying pan, add onion and garlic and saute until onion is softened. Add liver and cook, turning once, until slices are firm, 5 to 7 minutes. Add wine and thyme and cook for 2 minutes longer. Arrange 2 toast triangles on each of 2 plates, top each portion of toast with half the liver mixture and sprinkle each with 1 teaspoon parsley.

Each serving provides: 4 Protein Exchanges, 1 Bread Exchange, ½ Vegetable Exchange, 1 Fat Exchange, 20 Calories Optional Exchange

•

— Liver, Peppers —
and Onions

SERVES 2

510 CALORIES PER SERVING

1 teaspoon vegetable oil

3oz (90g) onion, sliced and separated into rings

3oz (90g) each green and red peppers, seeded and cut into rings

½ teaspoon marjoram

3 tablespoons flour

½ teaspoon salt

pinch freshly ground pepper

10oz (300g) calf liver, thinly sliced

4 teaspoons low-fat spread

8oz (240g) cooked long grain rice, hot

Heat oil in non-stick frying pan, add onion and pepper rings and cook, stirring occasionally, just until tender. Remove vegetables from pan and sprinkle with marjoram. Set aside and keep warm. Mix flour, salt and pepper and dredge liver in seasoned flour, using all the mixture to coat liver on all sides. Heat low-fat spread in same pan, add liver and saute briefly, just until golden brown on all sides. Arrange rice on serving dish, top with liver slices and decorate with onion and pepper rings.

Each serving provides: 4 Protein Exchanges, 2 Bread Exchanges, 1 Vegetable Exchange, 1½ Fat Exchanges

•

— Liver with Fruit— and Rice Stuffing

SERVES 2

530 CALORIES PER SERVING

4 teaspoons margarine

2oz (60g) onion, sliced

1oz (30g) celery, chopped

1 garlic clove, crushed

4 tablespoons dry sherry

1 medium apple, cored, peeled and chopped

1oz (30g) raisins

½ teaspoon salt

pinch each white pepper, sage and nutmeg

4oz (120g) cooked long grain rice

2 slices calf or ox liver, each 5oz (150g)

2 tablespoons buttermilk

3 tablespoons dried breadcrumbs

Heat 2 teaspoons margarine in a frying pan, add onion, celery and garlic and saute until onion is transparent, about 5 minutes. Add sherry, then apple, raisins and seasonings. Cover and cook, stirring occasionally, until most of liquid evaporates, about 5 minutes. Add rice, stir to combine, remove from heat and set aside. Dip each slice of liver into buttermilk, coating both sides, then into breadcrumbs, being sure to use all the buttermilk and crumbs. Grease a baking tin with 1 teaspoon margarine. Place 1 slice of breaded liver in pan and top with fruit mixture, then second liver slice. Secure with cocktail sticks (some stuffing may fall into pan). Dot liver with remaining teaspoon margarine. Bake at 375°F, 190°C, Gas Mark 5, for about 20 minutes, or until liver is cooked but still slightly pink on the inside when pierced with a fork.

Each serving provides: 4 Protein Exchanges, 1½ Bread Exchanges, ½ Vegetable Exchange, 2 Fat Exchanges, 1 Fruit Exchange, 40 Calories Optional Exchange

— Calf Liver — with Vegetables Julienne

SERVES 2

345 CALORIES PER SERVING

1 tablespoon flour

pinch each salt and pepper

2 slices calf liver, each 5oz (150g)

1 tablespoon vegetable oil

4oz (120g) onion, thinly sliced

2oz (60g) each carrots and celery, cut into thin strips

8oz (240g) canned tomatoes, drained and chopped (reserve liquid)

Mix flour, salt and pepper and dredge liver in flour mixture, coating both sides. Heat oil in non-stick frying pan, add liver and brown quickly on both sides. Remove liver from pan and set aside. Reduce heat to moderate and add onions, carrot and celery to same pan. Saute, stirring to prevent sticking, until onions are browned. Add reserved tomato liquid, reduce heat to low, cover and simmer until vegetables are tender, about 5 minutes. Stir tomatoes into vegetable mixture, top with liver, cover and simmer until mixture is hot, about 5 minutes.

Each serving provides: 4 Protein Exchanges, 3 Vegetable Exchanges, 1½ Fat Exchanges, 15 Calories Optional Exchange

— Liver and — Vegetables with Rosemary

SERVES 2

305 CALORIES PER SERVING

2 teaspoons vegetable oil

3oz (90g) mushrooms, chopped

2oz (60g) carrot, cut into thin strips

1½oz (45g) green pepper, seeded and cut into thin strips

1 garlic clove, crushed

10oz (300g) calf liver, cut into 1-inch (2.5-cm) wide strips

4fl oz (120ml) chicken stock, prepared according to package directions

2 teaspoons flour

2 medium tomatoes, blanched, peeled, seeded and chopped

¼ teaspoon rosemary

pinch each salt and pepper

1 tablespoon chopped parsley for garnish

Heat oil in frying pan, add mushrooms, carrot, green pepper and garlic and saute until vegetables are tender-crisp, about 5 minutes. Add liver and cook, stirring quickly, until all pink has disappeared, about 5 minutes. Mix 1 tablespoon stock with the flour, stirring well, and add to liver mixture with all remaining ingredients except parsley. Cook, stirring constantly, until sauce is thickened. Serve sprinkled with parsley.

Each serving provides: 4 Protein Exchanges, 2 Vegetable Exchanges, 1 Fat Exchange, 10 Calories Optional Exchange

— Chicken Livers —
in Creamy Mushroom Sauce

SERVES 2

330 CALORIES PER SERVING

2 teaspoons margarine

10oz (300g) chicken livers

6oz (180g) mushrooms, sliced

1 packet low-calorie chicken soup powder

¼ teaspoon each paprika and salt

pinch pepper

3fl oz (90ml) water

2 tablespoons low-fat natural yogurt

2 slices white bread, toasted and cut into 4 triangles each

2 tablespoons chopped parsley for garnish

Heat margarine in a small frying pan, add chicken livers, mushrooms, soup powder, paprika, salt, pepper and water. Cover and cook for 15 minutes, stirring occasionally. Remove pan from heat and stir in yogurt. Arrange 4 toast triangles on each of 2 plates. Spoon half the liver mixture over each portion of toast and sprinkle each serving with 1 tablespoon chopped parsley.

Each serving provides: 4 Protein Exchanges, 1 Bread Exchange, 1 Vegetable Exchange, 1 Fat Exchange, 30 Calories Optional Exchange

—Italian-Style—
Liver and Onions

SERVES 2

460 CALORIES PER SERVING

6 tablespoons dried breadcrumbs

4 teaspoons grated Parmesan cheese

1 tablespoon chopped parsley

½ teaspoon oregano

¼ teaspoon garlic powder

pinch each salt and pepper

10oz (300g) chicken livers, cut into chunks

3 tablespoons buttermilk

3 teaspoons margarine

4oz (120g) onions, sliced

Mix breadcrumbs, cheese, parsley, oregano, garlic powder, salt and pepper together in a shallow dish. Dip liver, one piece at a time, into buttermilk then into crumb mixture, being sure to use all the buttermilk and crumb mixture. Grease a baking sheet with 1 teaspoon margarine, transfer liver to sheet and bake at 350°F, 180°C, Gas Mark 4, until lightly browned, 15 to 20 minutes. While liver is baking, heat remaining 2 teaspoons margarine in a non-stick frying pan, add onions and saute until golden. Serve with the liver.

Each serving provides: 4 Protein Exchanges, 1 Bread Exchange, 1 Vegetable Exchange, 1½ Fat Exchanges, 35 Calories Optional Exchange

— Chicken Livers —
with Green Pepper

SERVES 2

255 CALORIES PER SERVING

2 teaspoons margarine

1½oz (45g) onion, chopped

1 small garlic clove, crushed

10oz (300g) chicken livers

1 medium green pepper, seeded and cut into thin strips

4 teaspoons dry sherry

4 tablespoons chicken stock, prepared according to package directions

pinch each pepper and thyme

Heat margarine in a frying pan, add onion and garlic and saute until onion is soft, about 2 minutes. Add livers and saute, turning occasionally, until browned, about 3 minutes. Add green pepper and sherry and saute for 1 minute longer. Stir in remaining ingredients and bring to the boil. Reduce heat, cover and simmer for 2 minutes.

Each serving provides: 4 Protein Exchanges, 1 Vegetable Exchange, 1 Fat Exchange, 10 Calories Optional Exchange

— Liver and Cheese — Spread

SERVES 4

165 CALORIES PER SERVING

2 teaspoons margarine

3oz (90g) onion, chopped

8oz (240g) chicken livers

2oz (60g) strong Cheddar cheese, grated

4 teaspoons pickle

4 lettuce leaves

Heat margarine in small non-stick frying pan, add onion and saute until transparent. Add livers and saute, stirring frequently, until browned on the outside but still pink on the inside. Transfer liver mixture to blender or food processor and puree until smooth. Transfer to a bowl, add cheese and pickle and stir until well combined. Transfer mixture to sheet of greaseproof paper and, rolling mixture in the paper, form into a cylinder about 6 inches (15 cm) long and 2 inches (5 cm) in diameter. Refrigerate, wrapped, until firm, at least 2 hours. When ready to serve, line a serving plate with lettuce leaves, unwrap liver and serve on lettuce.

Each serving provides: 2 Protein Exchanges, ½ Vegetable Exchange, ½ Fat Exchange, 10 Calories Optional Exchange

— Oriental Liver — and Vegetables

SERVES 2

265 CALORIES PER SERVING

2 teaspoons peanut or vegetable oil

3oz (90g) onion, chopped

1 garlic clove, crushed

10oz (300g) chicken livers

3oz (90g) mushrooms, sliced

2oz (60g) celery, sliced, or green pepper, seeded and coarsely chopped

5 tablespoons water

2 teaspoons soy sauce

1 teaspoon cornflour

pinch pepper

Heat oil in a frying pan, add onion and garlic and saute until onion is transparent. Add livers, mushrooms and celery or green pepper and saute over fairly high heat for 5 minutes. Mix water, soy sauce and cornflour, stirring well. Stir into liver mixture and sprinkle with pepper. Stirring constantly, cook until mixture thickens.

Each serving provides: 4 Protein Exchanges, 1½ Vegetable Exchanges, 1 Fat Exchange, 5 Calories Optional Exchange

— Polynesian — Chicken Livers

SERVES 2

275 CALORIES PER SERVING

1 teaspoon vegetable oil

10oz (300g) chicken livers

1oz (30g) green pepper, seeded and diced

1½oz (45g) spring onion, thinly sliced

4oz (120g) canned pineapple chunks, no sugar added (drain and reserve juice)

1 tablespoon each wine vinegar and soy sauce

1½ teaspoons brown sugar

1 teaspoon cornflour

Heat oil in a frying pan. Add livers, green pepper and spring onion and cook over high heat, stirring constantly, until livers are browned. Remove from heat and set aside. Heat pineapple chunks, vinegar, soy sauce and sugar together in a small saucepan. Mix cornflour with reserved pineapple juice, add to the hot fruit and cook, stirring constantly, until mixture is thickened. Pour over liver mixture in pan, return pan to moderate heat and cook for 1 minute.

Each serving provides: 4 Protein Exchanges, ½ Vegetable Exchange, ½ Fat Exchange, ½ Fruit Exchange, 20 Calories Optional Exchange

— Chicken Liver — Pate

SERVES 2

365 CALORIES PER SERVING

10oz (300g) chicken livers

1 packet low-calorie chicken soup powder

4 teaspoons dry sherry

6oz (180g) peeled cooked potatoes, cut into chunks

1½oz (45g) onion, chopped

½oz (15g) low-fat dry milk, mixed with 2 tablespoons water

2 teaspoons margarine

½ teaspoon French mustard

¼ teaspoon each salt and nutmeg

pinch pepper

Stir chicken livers and soup powder together in a non-stick frying pan and cook, stirring frequently, until livers are browned on the outside but still pink on the inside, about 5 minutes. Add sherry and set aside. Puree remaining ingredients in blender or food processor until smooth, add livers and pan juices and process until just blended. Transfer mixture to a non-stick loaf tin, cover and chill overnight or at least 3 hours. To serve, loosen edges of pate and invert onto serving dish.

Each serving provides: 4 Protein Exchanges, 1 Bread Exchange, ¼ Vegetable Exchange, 1 Fat Exchange, ¼ Milk Exchange, 30 Calories Optional Exchange

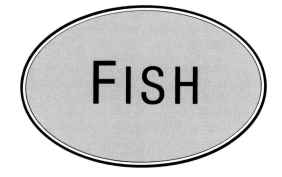

FISH

*H*igh in protein, low in fat and good to eat, fish is easy to cook, too, particularly now that so many excellent packs of frozen fish are available. If you buy fresh fish, make sure that it's really fresh and cook it as soon after purchase as possible, then you will enjoy the full flavour of dishes such as Portuguese Cod Fillets and Baked Fish with Mushroom-Wine Sauce. Canned fish is an excellent buy, too, particularly for salads and sandwiches and cold buffet dishes such as Savoury Jelly Ring with Tuna-Cheese Salad.

— Scallops en — Brochette

SERVES 2

245 CALORIES PER SERVING

10oz (300g) scallops, cut into 1-inch (2.5-cm) pieces

4 tablespoons dry white wine

12 small mushroom caps (about 1-inch/2.5-cm diameter)

½ each medium green and red peppers, seeded and cut into 1-inch (2.5-cm) squares

2 teaspoons margarine, melted

¼ teaspoon paprika

lemon slices and parsley sprigs for garnish

4oz (120g) cooked long grain rice, hot

Soak scallops in wine for 30 minutes. Drain, reserving wine. Thread 1 mushroom cap on to each of six 8 or 9-inch (20 or 23-cm) wooden skewers. Alternating ingredients, thread ⅙ of the scallops and pepper squares on to each skewer, then thread each with 1 of the remaining mushroom caps. Preheat grill. Arrange skewers in a single layer in a baking tin and pour wine over skewers. Drizzle margarine over scallops only. Dust all ingredients with paprika and grill until scallops turn opaque, 4 to 5 minutes. Serve immediately with hot rice, spooning pan juices evenly over the skewers and garnishing with lemon slices and parsley sprigs.

Each serving provides: 4 Protein Exchanges, 1½ Vegetable Exchanges, 1 Fat Exchange, 1 Bread Exchange, 30 Calories Optional Exchange

— Savoury Jelly — Ring with Tuna-Cheese Salad

SERVES 4

265 CALORIES PER SERVING

Jelly Ring

1 teaspoon vegetable oil

1 tablespoon unflavoured gelatine

8fl oz (240ml) boiling water

8oz (240g) canned tomatoes, crushed

2 tablespoons lemon juice

2oz (60g) green peppers, seeded and chopped

2 tablespoons chopped onion

½ teaspoon salt

¼ teaspoon Worcestershire sauce

3 drops hot pepper sauce

Salad

8oz (240g) drained canned tuna, flaked

2 tablespoons each chopped onion and celery

2 tablespoons mayonnaise

pinch each salt and pepper

2oz (60g) lettuce, shredded

4oz (120g) Cheddar cheese, cut into 4 equal squares

To Prepare Jelly Ring: Oil a ring mould lightly with the vegetable oil. Sprinkle gelatine over boiling water and stir until dissolved. Add all remaining ingredients for jelly ring to gelatine mixture and stir to combine. Pour mixture into ring mould, cover with cling film and refrigerate for at least 3 hours or until set.

To Prepare Salad and Serve: Mix flaked tuna with the onion, celery, mayonnaise, salt and pepper. Turn jelly ring out onto large serving dish and fill centre of ring with tuna mixture. Arrange shredded lettuce round outside of ring. Cut each cheese square in half diagonally, forming 8 triangles, and arrange triangles on shredded lettuce.

Each serving provides: 3 Protein Exchanges, 1 Vegetable Exchange, 1½ Fat Exchanges, 15 Calories Optional Exchange

— Sole Florentine —

SERVES 2

235 CALORIES PER SERVING

1½oz (45g) onion, chopped

1 garlic clove, crushed

1½oz (45g) mushrooms, sliced

6oz (180g) well drained cooked chopped spinach

pinch each salt and pepper

2 lemon sole fillets, skinned, each 5oz (150g)

4 teaspoons mayonnaise

2 teaspoons French mustard

2 tablespoons each lemon juice and chopped parsley

Place onion and garlic in a non-stick frying pan, cover and cook until onion is soft. Add mushrooms and cook, stirring constantly, until all liquid has evaporated. Add spinach, salt and pepper and stir to combine. Preheat oven to 400°F, 200°C, Gas Mark 6. Spoon half the spinach mixture on to centre of each fillet. Roll fillets to enclose filling and place seam-side down in shallow casserole. Mix mayonnaise, mustard, lemon juice and parsley and spread evenly over fish rolls. Bake until fish is lightly browned, 15 to 20 minutes. Serve at once.

Each serving provides: 4 Protein Exchanges, 1½ Vegetable Exchanges, 2 Fat Exchanges

— Sauteed Prawns — with Green Sauce

SERVES 2

260 CALORIES PER SERVING

2 teaspoons olive oil

2 garlic cloves, crushed

½oz (15g) fresh basil, pureed in blender

2 tablespoons parsley, pureed in blender

8oz (240g) shelled prawns

6fl oz (180ml) water

½ chicken stock cube, crumbled

pinch freshly ground pepper

4oz (120g) cooked long grain rice, hot

2 teaspoons grated Parmesan cheese

Heat oil in frying pan, add garlic and saute briefly. Do not brown. Stir in basil and parsley. Add prawns and saute for 2 minutes. Add water, stock cube and pepper and cook until hot, 3 to 5 minutes. Spoon prawn mixture over rice and sprinkle with Parmesan cheese.

Each serving provides: 4 Protein Exchanges, 1 Fat Exchange, 1 Bread Exchange, 10 Calories Optional Exchange

— Crab and — Artichoke Appetiser

SERVES 2

160 CALORIES PER SERVING

Artichokes

2 globe artichokes, each about 8oz (240g), prepared for cooking as directed in Parmesan-Stuffed Artichokes (see page 45)

1 tablespoon lemon juice

½ teaspoon salt

Filling

2 tablespoons low-fat natural yogurt

4 teaspoons mayonnaise

1 tablespoon chopped chives

2 teaspoons chilli sauce

1 teaspoon each horseradish relish and Worcestershire sauce

½ teaspoon French mustard

dash hot pepper sauce

4oz (120g) drained crab meat (canned or thawed frozen)

To Prepare Artichokes: Pour about 3 inches (8 cm) water into a saucepan just large enough to hold artichokes. (Do not use aluminium or cast iron pan). Add lemon juice and salt and stand artichokes upright in pan. Cover and simmer until bases of artichokes can be pierced easily with a fork, about 35 minutes. Remove artichokes from liquid and stand upside down to drain. When well drained, cut each half lengthwise. Remove and discard choke and tough outer leaves.

To Prepare Filling: Mix all ingredients for filling except crab meat. Stir in crab meat, stirring until well coated with dressing. Stuff each artichoke half with ¼ of the filling. Transfer to serving plate, cover with cling film and chill lightly in refrigerator before serving.

Each serving provides: 2 Protein Exchanges, 2 Vegetable Exchanges, 2 Fat Exchanges, 30 Calories Optional Exchange

— Seafood Bake —

SERVES 8

325 CALORIES PER SERVING

1lb (480g) peeled prawns

1lb (480g) frozen white crab meat, thawed

16 tablespoons low-calorie mayonnaise

1 green pepper, seeded and chopped

1 small onion, chopped

4 sticks celery, chopped

1 tablespoon Worcestershire sauce

salt and pepper

6oz (180g) cornflakes, crushed

paprika

Preheat oven to 400°F, 200°C, Gas Mark 6. Place prawns and crab meat into a large mixing bowl, add mayonnaise, green pepper, onion, celery, Worcestershire sauce, salt and pepper. Mix ingredients thoroughly together. Spoon into an ovenproof casserole, sprinkle with cornflakes and dust with paprika. Place in centre of oven and bake for 25 minutes.

Each serving provides: 4 Protein Exchanges, ½ Vegetable Exchange, 3 Fat Exchanges, 1 Bread Exchange

Top: Seafood Bake
Bottom: Crab and Artichoke Appetiser

— Artichoke-Stuffed —
Red Snapper

SERVES 6

205 CALORIES PER SERVING

1 tablespoon vegetable oil

4oz (120g) onion, finely chopped

14oz (420g) canned artichoke hearts, drained and chopped

3 slices white bread, toasted and made into fine crumbs

2 tablespoons each chopped parsley and lemon juice

1 teaspoon salt

½ teaspoon pepper

*1 red snapper (3lb/1kg 440g), cleaned, with head and tail left on

2 teaspoons margarine

8fl oz (240ml) mixed vegetable juice

Preheat oven to 350°F, 180°C, Gas Mark 4. Heat oil in a frying pan, add onions and saute until transparent. Add artichoke hearts and saute for 3 minutes longer. Stir in breadcrumbs, parsley, lemon juice, salt and pepper. Remove from heat and allow mixture to cool slightly. Stuff fish with artichoke mixture, using cocktail sticks or wooden skewers to close cavity. Grease a baking tin with margarine (tin should be big enough for the fish to lie flat). Transfer stuffed snapper to tin and pour vegetable juice over fish. Bake, basting frequently with pan juices, until fish flakes easily with a fork, 40 to 50 minutes.

*A 3lb (1kg 440g) red snapper will yield about 1lb 8oz (720g) cooked fish.

Each serving provides: 4 Protein Exchanges, ½ Bread Exchange, 1 Vegetable Exchange, ½ Fat Exchange, 25 Calories Optional Exchange

— Batter 'Fried' —
Fish with Sweet-and-Sour
Sauce

SERVES 2

340 CALORIES PER SERVING

Sweet-and-Sour Sauce

2oz (60g) carrots, thinly sliced

4fl oz (120ml) water

4oz (120g) canned pineapple chunks, no sugar added (drain and reserve juice)

2oz (60g) each red and green peppers, seeded and chopped

2 teaspoons each brown sugar and soy sauce

1 teaspoon each cornflour and wine vinegar

pinch salt

Batter and Fish

3 tablespoons flour

¼ teaspoon baking powder

pinch salt

3 tablespoons water

10oz (300g) cod fillets, cut into 1-inch (2.5-cm) pieces

4 teaspoons vegetable oil

To Prepare Sweet-and-Sour Sauce: Place carrots and water in a saucepan and bring to the boil. Reduce heat, cover and simmer until carrot slices are tender, about 3 minutes. Stir in pineapple chunks and red and green peppers and cook until mixture is hot. Mix reserved pineapple juice with remaining ingredients for sauce, stirring well. Pour over carrot mixture and cook, stirring constantly, until mixture is hot and thickened. Set aside.
To Prepare Batter and Fish: Mix dry ingredients, add water and stir until batter is smooth. Add fish pieces to batter and turn until well coated. Heat oil in non-stick frying pan, add fish and cook until golden brown on underside, 3 to 4 minutes. Carefully turn pieces over and cook until other side is browned. Remove to a serving dish and top with warm sweet-and-sour sauce.

Each serving provides: 4 Protein Exchanges, 1 Vegetable Exchange, 2 Fat Exchanges, ½ Fruit Exchange, 70 Calories Optional Exchange

— Portuguese —
Cod Fillets

SERVES 2

210 CALORIES PER SERVING

1 tablespoon olive oil

1½oz (45g) onion, chopped

1 garlic clove, crushed

2oz (60g) green pepper, seeded and chopped

6oz (180g) canned tomatoes, crushed

2 tablespoons white wine

4 black olives, stoned and sliced

10oz (300g) cod fillets

pinch each salt and pepper

2 teaspoons chopped parsley for garnish

Heat 1 teaspoon oil in saucepan, add onion and garlic and saute until onion is softened. Add green pepper and saute for 3 minutes longer. Add tomatoes, wine and olives, cover and simmer, stirring occasionally, for 10 minutes. Sprinkle both sides of cod fillets with salt and pepper. Heat remaining 2 teaspoons oil in a frying pan, add fish and cook for 3 to 4 minutes. Turn fish over and top with vegetable mixture. Simmer until fish flakes easily when tested with a fork and vegetables are hot, about 3 minutes. Transfer to a dish and serve.

Each serving provides: 4 Protein Exchanges, 1½ Vegetable Exchanges, 1½ Fat Exchanges, 25 Calories Optional Exchange

— Golden Grilled —
Scallops

SERVES 4

140 CALORIES PER SERVING

1lb 4oz (600g) scallops, cut into 1-inch (2.5-cm) pieces

4 tablespoons lemon juice

8 teaspoons margarine, melted

½ teaspoon each paprika and pepper

4 each lemon wedges and parsley sprigs for garnish

Preheat grill. In each of 4 shallow individual flameproof dishes, arrange 5oz (150g) scallops in a single layer. Pour 1 tablespoon lemon juice and ¼ of the margarine over each portion and toss to coat. Sprinkle evenly with seasonings and grill until golden, about 2 minutes. Serve garnished with lemon and parsley.

Each serving provides: 4 Protein Exchanges, 2 Fat Exchanges

— Tuna Puff —
Appetisers

SERVES 8

180 CALORIES PER SERVING

2 teaspoons margarine

6oz (180g) spring onions, chopped

2oz (60g) celery, chopped

3oz (90g) red pepper, seeded and chopped

3oz (90g) mushrooms, chopped

5oz (150g) tuna, drained

1 slice white bread, made into crumbs

2 tablespoons chopped parsley

4 teaspoons low-calorie mayonnaise

1 tablespoon lemon juice

1 teaspoon Worcestershire sauce

1 teaspoon spicy brown mustard

½ teaspoon each salt and white pepper

24 puff shells (see Vegetable-Cheese Puffs, page 48)

parsley sprigs to garnish

Heat margarine in non-stick frying pan, add spring onions, celery and red pepper and saute until vegetables are soft. Add mushrooms and cook over moderate heat until most of liquid has evaporated, about 5 minutes. Transfer mixture to a bowl, add all remaining ingredients except puff shells and mix well. Using a sharp knife, slice off top of each puff shell and spoon an equal amount of filling (about 2 tablespoons) into each. Replace tops and place puffs on warm serving dish.

Each serving (including Vegetable-Cheese Puffs) provides: 1 Protein Exchange, ½ Vegetable Exchange, 2 Fat Exchanges, 35 Calories Optional Exchange

— Spanish Prawn —
Cocktail

SERVES 4

100 CALORIES PER SERVING

3oz (90g) green pepper, seeded and chopped

3oz (90g) cucumber, peeled, seeded and chopped

½ medium tomato, blanched, peeled, seeded and chopped

8 teaspoons chilli sauce

2 tablespoons chopped onion

4 teaspoons tomato ketchup

2 teaspoons olive or vegetable oil

2 teaspoons horseradish sauce

1 teaspoon cider vinegar

¼ teaspoon Worcestershire sauce

1 small garlic clove, crushed

12 small lettuce leaves

4oz (120g) shelled prawns, roughly chopped

4 Mediterranean prawns to garnish (approx 4oz/120g)

coriander sprigs to garnish

Place all ingredients except lettuce and prawns in food processor or blender and process until finely chopped. Do not puree. Pour into a container, cover and refrigerate until chilled. Chill 4 cocktail glasses. In each glass place 3 lettuce leaves. Stir dressing, add chopped prawns and spoon ¼ of mixture into centre of each portion. Garnish with the unshelled prawns and coriander sprigs.

Each serving provides: 2 Protein Exchanges, 1 Vegetable Exchange, ½ Fat Exchange, 20 Calories Optional Exchange

Top: Spanish Prawn Cocktail
Bottom: Tuna Puff Appetisers

— Quick — Tomato-Prawn Rice

SERVES 4

335 CALORIES PER SERVING

4 teaspoons each vegetable oil and margarine

4oz (120g) celery, chopped

6oz (180g) onions, chopped

4oz (120g) green peppers, seeded and chopped

4 small garlic cloves, mashed

2lb (960g) canned tomatoes, crushed

12oz (360g) shelled prawns

8oz (240g) cooked long grain rice

4oz (120g) ham, diced

2 bay leaves

½ teaspoon each chilli powder, pepper and thyme

Heat oil and margarine together in large non-stick frying pan, add diced vegetables and garlic and saute over moderate heat until vegetables are soft. Reduce heat to low, add remaining ingredients and simmer, stirring occasionally, until hot. Remove bay leaves before serving.

Each serving provides: 4 Protein Exchanges, 3½ Vegetable Exchanges, 2 Fat Exchanges, 1 Bread Exchange

— Haddock Florentine —

SERVES 2

165 CALORIES PER SERVING

2 teaspoons margarine

10oz (300g) haddock fillets

½ teaspoon salt

½ garlic clove, crushed

6oz (180g) well drained cooked chopped spinach

1 tablespoon lemon juice

pinch pepper

Preheat oven to 350°F, 180°C, Gas Mark 4. Grease a shallow casserole with 1 teaspoon margarine. Arrange fish in casserole and sprinkle with half the salt. Bake until fish flakes easily when tested with a fork, 10 to 12 minutes. While fish is baking, heat remaining margarine in small non-stick frying pan, add garlic and saute briefly. Do not brown. Add spinach, lemon juice, pepper and remaining salt and cook for 2 to 3 minutes. When fish is done, spoon spinach mixture over fillets, return to oven and bake until hot, 3 to 5 minutes.

Each serving provides: 4 Protein Exchanges, 1 Vegetable Exchange, 1 Fat Exchange

— Salmon-Cheese — Pate

SERVES 4

175 CALORIES PER SERVING

7½oz (225g) low-fat soft cheese

5oz (150g) skinned and boned, drained canned salmon, flaked

2 tablespoons each finely chopped spring onion and lemon juice

4 teaspoons mayonnaise

2 teaspoons each horseradish relish and French mustard

8 lettuce leaves

3 medium tomatoes, thinly sliced

2 tablespoons chopped fresh dill (optional)

Mix cheese, salmon, spring onion, lemon juice, mayonnaise, horseradish and mustard and stir until thoroughly combined. Place cheese mixture in a small bowl, cover and refrigerate for at least 2 hours. To serve, line serving dish with lettuce leaves and top with tomato slices, arranged in a circular pattern with slices overlapping. Turn cheese mixture out onto tomatoes. If desired, sprinkle dill evenly over the cheese mixture and gently pat down.

Each serving provides: 2 Protein Exchanges, 1 Vegetable Exchange, 1 Fat Exchange

— Grilled Prawns —

SERVES 4

160 CALORIES PER SERVING

1lb (480g) shelled prawns

3 tablespoons lemon juice

4 teaspoons margarine, melted

2 large or 4 small garlic cloves, crushed

½ teaspoon each salt, pepper and paprika

parsley sprigs for garnish

Preheat grill. Arrange 4oz (120g) prawns in each of 4 individual flameproof dishes. Mix all remaining ingredients except parsley, pour ¼ of mixture over each portion of prawns and toss to coat. Grill 3 to 4 inches (8 to 10 cm) from heat source until prawns are golden brown, 1 to 2 minutes. Serve garnished with parsley.

Each serving provides: 4 Protein Exchanges, 1 Fat Exchange

— Mushroom-Stuffed — Plaice

SERVES 2

180 CALORIES PER SERVING

2 teaspoons olive oil

3oz (90g) spring onions, chopped

1 garlic clove, crushed

3oz (90g) mushrooms, chopped

1 teaspoon salt

pinch each pepper and thyme

2 plaice fillets, each 5oz (150g)

1 teaspoon each lemon juice and chopped parsley

½ teaspoon grated lemon peel

Heat 1 teaspoon oil in a small frying pan, add spring onions and garlic and saute until softened. Add mushrooms, ¼ teaspoon salt and the pepper and thyme and saute for 5 minutes. Preheat oven to 400°F, 200°C, Gas Mark 6. Sprinkle fillets with lemon juice and remaining ¾ teaspoon salt. Spoon half the mushroom mixture onto centre of each fillet and roll to enclose filling. Secure each with a cocktail stick. Transfer rolls seam-side down to shallow flameproof casserole and sprinkle each roll with ½ teaspoon parsley and ¼ teaspoon lemon peel, then ½ teaspoon oil. Bake until fish flakes easily when tested with a fork, about 15 minutes. Carefully transfer rolls to serving dish and remove cocktail sticks before serving.

Each serving provides: 4 Protein Exchanges, 1 Vegetable Exchange, 1 Fat Exchange

•

— Hot Devilled — Crab

SERVES 4

270 CALORIES PER SERVING

2 tablespoons margarine

2 tablespoons each chopped onion and red pepper

1 teaspoon flour

8fl oz (240ml) skimmed milk

11oz (330g) frozen crab meat, thawed and well drained

1 egg, beaten

3 tablespoons lemon juice

1 tablespoon chopped parsley

2 teaspoons French mustard

4 drops hot pepper sauce

2 teaspoons vegetable oil

6 tablespoons dried breadcrumbs

lemon crowns and dill sprigs for garnish

Heat 2 teaspoons margarine in non-stick frying pan, add onion and pepper and saute until onion is golden. Sprinkle vegetables with flour and cook, stirring constantly, for 1 minute. Gradually stir in milk and, stirring constantly, bring to the boil. Reduce heat and simmer, stirring, until mixture thickens. Stir in crab meat and remove from heat. Mix egg with 2 tablespoons lemon juice and the parsley, mustard and hot sauce. Add 2 to 3 tablespoons hot crab mixture to egg mixture, stirring well. Pour egg mixture into pan containing remaining crab mixture and cook over low heat, stirring constantly, until hot. Do not boil. Remove from heat. Preheat grill. Grease 4 large flameproof scallop shells with vegetable oil and spoon an equal amount of crab mixture into each shell. Mix remaining 4 teaspoons margarine with breadcrumbs and remaining tablespoon lemon juice. Sprinkle an equal amount of crumb mixture round edge of each shell and grill until crumbs are browned and

crab mixture is hot, 1 to 2 minutes. Serve garnished with lemon and dill.

Each serving provides: 3 Protein Exchanges, ½ Vegetable Exchange, 2 Fat Exchanges, ½ Bread Exchange, 25 Calories Optional Exchange

•

— Tuna Italienne —

SERVES 4

420 CALORIES PER SERVING

4 teaspoons vegetable oil

4oz (120g) onions, sliced

3 garlic cloves, crushed

12oz (360g) tomatoes, chopped

2 tablespoons tomato puree

pinch each oregano leaves, salt and pepper

dash hot pepper sauce

8oz (240g) drained canned tuna, flaked

1lb (480g) cooked noodles

4oz (120g) Cheddar cheese, grated

shredded lettuce for garnish

Heat oil in frying pan, add onions and garlic and saute until onions are transparent, about 5 minutes. Add tomatoes, tomato puree and seasonings. Cook, stirring occasionally, for 5 minutes. Stir in tuna and cook until heated through. Place cooked noodles in large serving dish. Top with tuna mixture and grated cheese. Garnish with shredded lettuce.

Each serving provides: 3 Protein Exchanges, 2 Bread Exchanges, 1½ Vegetable Exchanges, 1 Fat Exchange, 5 Calories Optional Exchange

•

— Tuna-Stuffed — Potato

SERVES 2

375 CALORIES PER SERVING

1 baking potato, 6oz (180g), cut in half lengthwise

6oz (180g) drained canned tuna

2 teaspoons margarine

1½oz (45g) onion, chopped

2 teaspoons flour

5fl oz (150ml) low-fat natural yogurt

2oz (60g) Cheddar cheese, grated

2 tablespoons chopped drained canned pimento

½ teaspoon salt

pinch each pepper and paprika

Preheat oven to 350°F, 180°C, Gas Mark 4. Place potato halves cut-side down on non-stick baking sheet and bake until tender but not soft, 35 to 40 minutes. Remove from oven and let cool. Scoop pulp from each potato half into bowl of food processor, leaving ¼-inch (5-mm) thick shell. Reserve shells. Add tuna to potato pulp and, using an on-off motion, process until finely minced, but do not puree. Set aside. If food processor is not available, potato pulp and tuna may be mashed well with a fork. Heat margarine in small non-stick frying pan, add onion and saute for about 1 minute. Sprinkle with 1 teaspoon flour and cook, stirring constantly, for about 1 minute. Remove from heat. Mix yogurt well with remaining teaspoon flour. Stir 2 tablespoons onion mixture into yogurt mixture, then add yogurt mixture to pan and stir to mix. Add 1oz (30g) cheese and the pimento, salt, pepper, paprika and reserved tuna mixture to yogurt mixture and stir to combine. Spoon

half the tuna mixture into each reserved potato shell, mounding mixture. Sprinkle each half with ½oz (15g) cheese and place on baking sheet. Bake at 350°F, 180°C, Gas Mark 4, until cheese is melted and potato is hot, 10 to 15 minutes.

Each serving provides: 4 Protein Exchanges, ½ Vegetable Exchange, 1 Fat Exchange, ½ Milk Exchange, 1 Bread Exchange, 10 Calories Optional Exchange

•

— Fish au Gratin —

SERVES 4

280 CALORIES PER SERVING

5 teaspoons margarine

15oz (450g) sole fillets

½ teaspoon each salt and pepper

1 teaspoon flour

8fl oz (240ml) skimmed milk

4oz (120g) extra strong Cheddar cheese, grated

parsley sprigs for garnish

Preheat oven to 350°F, 180°C, Gas Mark 4. Grease a flameproof casserole with 1 teaspoon margarine. Arrange fillets in casserole and sprinkle evenly with salt and pepper. Bake until fish flakes easily when tested with a fork, 10 to 15 minutes. While fish is baking, prepare sauce. Melt remaining margarine in a non-stick saucepan, add flour and cook, stirring constantly, for 1 minute. Gradually stir in milk and, stirring constantly, heat just to boiling point. Reduce heat, add cheese and simmer, stirring constantly, until mixture thickens and cheese is melted. Pour cheese sauce over fish and grill until sauce is browned, 1 to 2 minutes. Serve garnished with parsley.

Each serving provides: 4 Protein Exchanges, 1 Fat Exchange, 35 Calories Optional Exchange

•

— Salmon with — Asparagus Sauce

SERVES 2

385 CALORIES PER SERVING

2 teaspoons olive oil

2 tablespoons chopped shallots

1 garlic clove, crushed

6oz (180g) cooked asparagus, chopped

½ teaspoon salt

¼ teaspoon white pepper

2 teaspoons mayonnaise

¼ teaspoon French mustard

1 salmon fillet, 10oz (300g)

4 tablespoons dry white wine

2 teaspoons grated Parmesan cheese

Heat oil in frying pan, add shallots and garlic and saute until shallots are transparent, being careful not to burn garlic. Transfer shallot mixture to blender. Add asparagus, ¼ teaspoon salt and pinch pepper, puree until smooth and set aside. Preheat oven to 400°F, 200°C, Gas Mark 6. Mix mayonnaise and mustard, spread on fish and sprinkle with remaining ¼ teaspoon salt and pinch pepper. Transfer salmon to non-stick baking tin, add wine and bake until fish flakes easily when tested with a fork, about 15 minutes (exact timing will depend upon thickness of fillet). Remove tin from oven and heat grill. Spread asparagus puree over fish and sprinkle with cheese. Grill just until heated through.

Each serving provides: 4 Protein Exchanges, 1 Vegetable Exchange, 2 Fat Exchanges, 40 Calories Optional Exchange

•

Salmon with Asparagus Sauce

— Baked Cod — a l'Italienne

SERVES 2

205 CALORIES PER SERVING

2 teaspoons olive oil

1½oz (45g) onion, chopped

1 garlic clove, crushed

1½oz (45g) mushrooms, chopped

4 tablespoons white wine

4oz (120g) canned tomatoes, chopped

¼ teaspoon each basil, oregano and salt

pinch pepper

10oz (300g) cod fillets

2 teaspoons grated Parmesan cheese

1 tablespoon chopped parsley

Preheat oven to 400°F, 200°C, Gas Mark 6. Heat oil in frying pan, add onion and garlic and saute until onion is transparent, about 1 minute. Add mushrooms and cook until mushrooms are just tender, about 2 minutes. Add wine and bring to the boil. Add tomatoes and seasonings and cook, stirring occasionally, until sauce thickens, about 2 minutes. Arrange fillets in shallow flameproof casserole and top with sauce. Sprinkle with cheese and bake until fish flakes easily with a fork, 15 to 20 minutes. Carefully remove fish from casserole to serving dish and keep hot. Place casserole over moderate heat and cook remaining pan juices until reduced and thickened, about 2 minutes. Pour over fish and serve sprinkled with parsley.

Each serving provides: 4 Protein Exchanges, 1½ Vegetable Exchanges, 1 Fat Exchange, 40 Calories Optional Exchange

— Prawn Quiche — with Rice Crust

SERVES 4

350 CALORIES PER SERVING

Crust

1 teaspoon vegetable oil

8oz (240g) cooked long grain rice

1 egg, beaten

1oz (30g) Cheddar cheese, grated

pinch each salt and pepper

Filling

2 teaspoons margarine

4oz (120g) red peppers, seeded and chopped

6oz (180g) onions, chopped

1 garlic clove, crushed

6oz (180g) frozen prawns, thawed

3 eggs, beaten

1oz (30g) Cheddar cheese, grated

1 tablespoon chopped parsley

Topping

2 teaspoons margarine

3 tablespoons dried breadcrumbs

To Prepare Crust: Preheat oven to 425°F, 220°C, Gas Mark 7. Grease a 9-inch (23-cm) flan dish or deep pie plate with vegetable oil. Mix cooked rice with beaten egg and press mixture over bottom and up sides of dish. Bake until firm and lightly browned, about 25 minutes. Remove from oven and set aside. Reduce oven temperature to 375°F, 190°C, Gas Mark 5.

To Prepare Filling: Heat margarine in small frying pan, add peppers, onions and garlic and saute, stirring occasionally, until vegetables are tender. Transfer to a bowl, add remaining ingredients for filling and stir to combine. Spoon into prepared crust.

To Prepare Topping and Bake: Heat margarine in same pan, add breadcrumbs and stir to combine. Sprinkle crumbs evenly over filling and bake until filling has set, 30 to 35

minutes. If crumb topping browns too fast, cover top of quiche with foil. Remove quiche from oven and let stand for 10 minutes before cutting.

Each serving provides: 3 Protein Exchange, 1 Vegetable Exchange, 1 Fat Exchange, 1 Bread Exchange, 40 Calories Optional Exchange

— Baked Fish with — Mushroom-Wine Sauce

SERVES 2

190 CALORIES PER SERVING

2 teaspoons margarine

3oz (90g) mushrooms, chopped

2 tablespoons lemon juice

1 small garlic clove, crushed

pinch each salt and pepper

10oz (300g) fish fillets

1½oz (45g) spring onion, chopped

4 tablespoons dry sherry

1 tablespoon chopped parsley (optional)

Preheat oven to 400°F, 200°C, Gas Mark 6. Heat margarine in small frying pan, add mushrooms, lemon juice and seasonings and saute over high heat, stirring occasionally, until most of liquid has evaporated. Place fish in a casserole and top with mushroom mixture, spring onions and sherry. Bake until fish is opaque and flakes easily when tested with a fork, about 10 minutes. If desired, sprinkle with parsley just before serving.

Each serving provides: 4 Protein Exchanges, 1 Vegetable Exchange, 1 Fat Exchange, 30 Calories Optional Exchange

— Green Pasta —
with Tuna Sauce

SERVES 4

285 CALORIES PER SERVING

2 tablespoons margarine

1 garlic clove, crushed

3oz (90g) mushrooms, thinly sliced

3oz (90g) onion, chopped

2oz (60g) green pepper, seeded and chopped

1 tablespoon flour

½ pint (300ml) skimmed milk

6fl oz (180ml) water

1 chicken stock cube, crumbled

12oz (360g) drained canned tuna, flaked

1 tablespoon each chopped fresh basil and parsley

8oz (240g) cooked green pasta, hot

4 teaspoons grated Parmesan cheese

Heat margarine in large non-stick frying pan, add garlic and saute until golden. Remove and discard garlic, using a slotted spoon. Saute mushrooms, onion and green pepper in the same pan until onion is lightly browned. Sprinkle vegetables with flour and cook, stirring constantly, for 1 minute. Gradually stir in milk. Add water and stock cube and, stirring constantly, bring to the boil. Reduce heat and simmer, stirring, until mixture thickens. Stir in tuna, basil and parsley and cook until hot. Pour sauce over hot pasta and sprinkle with cheese.

Each serving provides: 3 Protein Exchanges, 1 Bread Exchange, 1 Vegetable Exchange, 1½ Fat Exchanges, ¼ Milk Exchange, 20 Calories Optional Exchange

— Rice-Stuffed Fish —
Rolls with Lemon Sauce

SERVES 2

230 CALORIES PER SERVING

1 tablespoon margarine

2oz (60g) cooked long grain rice

1½oz (45g) carrots, chopped

2 tablespoons chopped parsley

¼ teaspoon salt

pinch pepper

2 fish fillets, each 5oz (150g)

paprika

1 teaspoon flour

2½fl oz (75ml) skimmed milk (at room temperature)

2 teaspoons lemon juice

Preheat oven to 350°F, 180°C, Gas Mark 4. Set aside 2 teaspoons margarine. Melt remaining teaspoon margarine and mix half with the rice, carrot, parsley, salt and pepper. Spoon an equal amount of mixture on to each fillet and roll fish to enclose filling. Place rolls seam-side down in shallow casserole and drizzle with rest of melted margarine. Sprinkle each roll with pinch paprika and bake until fish flakes easily with a fork, 15 to 20 minutes. While fish is baking, heat remaining 2 teaspoons margarine in small non-stick saucepan, add flour and stir until combined. Gradually stir in milk and cook, stirring constantly, until mixture thickens, 2 to 3 minutes. Stir in lemon juice and pinch paprika and cook until hot. Do not boil. Carefully transfer fish rolls to serving dish and top with sauce.

Each serving provides: 4 Protein Exchanges, ½ Bread Exchange, ½ Vegetable Exchange, 1½ Fat Exchanges, 20 Calories Optional Exchange

OPTIONAL

There is already lots of variety in the Food Plan, but now you can add even more zest and interest with the Optional Exchange. Just juggle your allowance of extra calories and you can include in your meals items you would never have expected – wine, sherry, honey and sugar. You can make Mexican Guacamole with avocado, use Sherry Marinade with poultry and fish, and even make treats like Wine Spritzer.

Sponge Fingers and Raspberries (P192)

— Guacamole —

SERVES 8

155 CALORIES PER SERVING

1 ripe avocado, 8oz (240g), peeled and stoned

3 tablespoons lemon juice

4oz (120g) ham, diced

2 medium tomatoes, blanched, peeled, seeded and chopped

2 tablespoons each chopped onion and drained canned mild green chillies

1 tablespoon chopped parsley

1 tablespoon chopped fresh coriander or ½ teaspoon ground

½ teaspoon salt

1 small garlic clove, crushed

pinch pepper

1lb (480g) hot cooked rice

Using a fork, mash avocado to a smooth pulp with the lemon juice and stir in all remaining ingredients except rice. Cover with cling film and refrigerate for at least 1 hour. Serve with hot cooked rice.

Each serving provides: ½ Protein Exchange, ⅓ Vegetable Exchange, 1 Bread Exchange, 50 Calories Optional Exchange

---

— Sponge Fingers — and Raspberries

SERVES 8

55 CALORIES PER SERVING

1 teaspoon vegetable oil

1½oz (45g) flour, sifted

½ teaspoon baking powder

2 eggs, separated

1 tablespoon sugar

¼ teaspoon each grated lemon peel and vanilla flavouring

pinch cream of tartar

1¼lb (600g) raspberries

Grease a baking sheet lightly with vegetable oil. Preheat oven to 350°F, 180°C, Gas Mark 4. Sift together flour and baking powder and set aside. Place egg yolks, sugar, lemon peel and vanilla in a mixing bowl and beat with electric mixer until thick and pale yellow, about 3 minutes. Beat in half the flour mixture. In another bowl, using clean beaters, beat egg whites with cream of tartar until stiff peaks form. Gently fold whites into yolk mixture alternately with remaining flour mixture. Using an icing bag fitted with ½-inch (1-cm) plain nozzle, pipe batter on to baking sheet to make 16 strips, each about 3 inches (8 cm) x 1 inch (2.5 cm). Bake for 10 to 12 minutes. Remove immediately from baking sheet, using a palette knife, and cool on wire rack. Serve each portion with 2½oz (75g) raspberries.

Each serving provides: ½ Fruit Exchange, 55 Calories Optional Exchange

---

— Sherry Marinade —

SERVES 4

22 CALORIES PER SERVING

4 tablespoons each dry sherry and lemon juice

1 teaspoon demerara sugar

1 garlic clove, chopped

½ bay leaf, crushed

½ teaspoon basil

pinch each salt and pepper

Place all ingredients in blender and puree until smooth. Use as a marinade for poultry or fish.

Each serving provides: 20 Calories Optional Exchange

— Courgette-Onion — Dip

SERVES 8

40 CALORIES PER SERVING

4 teaspoons olive or vegetable oil

3oz (90g) onion, chopped

1 garlic clove, crushed

12oz (360g) courgettes, chopped

1 teaspoon salt

pinch pepper

dash lemon juice

5fl oz (150ml) low-fat natural yogurt

Heat oil in non-stick frying pan, add onion and garlic and saute until onion is transparent. Add courgettes and saute, stirring constantly, until softened, about 5 minutes. Transfer onion mixture to food processor or blender, add salt, pepper and lemon juice and puree. Pour mixture into bowl and stir in yogurt. Cover and refrigerate until chilled. Serve with raw vegetables such as blanched broccoli and cauliflower florets, strips of carrot and peppers, quartered tomatoes, cucumber and mushroom slices etc.

Each serving provides: ½ Vegetable Exchange, ½ Fat Exchange, 25 Calories Optional Exchange

---

— 'Sour Cream' —

SERVES 2

55 CALORIES PER SERVING

2½oz (75g) low-fat soft cheese

1 tablespoon low-fat natural yogurt

2 teaspoons lemon juice

pinch each salt and white pepper

Puree all ingredients in blender at low speed until smooth. Serve on baked potatoes or with a mixed green salad.

Each serving provides: ½ Protein Exchange, 10 Calories Optional Exchange

— Melba Snowballs —

SERVES 2

265 CALORIES PER SERVING

4 teaspoons raspberry jam

4oz (120g) vanilla ice cream, slightly softened

2 digestive biscuits, made into crumbs

4 teaspoons desiccated coconut, toasted

Force jam through sieve into small bowl to remove seeds. Add ice cream and, using a fork, stir jam lightly through ice cream to create swirl effect. Using small ice cream scoop, form 4 balls and place on baking sheet. Cover lightly with cling film and freeze until hard. Mix crumbs and coconut and roll each ball in mixture until well coated on all sides. Serve immediately or cover and freeze for future use.

Each serving provides: 1 Bread Exchange, 150 Calories Optional Exchange

•

— Caramel Sauce —

SERVES 4

105 CALORIES PER SERVING

4 tablespoons brown sugar

4 teaspoons margarine

2 teaspoons low-fat dry milk, mixed with 2 tablespoons water

Melt sugar and margarine together in a small saucepan over moderate heat, stirring constantly. Gradually stir in the milk and cook, still stirring, for about 1 minute or until thick and syrupy.

Each serving provides: 1 Fat Exchange, 75 Calories Optional Exchange

— Sweet and Sour — Salad Dressing

SERVES 4

20 CALORIES PER SERVING

1 tablespoon cornflour

8fl oz (240ml) water

2 tablespoons each lemon juice and wine vinegar

1 tablespoon finely chopped parsley

2 teaspoons chilli sauce

1 teaspoon each honey and Worcestershire sauce

1 garlic clove, crushed

pinch each salt and pepper

1 teaspoon caster sugar

Mix cornflour with water and, stirring constantly, bring to the boil. Continue cooking and stirring for 1 minute longer. Transfer to a bowl and add remaining ingredients. Mix well. Cover and refrigerate until required. Stir again just before serving. May also be used as a marinade for cold cooked vegetables such as broccoli, cauliflower and green beans

Each serving provides: 20 Calories Optional Exchange

•

— Wine Spritzer —

SERVES 2

40 CALORIES PER SERVING

6fl oz (180ml) chilled soda water

4fl oz (120ml) chilled dry white wine

4 to 6 ice cubes

2 strips lemon peel

Chill 2 tall glasses. Mix soda water and wine in a jug and divide into chilled glasses. Add 2 or 3 ice cubes and 1 strip lemon peel to each glass and serve immediately.

Each serving provides: 50 Calories Optional Exchange

— Blender — Cream of Tomato Soup

SERVES 4

130 CALORIES PER SERVING

4 teaspoons margarine

4oz (120g) onion, chopped

1 tablespoon flour

16fl oz (480ml) tomato juice

½ bay leaf

2oz (60g) low-fat dry milk, mixed with ½ pint (300ml) water

½ teaspoon Worcestershire sauce

pinch each salt and pepper

Heat margarine in a saucepan, add onion and saute until softened. Sprinkle with flour and cook, stirring constantly, for 2 minutes. Gradually stir in tomato juice. Add bay leaf and, stirring constantly, bring mixture to the boil. Reduce heat and simmer for 5 minutes. Remove from heat and let cool slightly. Remove bay leaf. Pour mixture into blender container and puree at low speed until smooth. Return mixture to saucepan and gradually stir in milk. Add Worcestershire sauce, salt and pepper and cook over low heat, stirring occasionally, until hot. Do not boil.

Each serving provides: ⅓ Vegetable Exchange, 1 Fat Exchange, ½ Milk Exchange, ½ Fruit Exchange, 10 Calories Optional Exchange

•

Vegetarian Full Exchange Menu Plan

	MONDAY	TUESDAY	WEDNESDAY
BREAKFAST	4fl oz (120ml) orange juice 2½oz (75g) low-fat soft cheese 1 slice wholemeal bread beverage	3oz (90g) grapes 2½oz (75g) low-fat soft cheese wholewheat crispbreads up to 80 calories spread with 1 teaspoon yeast extract beverage	½ medium banana, sliced ¾oz (20g) muesli ¼ pint (150ml) skimmed milk beverage
LUNCH	1oz (30g) chopped mixed nuts 1oz (30g) sultanas ¾oz (20g) wheatflakes mixed together with 5fl oz (150ml) low- fat natural yogurt with vanilla flavouring to taste beverage	9oz (270g) baked beans 1oz (30g) wholemeal bread, toasted 1 teaspoon margarine 2 medium tomatoes, halved and grilled 1 medium orange beverage	CHEESY DUMPLINGS IN TOMATO SAUCE 5oz (150g) strawberries, pureed in blender with sweetener to taste and poured over 3oz (90g) tofu, mashed beverage
DINNER	SPANISH OMELETTE mixed salad 5oz (150g) strawberries mixed with 2½oz (75g) low-fat soft cheese beverage	CHEESE AND TOMATO BAKE mixed salad 2 teaspoons mayonnaise 4oz (120g) canned sliced peaches 5fl oz (150ml) low-fat natural yogurt beverage	1 egg, scrambled with 1oz (30g) grated cheese, 1 teaspoon vegetable oil (to cook with) sliced tomato and onion mixed salad 2 teaspoons mayonnaise 2″ wedge honeydew melon beverage
SNACKS OR DRINKS TO BE USED THROUGHOUT THE DAY	½ pint (300ml) skimmed milk	½ pint (300ml) skimmed milk	¾ pint (450ml) skimmed milk

THURSDAY	FRIDAY	SATURDAY	SUNDAY
3oz (90g) grapes, halved and seeded over ¾oz (20g) bran flakes ¼ pint (150ml) skimmed milk beverage	¾oz (20g) porridge oats ½oz (15g) finely chopped nuts ½ medium apple, cored and sliced ½oz (15g) sultanas, all mixed together ¼ pint (150ml) skimmed milk, mixed with 1 teaspoon honey and poured over muesli beverage	4fl oz (120ml) orange juice 2½oz (75g) low-fat soft cheese 2 rice cakes beverage	½ medium grapefruit 3oz (90g) baked beans 1oz (30g) wholemeal bread, toasted 1 teaspoon margarine beverage
Banana Crunch Open Sandwich – spread 1 slice wholemeal bread with 2 tablespoons crunchy peanut butter, topped with ½ medium banana, sliced mixed salad beverage	BEAN AND NOODLE SOUP ½ medium banana 2oz (60g) vanilla ice cream, topped with 1 teaspoon chocolate sauce beverage	3 tablespoons crunchy peanut butter, spread on 1 slice wholemeal bread and topped with sliced tomato, cucumber and chopped fresh chives 5oz (150g) strawberries 5fl oz (150ml) low-fat natural yogurt beverage	EGG AND BEAN SALAD 4oz (120g) canned pineapple 5fl oz (150ml) low-fat natural yogurt beverage
HERBY BEAN BAKE 3oz (90g) green beans 3oz (90g) courgettes 4oz (120g) canned orange sections 2½oz (75g) low-fat soft cheese, mixed with juice from orange sections and spooned over fruit beverage	5oz (150g) cottage cheese, mixed with dash curry powder mixed salad 2 teaspoons mayonnaise 1 slice wholemeal bread, spread with 1 teaspoon low-fat spread 1 medium orange beverage	SAVOURY MACARONI PUDDING 1 medium pear beverage	6oz (180g) potato, baked in its jacket: scoop out potato and mix with 2½oz (75g) low-fat soft cheese, 2 teaspoons chopped chives and 1oz (30g) Cheddar or Edam cheese, diced. Spoon mixture back into potato shells and grill until top is golden. Serve with mixed salad 3oz (90g) grapes 4fl oz (120ml) wine beverage
¾ pint (450ml) skimmed milk	¾ pint (450ml) skimmed milk	½ pint (300ml) skimmed milk	½ pint (300ml) skimmed milk

— Egg and Bean — Salad

SERVES 1

330 CALORIES PER SERVING

4 teaspoons low-calorie mayonnaise

½ teaspoon prepared mustard

2 tablespoons chopped onion

2 tablespoons chopped celery

6oz (180g) drained canned red kidney beans

2-inch (5-cm) chunk cucumber, peeled and chopped

lettuce, shredded

1 hard-boiled egg, quartered

2-inch (5-cm) chunk cucumber, peeled and sliced

1 medium tomato, sliced

In a bowl combine first 4 ingredients. Add kidney beans and diced cucumber. Chill. Spoon onto lettuce leaves. Surround with egg, tomato and cucumber slices.

Each serving provides: 3 Protein Exchanges, 3 Vegetable Exchanges, 2 Fat Exchanges

●

— Savoury — Macaroni Pudding

SERVES 1

290 CALORIES PER SERVING

2oz (60g) cooked wholemeal macaroni

1oz (30g) Cheddar cheese, grated

1 egg, beaten

1 small onion, chopped

½ teaspoon mixed herbs

salt and pepper to taste

Mix all ingredients together well. Bake in a medium-sized loaf tin for 1 hour at 350°F, 180°C, Gas Mark 4.

Each serving provides: 2 Protein Exchanges, 1 Vegetable Exchange, 1 Bread Exchange

— Bean and — Noodle Soup

SERVES 1

385 CALORIES PER SERVING

¾ pint (450ml) vegetable stock, made with 1 cube

3oz (90g) canned red kidney beans

3oz (90g) cut French beans

1 garlic clove, crushed

1 teaspoon fresh chopped basil or pinch dried

pepper to taste

3oz (90g) canned butter beans

1 small courgette, chopped

1 medium tomato, skinned and chopped

2oz (60g) cooked noodles

1oz (30g) cheese, grated

Heat stock in large saucepan. Add kidney beans, French beans, garlic, basil and pepper to taste. Bring to the boil and cook for 20 minutes. Add rest of ingredients except cheese and cook for a further 3 minutes. Serve at once with grated cheese sprinkled over.

Each serving provides: 3 Protein Exchanges, 2 Vegetable Exchanges, 1 Bread Exchange

●

— Herby Bean — Bake

SERVES 1

390 CALORIES PER SERVING

1 teaspoon vegetable oil

6oz (180g) drained canned butter beans

1 teaspoon yeast extract

1 tablespoon tomato puree

1 teaspoon chopped basil or other fresh herb

1 egg

¾oz (30g) wheatflakes, crushed

pepper to taste

Rub medium-sized loaf tin with vegetable oil. Mash butter beans and thoroughly mix in other ingredients. Spoon mixture into loaf tin and bake at 350°F, 180°C, Gas Mark 4 for 30 minutes. Serve hot or cold.

Each serving provides: 3 Protein Exchanges, 1 Fat Exchange, 1 Bread Exchange, 20 Calories Optional Exchange

●

— Cheesy —
Dumplings in Tomato Sauce

SERVES 1

355 CALORIES PER SERVING

3oz tofu, mashed

1 slice wholemeal bread, made into crumbs

1 garlic clove, crushed

1 tablespoon chopped onion

1 egg, lightly beaten

1oz (30g) Cheddar cheese, grated

2 teaspoons prepared mustard

1 teaspoon Worcestershire sauce

1 tablespoon chopped fresh parsley

pinch each basil, fennel seeds and marjoram

salt and pepper to taste

6oz (180g) canned tomatoes, chopped

Combine all ingredients except tomatoes in a large bowl and mix well. Shape into dumplings and brown over gentle heat in non-stick pan. Add chopped tomatoes and simmer for 10 to 15 minutes until sauce and dumplings are well heated.

Each serving provides: 3 Protein Exchanges, 2 Vegetable Exchanges, 1 Bread Exchange

— Cheese —
and Tomato Bake

SERVES 1

320 CALORIES PER SERVING

3oz (90g) potatoes, peeled and chopped

3oz (90g) onions, chopped

1 teaspoon yeast extract

1 teaspoon dry mustard

2½oz (75g) low-fat soft cheese

salt and pepper to taste

1 teaspoon fresh chopped basil or ½ teaspoon dried

1oz (30g) Cheddar cheese, grated

1 medium tomato, sliced

Preheat oven to 425°F, 220°C, Gas Mark 7. Cook potatoes and onions in boiling salted water for 10 to 15 minutes. Mix yeast extract and mustard with 2 teaspoons hot water. Drain cooked potatoes and onions and mash with low-fat soft cheese, salt and pepper, mustard mixture and basil. Turn into small ovenproof dish, sprinkle with grated cheese and arrange sliced tomato on top. Bake for 10 to 15 minutes. Remove from oven and serve immediately.

Each serving provides: 2 Protein Exchanges, 2 Vegetable Exchanges, 1 Bread Exchange, 10 Calories Optional Exchange

—Spanish —
Omelette

SERVES 1

280 CALORIES PER SERVING

2 teaspoons vegetable oil, divided

2 eggs

4 tablespoons water

2 tablespoons diced green pepper

2 tablespoons diced red pepper

4 finely chopped button mushrooms

1 teaspoon soy sauce

Heat 1 teaspoon oil in non-stick pan. Beat eggs with water, pour into pan, tipping pan to make sure egg mixture covers base. Cook until top is risen and firm. Meanwhile heat remaining oil in small non-stick saucepan, add peppers and mushrooms and saute until tender but still crisp. Stir in soy sauce. Slide cooked omelette onto a hot plate, spoon pepper mixture over half omelette and fold over.

Each serving provides: 2 Protein Exchanges, 2 Vegetable Exchanges, 2 Fat Exchanges

Fast Finish Menu Plan

	MONDAY	TUESDAY	WEDNESDAY
BREAKFAST	1 medium orange ¾oz (20g) cornflakes ¼ pint (150ml) skimmed milk tea or coffee	4fl oz (120ml) orange juice 1 egg 1oz (30g) slice wholemeal bread 1 teaspoon margarine tea or coffee	1oz (30g) sultanas ¾oz (20g) cornflakes ¼ pint (150ml) skimmed milk tea or coffee
LUNCH	2oz (60g) tuna, mixed with 2½oz (75g) cottage cheese and a pinch of curry powder large mixed salad 2 teaspons mayonnaise 4oz (120g) canned peaches (Mix 2 tablespoons juice with 2½fl oz (75ml) low-fat natural yogurt and pour over peaches) tea or coffee	6oz (180g) baked beans 1oz slice toast 2 medium tomatoes halved and grilled 4oz (120g) pineapple tea or coffee	Open sandwich made with 1oz (30g) slice wholemeal bread spread with 1 teaspoon margarine topped with mixture of salad vegetables and 2oz (60g) turkey 2 teaspoons pickle 1 medium orange tea or coffee
DINNER	3oz (90g) chicken 3oz (90g) carrots 3oz (90g) broccoli 3oz (90g) peas 3oz (90g) potato 1 teaspoon margarine 1 medium pear tea or coffee	3oz (90g) prawns (Mix together 2 teaspoons mayonnaise and 1 tablespoon tomato puree to make sauce) mixed salad 3oz grapes tea or coffee	5oz (150g) liver and 3oz (90g) onions, sauteed in 2 teaspoons vegetable oil 3oz (90g) cauliflower 3oz (90g) green beans 5oz (150g) strawberries 2½fl oz (75ml) low-fat natural yogurt tea or coffee
SNACKS OR DRINKS TO BE USED THROUGHOUT THE DAY	½ pint (450ml) skimmed milk	1 pint (300ml) skimmed milk	½ pint (450ml) skimmed milk

Please Note: Amounts given for meat, fish and poultry are cooked weights.

THURSDAY	FRIDAY	SATURDAY	SUNDAY
½ medium grapefruit 2½oz (75g) cottage cheese, grilled on 1oz (30g) slice toast sliced tomato tea or coffee	4oz (120g) grapefruit sections ¾oz (20g) wheatflakes ¼ pint (150ml) skimmed milk tea or coffee	2″ wedge or 5oz (150g) chunks honeydew melon 1 egg 1oz (30g) slice wholemeal bread 2 teaspoons low-fat spread tea or coffee	4fl oz (120ml) orange juice ¾oz (20g) muesli mixed with 2½fl oz (75ml) low-fat natural yogurt tea or coffee
3oz (90g) smoked mackerel mixed salad 2 teaspoons salad cream 2 cream crackers 1 teaspoon margarine 4oz (120g) orange sections 2½fl oz (75ml) low-fat natural yogurt tea or coffee	5oz (150g) low-fat soft cheese crispbread, up to 80 calories mixed salad 2 teaspoons mayonnaise 1 medium apple tea or coffee	3oz (90g) chicken 3oz (90g) potato, baked in jacket 1 teaspoon margarine mixed salad 5oz (150g) blackberries 2½fl oz (75ml) low-fat natural yogurt tea or coffee	Spread 2 teaspoons mayonnaise over 2 halved hard-boiled eggs mixed salad mix 1 teaspoon vegetable oil and vinegar together for dressing 3oz (90g) grapes tea or coffee
2 egg omelette, cooked in 1 teaspoon vegetable oil filled with 3oz (90g) mushrooms and 1 teaspoon grated Parmesan cheese 3oz (90g) courgettes 3oz (90g) canned tomatoes 1 medium pear tea or coffee	4oz (120g) grilled trout, brushed with 1 teaspoon vegetable oil 3oz (90g) Brussels sprouts 3oz (90g) carrots 4oz (120g) pineapple tea or coffee	cauliflower cheese made with 6oz (180g) cauliflower 2oz (60g) grated Edam cheese Sauce made with 1 teaspoon vegetable oil, 2 teaspoons cornflour and ¼ pint (150ml) skimmed milk sliced tomatoes and onions 1 medium orange tea or coffee	4oz (120g) beef 3oz (90g) green beans 3oz (90g) carrots 3oz (90g) potato 1 teaspoon horseradish relish 4oz (129g) fruit salad 2½fl oz (75ml) low-fat natural yogurt tea or coffee
¾ pint (450ml) skimmed milk	¾ pint (450ml) skimmed milk	½ pint (300ml) skimmed milk	½ pint (300ml) skimmed milk

LIST OF PHOTOGRAPHS

INDEX

Hot Cross Buns (P66)

Auchtermuchty Newmills

Mrs. Brown

Asst. Director of Obst. of Places.

First Park.

153581

153581